WORDS TO LIVE BY

Designed by Frank Strack
Cover design by Gerald Lee Monks
Cover photos from iStockphoto | chinaface. Also, Dreamstime for the *Words to Live By*
cover icons.

Additional copies of this book can be obtained by calling toll-free 1-800-765-6955 or
by visiting http://www.AdventistBookCenter.com.

ISBN 978-0-8163-6296-7

July 2017

WORDS TO LIVE BY

JACK BLANCO

Pacific Press®
Publishing Association
Nampa, Idaho | Oshawa, Ontario, Canada
www.pacificpress.com

INTRODUCTION

This devotional is written for busy people who are under the pressures of modern life and want to grow spiritually. Also it is written to bring spiritual help to prisoners. The insights from Scripture and the writings of Ellen G. White were selected for their spiritual focus. I have not quoted Ellen White's works verbatim but have summarized the thoughts found in the original work. These short daily devotionals were written for easy reading, understanding, and personal application. Each day is followed by suggested questions to help engage heart and mind. I wish to thank Star Stevens for her editorial help.

As all of us know, spiritual improvement is necessary for a growing relationship with Jesus, just as a plant that, if not watered and nurtured, will wither and die. Each day we all need to take time for devotions with Jesus in order to maintain and strengthen our relationship with Him. We may feel comfortable in knowing Him, but just knowing Him is different from having a love relationship with Him, and a deepening relationship.

In addition to their developing a closer relationship with Jesus, it is my hope and prayer that my family and friends will gain a deeper and more trusting relationship with the Father. Jesus came to reveal the Father and His love for us. When Philip asked Jesus to show him the Father, Jesus answered, "Have I been so long with you, and yet you have not known Me, Philip? You must believe me when I tell you that I am the Father in action, and the Father is living out His life in me" (paraphrased; see John 14:8–11).

Pray, focus, and visualize the depicted actions of what all of us are reading to transfer them to our hearts and minds. Also pray for the Holy Spirit to enlighten you and help you grow as a true and loyal follower of Jesus. He is the One who died for us on Calvary and offers us the free gift of His grace to strengthen us. Our personal faith or our works alone will not save us, but Jesus the One who loves us will save us by His grace (see Ephesians 2:8). We need to live for Him and to show our love and gratitude to Him for what He has done for us. Do not say, as some do, "I am saved, I am saved," for that can lead to a false sense of security. We are growing in Jesus as a child grows and develops, and we are as secure as when a child is being held in the arms of loving and caring parents and wishes to show them its love by carrying out their wishes.

The Promises of God

Insights From Scripture

Listen to my words,

O L<small>ORD</small>,

Consider my inmost thoughts;

Heed my cry for help,

My king and my God.

In the morning,

When I say my prayers,

Thou wilt hear me.

Psalm 5:1–3, NEB

January 1

It is impossible for God to lie.—Hebrews 6:18, NKJV

God Kept His Promises

Genesis 3:15. After Adam and Eve sinned, the Lord said to the serpent: "I will put hostility between them and you, between Eve's Seed and you. You will strike His heel, but He will crush your head."

Genesis 9:11–17. God said to Noah, "I promise not to bring another worldwide flood on the earth again. I will set a rainbow in the clouds as evidence for everyone to see. This is the agreement that I am making with you and with those who will come after you."

Genesis 12:1, 2. The Lord said to Abraham, "Take your family and leave the area where you're living now and go to the land that I will show you. I will bless you, and all nations of the earth will be blessed because of you."

2 Samuel 7:8–28. The Lord sent a message to David and said, "I took you from taking care of sheep to be ruler of my people." David said, "Lord, what You promise comes true."

Isaiah 7:14. "The Lord Himself will give you a sign. A virgin shall conceive and bear a son, and His name will be called Immanuel, meaning 'God With Us.' "

Questions: Jesus promised He would come again. Do you believe that, and if so, are you living as if you really believe it?

January 2

For all the promises of God in Him are Yes, and in Him Amen.
—2 Corinthians 1:20, NKJV

God's Promises for Today

Genesis 28:15. I am the God of Abraham; behold, I am with you. I will not leave you or forsake you, but keep My promise to go with you and be with you.

Exodus 6:6, 7. I am the Lord. I will take you to Myself to be part of My people, and you will know that I brought you out from the burdens you were carrying.

Exodus 19:5. If you will obey and keep My commandments, then you will continue to be My treasure. The whole world is Mine, but My people are special and you will be part of them, a kingdom of men and women committed to Me forever.

Questions: How committed are you to Jesus Christ? Totally? Are you sure?

January 3

*Commit your way to the L*ORD*, trust also in Him.*—Psalm 37:5, NKJV

Deuteronomy 26:16–18. I, the Lord your God, am asking you to keep My commandments and to live by them with all your heart. When you do this, I promise that you will be a special people to Me, and I will value you above all nations as belonging to Me.

Joshua 1:7–9. The Lord promised: I will be with you. I will not fail you or forsake you. So be strong and of good courage. Be strong and very courageous. Read from My Book; keep what is written and meditate on what it says—then you will be blessed. Don't be afraid or dismayed, for the Lord your God is with you wherever you go.

Ruth 1:16; 3:5; 4:17. Ruth, a Moabite, had lost her Jewish husband and said to Naomi, her mother-in-law, who was returning to Judah, "Wherever you go, I will go. Wherever you live, I will live. Your people will be my people, and your God will be my God. Whatever you tell me to do, I will do." Then the Lord blessed Ruth, gave her a righteous husband, and helped her conceive. She had a son whom she named Obed, who was the grandfather of David.

Questions: Can you say what Ruth said and mean it? Will God's people be your people?

JANUARY 4

The Lord shall be thy confidence.—Proverbs 3:26, KJV

1 Samuel 2:30. The Lord said, "I will bless your house and your father's house, that you should walk with Me forever. Those who honor Me, I will honor, but those who disrespect Me I cannot honor."

1 Samuel 12:20, 22, 24. Do not turn away from following the Lord, but serve Him with all your heart. The Lord will not forsake His people, and it pleases Him to make you part of His people. Respect the Lord, and don't forget the things He has done for you.

1 Samuel 16:7. The Lord is not impressed by how a man looks, how tall he is, what position he holds, or how well dressed he is, but the Lord looks at a man's heart to know how much he loves Him.

Questions: When the Lord looks at your heart, what does He see? Do you appreciate what He has done for you? Have you told Him so?

January 5

The LORD grants wisdom! . . . He grants good sense to the godly—his saints.
—Proverbs 2:6, 7, TLB

2 Samuel 7:18–22. David said to the Lord, "Who am I, O Lord God? And what is my family that you have brought us this far? You have done all these things according to Your own heart of love and have let us know them. How great You are, Lord! There is no one like You; we have not heard of anyone like You."

1 Kings 3:9–12. Solomon prayed, "O Lord my God, give me an understanding heart so I can know the difference between what is good and what is bad." Solomon's request pleased the Lord, and He said, "Because you didn't ask for riches, a long life, or the destruction of your enemies, I will give you an understanding heart for which you asked. There will never be anyone like you either past, present, or future."

1 Kings 8:56–60. Solomon blessed the people and said, "Not one word that the Lord has promised has failed. God will be with us as He was with our fathers; He will not leave us or forsake us. Walk in His ways and keep His commandments, that all the people of the earth may know that the Lord is God and there is no other."

Questions: What is your reason for keeping God's commandments? Is it because you want to get to heaven or because you love Jesus?

January 6

As long as I live, I will call on him when I need help.—Psalm 116:2, NET

2 Chronicles 34:31. Josiah the king made a covenant and promised to walk in the way of the Lord, to keep His commandments and His testimonies with all his heart and soul, which are written in the Book.

Job 13:15–18. Job said, "I will trust the Lord, though He decides to take my life, and I will watch my ways before Him. He is my salvation, and I know that I shall be justified."

Job 19:25–27. Job further said, "I know that my Redeemer lives and that He will stand on the earth when the end comes. Even if I die before then and my body turns to ashes, yet in my new body I will see God. And I will see Him for myself and not by another."

Questions: When you need help, do you only go to people, or do you also ask the Lord for help? Where do you begin?

January 7

The guardian of Israel does not doze or sleep.—Psalm 121:4, JB

Psalm 8:1–5. O Lord, how excellent is Thy name. When I consider the heavens, the moon and the stars which You made, what is man, that You are mindful of him and visit him? You made him only a little lower than the angels and crowned him with glory and honor.

Psalm 19:7–10. The law of the Lord is sure, making wise those who love Him and have simple faith. The instructions of the Lord are dependable, His commandments are pure. They enlighten the mind and bring joy to the heart. They are more valued than gold and are as sweet as honey.

Psalm 23:1–4. The Lord is my shepherd. He leads me to green pastures and quiet waters. He restores and refreshes my soul. He leads me in the way of righteousness. Though I have to walk through the valley of death, I will not fear, because You are with me and comfort me.

Questions: How much confidence do you have in the Bible? Would you be willing to sacrifice your life for your faith in the Bible? Are you sure?

January 8

*They that trust in the L*ORD *shall be as mount Zion, which cannot be removed.*
—Psalm 125:1, KJV

Psalm 37:3–7. Trust in the Lord, and do good. Delight yourself in the Lord, and He will listen to the desires of your heart. Commit your ways to the Lord and trust Him. Rest in the Lord and wait patiently for Him to bring about justice and make things right.

Psalm 51:6–12. Lord, you want to see truth in my heart, but You are the only one who can give wisdom to know right from wrong. Wash my sins away. Create in me a clean heart, O God, and renew a right spirit within me. Don't turn me away from Your presence or take the Holy Spirit from me. Restore in me the joy of salvation, and uphold me with Your free spirit.

Psalm 84:10–12. Lord, one day with You in heaven is better than a thousand years here. I would rather be a doorkeeper there than to live here among the wicked. The Lord is like the light of the sun and a shield from evil. He will give us of His grace and not withhold one spiritual thing from us as we walk uprightly. O Lord, blessed are the men and women who put their trust in You.

Questions: Have you asked the Lord to give you a good heart? Are you trying to be good by yourself?

JANUARY 9

Unto You I lift up my eyes.—Psalm 123:1, NKJV

Psalm 91:2–5. I will say to the Lord, "You are my fortress, my God, in whom I will trust." The Lord will cover you with His feathers and wings, and you can trust Him. His truth will be like a shield to you, protecting you from evil and from being deceived. You don't have to be afraid of such darkness or of what comes to you during the day.

Psalm 101:1–3. I will sing of Your mercy, O Lord. Yes, I will sing of Your love and kindness. I will behave myself and walk wisely in my house. I will set no evil thing before my eyes. I hate those evil things and will not let them stay in my mind.

Questions: Do you enjoy singing to the Lord? Do you do it at home, too, or just when you're in church?

JANUARY 10

I wait for the LORD, . . . in His word do I hope.—Psalm 130:5, KJV

Psalm 119:33–37. Teach me to walk in the way of Your law, and give me understanding of how to keep Your commandments. I will do with my whole heart what You have told me to do. I delight to do Your will. Help my heart to lean toward Your testimonies, and turn my eyes away from the world's riches.

Psalm 119:97–99, 105. O Lord, I do love Your law. I think about it all through the day. Through Your commandments You have made me wise, and they are ever with me. I have more understanding than all my teachers, for Your testimonies are my meditation. Your word is a lamp unto my feet and a light shining on my path.

Psalm 139:1–10. Lord, You have searched me and known me. You know when I sit down and when I get up. You read my thoughts before I speak. You are acquainted with all my ways. There is not a word in my mouth that You don't know. Such knowledge is beyond me—I can't understand it. Where can I go where You are not there? If I go up into the sky and fly to a place across the ocean, You are there. If I climb down into the earth, You are there. Your right hand is always holding onto me.

Questions: Do you realize that the Lord knows everything you say and the words you use to say it? Do you need to change? If so, how will you do it?

January 11

My son, forget not my law.—Proverbs 3:1, KJV

Proverbs 1:24, 28, 33. The Lord said, "I called and stretched out My hand to you, but you refused to come to Me. You set aside all My counsel. So when you call to Me, I will not answer. You will look for Me but will not find Me. But those who listen to Me will quietly rest in My love and feel that they are kept in My care for eternity."

Proverbs 3:5, 6. Trust in the Lord with all your heart, and don't lean on your own understanding. Acknowledge Him in all your ways, and He will direct your paths.

Proverbs 28:7–14, 26. Whoever keeps the law of the Lord is wise. For he who turns away from hearing the law, even his prayers will not be heard. The rich man feels that he is wise in walking in his own conceit, but the poor man who has understanding keeps thinking things through. He who covers his sins is not wise, but he who forsakes them will have mercy. Happy is the man who respects and honors the Lord, but he who hardens his heart will fall into sin.

Questions: What place does the Lord have in your heart? What place does He have in your life?

January 12

The fool has said in his heart, "There is no God."—Psalm 53:1, NKJV

Ecclesiastes 5:1–5. When you go into the house of God to worship, don't be so foolish as not to listen, but hear what's being said. Don't be rash but be careful what you say, for God is in heaven and you're on this earth. If you make a vow and promise to do something, carry it out. God has no pleasure in fools who just talk and don't do. It's better not to promise to do something than to promise and not do it.

Ecclesiastes 12:13, 14. Let's hear the conclusion of the whole matter: Respect God and keep His commandments. This is the whole duty of man, and God will look at what we do and decide whether it's good or bad.

Questions: Is all your religion just talk? What are you doing for the Lord?

January 13

A book of remembrance was written before Him for those who . . .
meditate on His name.—Malachi 3:16, NKJV

Isaiah 1:18, 19. "Come, let us reason together," says the Lord. "Even if your sins are like scarlet, they will be as white as snow; even if they are red like crimson, they will be like clean wool. If you are willing and obedient, you will eat the fruit from the good land that is waiting for you."

Isaiah 49:15, 16. Can a woman forget her nursing child and not have compassion on the son of her womb? She may forget about him and have no compassion for him. But I will not forget you and will never lose My compassion for you. I have scars in My hands to prove it.

Isaiah 66:22, 23. "As the new heavens and the new earth which I will make will remain," says the Lord, "so will your name remain. And it will be that from one new month to another and from one Sabbath to another, all the redeemed will come together to worship Me."

Questions: Do you realize that by keeping the Sabbath here, you are saying that you will be keeping the Sabbath in heaven? Does this make a difference in your life?

January 14

I will praise You, O L<small>ORD</small>, with my whole heart.—Psalm 9:1, NKJV

Jeremiah 24:7. I will give My people a heart to really know Me, to know that I am the Lord and that they are My people. And they will turn to Me with their whole hearts.

Jeremiah 29:11–13, "I know the thoughts I think toward you," says the Lord. "They are thoughts of peace and not anger, to give you a good future that has no ending. When you seek Me, you will find Me, if you search for Me with all your heart."

Jeremiah 31:33, 34. This is the agreement that I will make with My people: I will put My law in their hearts and be their God, and they will be My devoted people. They will no longer have to teach their neighbors and tell them about Me, for they will all know Me, from the least to the greatest. I will forgive their wickedness and will not remember their sins anymore.

Questions: Do you love God more than anything else in the world? Do you love Him more than anyone else in the world?

January 15

Jesus said . . . , "I am the resurrection and the life."—John 11:25, NKJV

Ezekiel 11:19, 20. I will give My people one heart and will put a new spirit within them. I will take out their stony hearts and give them hearts that are tender. Then they will follow my instructions and walk together as they do them. They will be My people, and I will be their God.

Ezekiel 37:1–14. The Lord picked me up and took me to a valley full of bones and said to me, "My people are saying that their hope is gone. But I will open the graves of the dead, and they will live. So prophesy to these dry bones and see them come alive." So I prophesied, and there was a great shaking. The bones came together, and flesh came on them, but they had no breath. Then the Lord said, "Prophesy to the wind." So I did, and breath came into the bones, and they lived. Then the Lord said, "I showed you this to give my people hope. I promise to open their graves, and they will come out alive."

Questions: On what does your hope rest of seeing your dead loved ones and friends? Can you substantiate that?

January 16

Weeping may endure for a night, but a shout of joy comes in the morning.
—Psalm 30:5, AMP

Daniel 3:17–25. The king of Babylon asked Daniel's three friends to bow down and worship a huge idol. If they refused, they would be thrown into a burning furnace. They said, "Our God can deliver us, but if not, we will not bow down and worship the idol." So the king ordered the guards to take them and throw them into the fire. The king was shocked when he saw that they were not burned, because he saw the Son of God in there with them. So the king ordered the three men to come out, and they did.

Daniel 6:10. When the Persians defeated the Babylonians and took over, Daniel knew that his enemies wanted to get rid of him by having him thrown into the lion's den. So Daniel went into his house, opened the windows, looked in the direction of Jerusalem, knelt on his knees, and prayed three times a day, as he had many times before. When he was thrown into the lion's den, the angel of the Lord protected him by closing the lions' mouths, and the king pulled him out unharmed.

Daniel 12:1–4. Daniel was told that at the time of the end, Michael will stand up, the Son of God, the great Prince who stands for His people. At that time, He will deliver His people, everyone whose name is written in the Book of Life.

Questions: How often do you pray in a day? What do you pray about?

JANUARY 17

Fine linen, clean and white . . . is the righteousness [given to] the saints.
—Revelation 19:8, KJV

Zechariah 3:1–4. The Lord gave me a vision, and I saw Joshua, our high priest who represents our people, stand before God, and Satan was standing next to Joshua, accusing him of many sins. Then the Lord rebuked Satan and said to the angel nearby, "Take away Joshua's filthy garments, dress him in a white robe, and put a crown on his head. I have taken away his sin and covered him with My righteousness."

Malachi 1:6. The Lord said, "A son honors his father, and a servant respects his master. I am your heavenly Father and also your Lord. Where is My honor and respect?"

Questions: How do you show God that you respect Him? Can you give some practical example?

January 18

"Take care that no one misleads you."—Matthew 24:4, NEB

Matthew 7:7, 8. Ask and it will be given to you; seek and you will find; knock and the door will opened to you. Everyone who asks receives, those who seek will find, and to those who knock on the door, it opens.

Matthew 11:28–30. Come to Me, all of you who work hard and are loaded down, and I will give rest to your hearts. Learn about Me, for I am meek and humble, and you will find what helped Me. My requirements are easy and light—they are not a burden.

Matthew 24:24–27. False teachers will come and do great things to make you believe them. They will try to deceive the very ones who belong to Me. I'm telling you this so that when they come and tell you that they saw Christ here or there, don't believe them. When I come back, it will be like the lightning that shines from east to west, and everyone will see it.

Questions: Do you believe everything you hear people say about the Bible? Do you take time to pray and study things out for yourself?

JANUARY 19

Add . . . to godliness brotherly kindness, and to brotherly kindness love.
—2 Peter 1:5–7, NKJV

Mark 3:33–35. Jesus asked the people, "Who is My mother, and who are My brothers and sisters?" Then He looked at the crowd and said, "Whoever does the will of My Father, he or she is My brother, sister, and mother."

Mark 9:21–27. They brought to Jesus a boy who was possessed by the devil and asked Jesus to heal him. Jesus asked the father how long this has been going on. The father said, "Since he was a child." Jesus was moved with compassion and said to the father, "If you believe, all things are possible to those who believe." Crying, the father responded and said, "Lord, I believe; please help my unbelief." Then Jesus healed the boy, who looked like he was dead. He reached out His hand, and the boy got up.

Luke 6:36–38. Be merciful to others, as your heavenly Father is merciful. Don't judge and condemn, but forgive. When you give to others, don't do so grudgingly, but with good measure, pressed down, and running over. Such a good spirit will come back to you in the same way by lifting your spirits.

Questions: Do you still love and trust God, even if He does not heal you? What if He does not heal the person for whom you earnestly prayed?

JANUARY 20

This is a faithful saying and worthy of all acceptance, that Christ Jesus came into the world to save sinners.—1 Timothy 1:15, NKJV

Luke 15:3–7. Jesus shared this parable: If a man has a hundred sheep and one is missing, he leaves the ninety-nine in the pen and goes to search for the lost sheep until he finds it. And when he does, he's thrilled, takes it in his arms, picks it up, puts it on his shoulder, and carries it back home. Then he calls his neighbors and friends to tell them the good news. That's how it is in heaven when one lost person is found and brought back to the Father.

Luke 22:39–42. Jesus went with His disciples to the garden by the Mount of Olives to pray. When they got there, He went a little farther, fell on His knees, and prayed, "Father, please don't let Me go through all this suffering and be crucified. However, not My will but Yours be done."

Luke 23:33, 34. After Jesus was arrested and taken to Pilate, He was crucified. As the soldiers were nailing Jesus to the cross, He prayed, "Father, forgive these men—they're just doing what they are told. They don't really know who it is whom they're crucifying."

Questions: Did you know that Jesus, the Son of God and equal with God, let Himself be stripped naked and publicly crucified for you that way? What kind of love is this? How do you explain it?

January 21

If Christ is not risen, then our preaching is empty and your faith is also empty.
—1 Corinthians 15:14, NKJV

John 20:1–20. Early in the morning on the first day of the week, Mary Magdalene went to the tomb where Jesus was buried and found it open. She ran back to tell Peter and John, and they ran to the tomb. When they got there they looked inside, but Jesus' body wasn't there. The burial wrappings were folded and carefully laid to one side. So they knew that no one had stolen His body. The two disciples went back, puzzled. Mary had gotten there and stayed there crying, and as she turned around, she saw a man standing there. She thought it was the caretaker, and with bowed head and still crying, she asked Him about the body. Then Jesus lovingly spoke her name, "Mary." She recognized His voice, was startled, and fell at His feet. But Jesus said, "Don't touch Me—I haven't yet ascended to My Father. Go and tell the disciples that I'll see them this afternoon." So Mary ran back and told the disciples that she had seen Jesus. That afternoon Jesus came back from the Father to see the disciples. They could hardly believe that it was Jesus! So He showed them His wounds, and they were overjoyed.

Questions: How firmly do you believe that Jesus died and is alive today? What would you say if someone challenged you on that?

JANUARY 22

After Jesus was baptized [as an example for us], . . . a voice from heaven said, "This is My beloved Son."—Matthew 3:16, 17, AMP

Acts 1:3, 9–14. Jesus spent some days with the disciples and appeared to many people, showing them unmistakably that He was alive. Then He went with His disciples to the Mount of Olives, just a little east of Jerusalem. As they were talking together, He was slowly lifted up and disappeared into the clouds. The disciples kept looking up, hoping to catch another glimpse of Jesus. Suddenly, two men dressed in white appeared and said to them, "Why are you standing here gazing up to heaven? One day Jesus will come back the same way you have seen Him go."

Acts 2:1–41. When the disciples were together in one place praying, the Holy Spirit came upon them, and they were given the gift of speaking in different languages. So Peter went to speak to the people about Jesus, who had been crucified but was resurrected and is now sitting on the right hand of God. When the people heard this, their hearts were moved and they said, "What should we do?" Peter said, "Repent and be baptized as a sign of the forgiveness of sins." That day, three thousand people were baptized!

Questions: Have you been baptized? If not, why not? If so, are you faithful to your baptismal vows?

January 23

"Blessed are you when people revile you and persecute you . . . for your reward is great in heaven."—Matthew 5:11, 12, NRSV

Acts 9:1–20. Now Saul, a zealous member of the Jewish high council, persecuted those who had accepted Christ and arrested many, and some were put to death. While on his way to Damascus to do the same there, suddenly an extremely bright light from heaven surrounded him, and a voice said, "Saul, why are you persecuting Me?" Saul asked, "Lord, who are You?" The voice said, "I am Jesus whom you are persecuting." When he opened his eyes, he couldn't see. Those with him had to lead him into Damascus, and three days later the Lord sent Ananias to talk to Saul and restore his eyesight. Then Saul was baptized and was known as Paul.

Acts 17:10–12. The Holy Spirit told Paul to go to Greece and preach in the cities there. So he went with Silas and preached there. In the city of Berea, those who responded were more earnest than in other cities. They received the Word of God very readily, and searched the Scriptures daily to make sure that what Paul said was true. Many accepted Christ and believed. Some were from the higher class of society, several honorable women and quite a few men.

Acts 23:1–11; 28:16, 30, 31. When Paul finally got back to Jerusalem, he was arrested and taken to the high priest, who ordered Paul to be slapped for claiming to have a good conscience. So the Roman commander stepped in and took him to the governor's castle to protect him. That night the Lord appeared to Paul and said, "Be of good courage, Paul. As you stood up for Me here in Jerusalem, so you will have to do the same in Rome." Paul was taken to Rome under guard. At first Paul was put under house arrest, with a soldier guarding him, until he could have a hearing by Caesar, after which he was executed.

Questions: Are you willing to be slapped, arrested, and executed for believing in Jesus? Are you sure? Would you stand firm and not deny your personal conversion and experience with Him?

January 24

So shall I keep thy law continually for ever and ever.—Psalm 119:44, KJV

Romans 1:16, 17. Paul wrote many letters to various people and churches. One letter was to the believers in Rome. He said, "I am not ashamed of the gospel of Christ, for it is the power of God unto salvation to everyone who believes, to the Jew and to the Greek."

Romans 2:28, 29. He is not a believer who is one just outwardly, but he is one who is a believer inwardly, in the heart and in the spirit. The praise of men is not important, but the praise of God is.

Romans 3:21–31. Righteousness that comes from God is by faith in Jesus Christ. All have sinned or come short of the glory of God. But we are justified freely by God's grace that comes to us in Jesus Christ. So where is boasting? There is no boasting. Should we then forget about God's law? No, we uphold His law.

Questions: Are you proud of your religious experience, or do you feel humble and thankful? Do you need to make a change? How will you do it?

January 25

I follow what is good.—Psalm 38:20, NKJV

Romans 8:28, 37–39. We know that God works all things together for good to them that love Him, to those who carry out His purpose for their life. We are more than conquerors through Him who loved us. Not death or life, angels, powers, things present, things to come, or things in the height or depth can separate us from the love of God which is in Christ Jesus our Lord.

Romans 14:12, 13; 15:13. Every one of us will have to give an account of himself to God. So let's not judge each other but, rather, make sure that you don't do something to give your brother an excuse to stumble in his faith. May the God of hope fill you with all joy and peace in believing, so that you may be filled with hope through the power of the Holy Spirit.

Questions: Are you thinking about the present only, or also about the future and Christ's second coming? Which is uppermost in your mind?

JANUARY 26

Stand fast in one spirit, with one mind striving together for the faith of the gospel.
—Philippians 1:27, KJV

1 Corinthians 4:7. Who makes each of you different from one another? What do you have that you did not receive? Now if you received it, why do you glory in what you have as if it weren't given to you and as though what you had was yours all along?

1 Corinthians 6:19, 20. Don't you know that your body is the temple of the Holy Spirit who is in you, whom God sent to help you, and that your body is not your own? You have been redeemed for a price, the death of the Lord Jesus Christ. So glorify God with your body and spirit.

1 Corinthians 12:4–11. There are different gifts that the Holy Spirit has given us. All these gifts are given by the same Holy Spirit as He wills. Although there are many parts to the body, it is still one body. All of us have been baptized into one body of faith, no matter what race of people we belong to, and we all drink from the same divine Source.

Questions: How much do you value your body? How do you treat your body? Have you forgotten that it belongs to God?

JANUARY 27

Let this mind be in you, which was also in Christ Jesus.—Philippians 2:5, KJV

2 Corinthians 5:14–17. It is the love of Christ that motivates us. So we do not live to serve ourselves but to serve Him who died for us and rose again. Therefore, if anyone is in Christ, he or she is a new creation through the power of the Holy Spirit. Old things are passed away—all things have become new.

2 Corinthians 10:12. We don't dare do what others are doing. They compare themselves among themselves and measure themselves by themselves. Those who do these things are not wise.

2 Corinthians 13:5, 6, 11. Examine yourself as to whether or not you're in the faith. Know yourself and prove yourself as to whether you are in Christ or not. Finally, brothers, farewell. Be mature, feel comfortable with each other, be of one mind, and live in peace; and the God of love and peace be with all of you.

Questions: Do you occasionally review and reevaluate your Christian experience? How important is this for you to do? Why?

JANUARY 28

"To him who overcomes I will give to eat from the tree of life."
—Revelation 2:7, NKJV

Galatians 2:20, 21. I am crucified with Christ, but I live. Yet it's not I who lives, but Christ who lives in me, because I live by faith in the Son of God who gave Himself for me. I don't nullify the grace of Christ by trying to earn my salvation by works. If that's the way of salvation, then why did Christ come to die?

Galatians 5:22, 23. The fruit that comes in our life from the Holy Spirit is love, joy, peace, patience, gentleness, goodness, faith, meekness, and temperance. There is no law against such living.

Questions: Is the fruit of the Holy Spirit seen in your life? Are you praying for the Holy Spirit to produce this kind of fruit in your life?

January 29

Fight the good fight of faith.—1 Timothy 6:12, KJV

Ephesians 2:8, 9. For by grace you are saved through faith, not because of what you do, but as a gift from God. If we could work our way to heaven, then men and women could boast.

Ephesians 4:1–6. Live worthy of your high calling as people whom God has redeemed. Live humbly in meekness and patience with each other, and do so with love. Keep the unity of faith through the Holy Spirit which holds you together, and be at peace. There is one body of believers, one Holy Spirit, one hope, one faith, one baptism, one Lord Jesus, and one God and Father who is in all of you.

Ephesians 6:10–18. Finally, brothers, put on the whole spiritual armor of God so that you will be able to stand against the weapons of the devil. We're not fighting against men but against spiritual forces, those who rule over the darkness of this world. Be sure to put on the whole armor of God, and stand your ground. Be dressed with the uniform of truth, have the shield of Christ's righteousness around your chest, wear the boots of the gospel of peace, and above all, hold the shield of faith in front of you to stop the bullets of the wicked one. Put on the helmet of salvation, and hold the sword of the Holy Spirit in your right hand, which is the Word of God. Always pray with your brothers and sisters for their safety and yours.

Questions: Are you willing to take a firm stand for what is truth? Whom would you need to help you to do so?

JANUARY 30

Be of good courage, and he shall strengthen your heart.—Psalm 31:24, KJV

Philippians 1:1–6. Paul wrote, "Grace and peace to you from God our Father, and from the Lord Jesus Christ. I thank God for all of you and in every prayer make requests for you with joy in my heart. I praise God for your fellowship in the gospel from the first day until now. Be confident of this very thing—that He who has begun a good work in you will carry it out until the day when Christ comes again."

Philippians 3:13–15. Brothers, I, Paul, don't consider that I have achieved perfection. But this one thing I do: I forget the past things in my life and press forward to the high calling of God in Jesus Christ. Let us all be like-minded, and God will lead you and show you the way.

Colossians 3:8–10. Put away such things as anger, rage, cursing, and filthy talk, and don't lie to one another. You have put off the old man of sin and put on the new man in Jesus Christ. You have new knowledge that you didn't have before, and you have been recreated in His image, so reflect Him.

Questions: Are you able to forget the past and work to be a better Christian? How earnest are you in doing this?

JANUARY 31

Jesus said . . . , "I am the resurrection and the life."—John 11:25, NKJV

1 Thessalonians 4:13–18. I would not have you be ignorant, my brothers, concerning those who have died in the Lord and are now sleeping. I don't want you to sorrow as others do who have no hope. We believe that Jesus died and rose again, so that's what will happen to those who have died in the Lord. When Jesus comes back, they will live again. He will descend from heaven with a shout, with the voice of leadership as Michael, the One in charge of the angels. The trumpet will sound, and those who died in Christ will come up first. They will be caught up in the air, we who are alive and remain will be caught up to meet them in the air, and together we will meet the Lord and be with Him forever. So comfort each other with these words.

2 Thessalonians 3:3–5. The Lord is faithful who will establish and strengthen you to keep you from evil. We have confidence in you, that you will do what the Lord says and what we have asked you to do. The Holy Spirit will direct your hearts deeper into the love of God and the patient waiting for the return of the Lord Jesus Christ.

Questions: Can you share your confidence with others that the Lord will come again? Does this include that He will raise the good people, and translate the good ones still living?

FEBRUARY 1

How shall a young man cleanse his way? By taking heed . . . according to Thy word.
—Psalm 119:9, KJ21

1 Timothy 4:12–14. Paul wrote to Timothy: "Let no one look down on you because you're young in the ministry. Be an example to the believers in your life, the spirit that you have, in what you say, and in love, faith, and purity. Until we get together again, give attention to your reading of Scripture, your encouragement to believers, and to the doctrine you're teaching them. Don't forget your ordination and the gifts that the Holy Spirit gave you when they laid their hands on you and you were ordained."

2 Timothy 3:1–5. Know this, that in the last days, dangerous days will come. People will only love themselves, be proud and boastful, be jealous of each other, curse, and be unthankful; and the young will not listen to their parents. They don't even have natural affection but break their word, falsely accuse others, are always angry at something or someone, and hate people who are good. They have no self-control and love pleasure more than they love God. Some have a form of godliness; don't be fooled by such people.

Titus 2:13, 14. Let's look forward to that blessed hope and the glorious appearing of our Father and the Lord Jesus Christ. He gave Himself for us, to redeem us from our sins and to purify for Himself a unique people who are full of good works.

Questions: Considering the last days we live in, are you able to live above such wickedness to the honor and glory of God? How do you do that?

FEBRUARY 2

Be of good courage . . . all you who hope in the LORD.—Psalm 31:24, NKJV

Hebrews 6:17–19. God, wanting to show His people the dependability of what He says, based it on two things: One, He cannot lie; and two, He took an oath to prove that what He said is the truth. Now He couldn't take an oath confirming it by some higher power, for there is no higher power, so He took an oath based on Himself. It's on these two things we have based our hope. This is our anchor, sure and steadfast.

Hebrews 11:1–16. By faith we are confident of what we hope for, and it's the evidence of things we can't see. This is how God's people lived, such as Abel, Enoch, Noah, Abraham, Sara, and others. They considered themselves pilgrims on this earth, and they died with hope in their hearts as they looked forward to when God, who is not ashamed of them, would fulfill His promise, and they would live in a new country, in a city especially prepared for them.

Hebrews 12:1–3. Considering that we have such a great number of examples of faith who lived before us, let us put away our sins and get rid of anything that's holding us back from taking part in the spiritual race that we are in as we head for home. And let us keep our eyes fixed on Jesus, the Author and Finisher of our faith, who, for the joy that was ahead of Him, endured the cross, despised the shame, and is now sitting on the right hand of God. Carefully consider this so that you don't grow weary and faint on the way.

Questions: What is the foundation of your hope? What is your anchor of faith gripping? How would you tell someone about it?

FEBRUARY 3

I saw a new heaven and a new earth . . . the former things are passed away.
—Revelation 21:1–4, KJV

James 2:14–20. What good is there in saying, "I have faith," but then not doing anything? Can faith alone save you? When someone is in need, help them; don't just talk about it. Can faith alone save you? Let us show our faith by what we do. If you believe in God, that's good, but the devil and his angels also believe. So faith in God without works is meaningless.

1 Peter 2:9, 10. You are a chosen lineage, a royal people, and a holy nation, special to the Lord. He wants you to praise Him for what He did for you by calling you out of spiritual darkness into His marvelous light. In the past you were not part of God's people, but through His mercy now you are God's people.

2 Peter 3:3–13. We know that in the last days scoffers will come, saying, "Where is the promise of His coming? Since our parents died and fell asleep, everything continues as it was from the beginning of creation." But they are ignorant of what is written. Beloved followers of Christ, those people are ignorant of one thing above others, that with God a thousand years is like one day to us. He has not lost His desire for people to be saved, and He has not forgotten His promise. We hold on to His promise and look for new heavens and a new earth, where only righteousness lives.

Questions: Do you believe that the time will come when only good people will live on this planet? How is that possible?

February 4

1 John 1:9, 10. If we confess our sins, God is faithful and just to forgive us our sins and wash away all unrighteousness. When we say that we have not sinned, we say that God is a liar and show that His word is not in our hearts.

1 John 2:1–4. My spiritual children, let me put what I want to say in writing. Don't sin, but if you sin, we have an advocate in heaven, Jesus Christ the Righteous. He is the One who paid for our sins, and not for ours only, but for the sins of the whole world. And this is how we know that we know Him—when we keep His commandments. He who says that he knows Jesus and doesn't keep His commandments is a liar, and the truth is not in him.

1 John 3:1, 2. Look at what love the Father has shown to us, that we should be called His sons and daughters. The world doesn't really know us; it didn't really know Jesus or who He was. We are the sons and daughters of God. It doesn't look as though we are, but when Jesus comes back, we will be changed to be like Him, because we will see Him as He is.

Questions: Is everything you do for the uplifting of the glory of God? How do you do that?

FEBRUARY 5

Draw near to my soul, and redeem it.—Psalm 69:18, NKJV

Revelation 1:1–7. This is the book of Revelation, which God the Father asked Jesus to give to us to show us things about the future that must take place. And Jesus gave it to His angel to share it with John the apostle. Blessed are those who read this prophecy and hold on to the things which are written, for it's time for them to know. So I, John, wrote what the Holy Spirit led me to write and sent these letters to the churches, for they are from Jesus, who died for our sins, rose again, and brought us back to God our Father. To Jesus our Savior be glory and praise forever and ever. Amen. He will come back in the clouds of heaven, and everyone on earth will see Him, including those who called for His crucifixion, for He promised them that they would be resurrected to see Him come. Even so, come Lord Jesus.

Revelation 3:14–22. I, John, sent a letter to the congregation that was located in the city of Laodicea just as it was given to me by the Amen, the One who created all things. The message said: "I know everything you do, but your faith is lukewarm. It would be better if you were cold or hot, but you are lukewarm, not good to the taste. You tell yourself that you are spiritually rich and don't need anything else. But you don't realize that you're blind and spiritually poor and naked. Come to Me for gold, and I will dress you in white robes, clean and white, and anoint your eyes with holy oil so you can see things clearly. Repent and be zealous for Me. I'm standing at your heart's door, knocking. If anyone opens his heart, I will come in and we will eat together. I will help him overcome, and I promise that he will sit by Me in heaven just as I sit by the Father. Those who have ears to hear, listen to what the Holy Spirit is telling you."

Questions: How can you tell when the Holy Spirit is speaking to you? How can you be sure? What do you do to double-check such impressions?

FEBRUARY 6

Praise the Lord, for the Lord is good; sing praises to His name.
—Psalm 135:3, NKJV

Revelation 12:17. The devil is angry, that evil dragon, and he is at war with the remnant of God's people, the last people living on earth who keep the commandments of God and have the testimony of Jesus Christ, which is the spirit of prophecy.

Revelation 19:1–9. Then I, John, heard the voices of many people in heaven saying, "Alleluia, salvation, glory, honor, and power unto God." And they fell on their knees before the throne of God. The voices of many people, which sounded like thunder, said, "Alleluia, the Lord God omnipotent reigns. Let us be glad and rejoice, for the marriage supper of the Lamb and His bride, the church, has come, and she's ready." She was dressed in a pure white robe, which is the righteousness of Christ given to her. Then I was told to write: "Blessed are those who have come to the marriage supper of the Lamb, having believed what was written."

Revelation 21:1–5. After this I, John, saw a new heaven and a new earth. And I saw the Holy City come down from God out of heaven looking beautiful, like a bride dressed for her wedding. Then I heard a great voice from heaven saying, "The dwelling place of God is with men, and He will live with them, for they are His people. He will wipe away all tears from their eyes, and there will be no more death, sorrow, crying, or pain, for the former things are passed away."

Questions: How can you be ready and dressed properly for the marriage supper? Do you believe that a city will be coming down from heaven?

Faith in God's Promises

Insights From "Faith and Acceptance" in
Ellen White's Book *Steps to Christ*

February 7

"Come, eat of my bread and drink of the wine I have mixed."
—Proverbs 9:5, NKJV

Faith in God's Promises. The words and promises of God are the only foundation of our faith. Take the word of God as a living, speaking voice to you personally. God is faithful in what He has promised. He is a reservoir of power. Come to Him in humility, open your Bibles, read His promises, and take your position on them. Tell Him that you will believe without any other evidence except His promise. This is not presumption but faith. We may have rich evidences of His love and mercy every day, and God will reward every good work done in His name and to His glory.

Help Promised. Jesus promised, "Ask, and it shall be given to you; seek, and you will find; knock, and it shall be opened to you. Everyone who asks will receive; and to the one who knocks, the door will be opened. If you give good gifts to your children, how much more will your heavenly Father give you what is best for you if you ask Him." The promises of God are full and abundant. To all who call on Him, God is near to give help. He is the only one who can fully understand us and give us the unerring counsel we need.

Meant for You. God's promises were meant for us individually. When we study the Bible, we should choose one verse and concentrate on it to determine the thought which God has put in that verse for us. The experiences written in God's Word are to be our experiences. Prayer and promise are to be ours. As our physical life is sustained by food, so our spiritual life is sustained by the promises of God in His word.

Questions: Do you have favorite Bible texts that have helped you before and are really helping you now? Are you willing to share them with others?

FEBRUARY 8

Herein is love, not that we loved God, but that he loved us, and sent his Son.
—1 John 4:10, KJV

Expressions of Love. The light from Calvary is now shining in clear, bright rays, revealing Jesus as our Sacrifice for sin. As you read the promises of God which are set before you, remember that they are the expressions of unutterable love and boundless compassion for you. So believe that God is on your side, no matter what happens. As you draw near to Him in confession and repentance, He will draw near to you with mercy and forgiveness.

Promises Are Like Roses. The promises in the Bible are like lilies, roses, and pink flowers. O that we might believe the promises of God! Let's not look into our hearts for joyful emotions as being evidence of God's acceptance of us. We are to take God's promises and say, "These promises are for me, I will receive them." By faith we should reach out and lay hold of Christ, who is our strength and our Savior. The promises in Scripture are to be received as God's word spoken to us. In these promises God is speaking to us individually, as directly as if we could listen to His voice. Feed on His promises, and be content to rely on them. Hang them in memory's hall. They are to be valued far above silver or gold.

Promises Can Be Trusted. Can't you trust your heavenly Father? Can't you depend on His promise? Precious promises! Can't you trust His promises, knowing that He is faithful and dependable? Let your faith take hold of them. Place your whole weight on them with an unwavering faith, for they will not and cannot fail.

Questions: How personal are God's promises? Do you really take them as given to you or just to people in general?

February 9

From childhood you have known the Holy Scriptures, which are able to make you wise for salvation.—2 Timothy 3:15, NKJV

Don't Dishonor God. Those who doubt God's promises and do not trust the assurance of His grace are dishonoring Him. We should not dishonor God by doubting His love and His promises. Comfort your soul with the promises of God, because His glory and reputation rests upon them.

Precious Grains of Gold. Over the field of revelation are scattered grains of gold. If you are wise, you will gather these precious grains of truth. So when tests and trials come, God's promises will be springs of heavenly comfort. Temptations often appear irresistible because we neglect prayer and forget God's promises. Let us commit the precious promises of God to memory, so when we are deprived of our Bibles, we may still have the Word of God in our hearts.

Questions: Do you have texts of Scripture so fixed in your mind that you can recall them any time you need them? Have you tried it to see?

FEBRUARY 10

All his commandments are sure. They stand fast for ever and ever.
—Psalm 111:7, 8, KJV

God's Commands Are Promises. When God spoke, the world came into existence. His word is power, and it creates life. The life thus imparted is also sustained by His word. Man shall live by every word that comes from God, for every command of His is a promise, and when He speaks, it happens. Let it be clear that the commandments of God are the way of life—they are not arbitrary. His laws, whether they are the laws of nature or the physical and moral laws He has given us, all imply a promise. If we live by them, blessings will follow.

False Claims. Some are making a mistake in waiting to claim God's promises. They are waiting to make themselves more worthy, which they believe they must do before they can claim the promises of God. By doing this, they are making a fatal mistake. Some have an idea that they must put forth some strong and wonderful effort to gain the favor of God. All this rests on self-dependence. It is only by connecting with Jesus through faith that we become hopeful, believing children of God and reach out to claim His promises.

Questions: How worthy are you to receive what God promised? Can you explain it to someone and tell them that God's promises apply to them as well?

FEBRUARY 11

You loyal followers of the Lord, trust in the Lord!—Psalm 115:11, NET

Promises Are Still Good. The promises of God have not lost their force. They are still as good today as they have always been. The availability of the Holy Spirit and the power of God that attended the early church have not changed. The Lord has bestowed great blessings on us and has committed the treasures of truth to us. Our obligation is to hold on to His promises and improve upon His blessings.

Promises for Us Individually. Through His promises God is speaking to us individually, speaking to us as directly as if we were listening to His voice. It is through these promises that Christ communicates to us His grace and power. They are like leaves from the tree of life. Received and assimilated, they are to be the strength of our character and the inspiration of our life. Nothing else can have such healing power and give courage, faith, and energy to us as the promises of God can do.

The Promise of Forgiveness. The Lord says, "Come now, let us think about this: Though your sins be many, if you give your heart to Me and are willingly obedient, you will be forgiven." You can trust the Lord to fulfill His word. Let His precious promises be placed in the framework of faith and placed in memory's hall. Not one of these promises can fail. God will do all that He has said He will do.

Questions: Is there any sin or sins that God cannot forgive? Are there any short or long term conditions? What are they?

February 12

Aren't there doctors there?—Jeremiah 8:22, GW

Depending on Promises. Neither life nor death can separate us from the love of God in Christ, not because we hold on to Him, but because He holds on to us. If our salvation depended on our own efforts, we could not be saved, for it depends on the One who is behind all His promises. Our hold on Him is weak, but His love holds on to us, and as long as we maintain our relationship with Him, no one can take us out of His hand.

Directing People to God's Promises. Physicians have opportunities to direct their patients to God's promises and to speak words of comfort and encouragement, as Jesus did during His earthly ministry. Let the physician study the Word of God, so that he may be familiar with God's promises and make his mind a storehouse of His promises so that he may repeat them to his patients. He should also talk of the works of healing by Christ and His love and tenderness. Never should he neglect to direct the minds of his patients to Christ as the chief Physician.

Questions: Are you holding on to God? If so, how firmly? Or is it better to place your hand in His and let Him hold on to you?

FEBRUARY 13

Nevertheless we, according to his promise, look for new heavens and a new earth.
—2 Peter 3:13, KJV

Promises Are Needed Today. Visions of the future given by God through the prophets are needed by the church today. The controversy of the ages is rapidly closing, and the promised blessings are soon to be realized. God's children in every age have been sustained by His promises as they looked forward to the time when He would fulfill them. These promises will be especially needed when the church goes through trials and suffers persecution. The Lord says, "Fear not, for I have redeemed you and called you by name. You are Mine and are precious in My sight."

Take God's Promises as Your Own. Do not forget that by accepting God as a father, you are admitting your relation to Him. His love for you is changeless. The gifts of our heavenly Father, who has all power in heaven and earth, are for His children. These gifts come to us through the costly sacrifice of His Son, our Savior, Jesus Christ, who shed His blood for us. We are God's children, so take God's promises as your own. Place them before Him as His own words to you and plead with Him, and you will receive His peace and joy.

Questions: Can you pray and talk to God this way? Do you feel comfortable doing this?

February 14

Moreover, we possess the prophetic word as an altogether reliable thing. You do well if you pay attention to this.—2 Peter 1:19, NET

Rest on God's Promises. Many who are seeking a closer relationship with God get discouraged and think it's because they lack faith, when the problem is that they mistake feeling for faith. Sometimes a deep sense of unworthiness comes over them, but this is no evidence that God has changed and forsaken them. They should turn their minds away from self, think about the mercy and love of God, and focus on His promises, believing He will fulfill them. Let us keep our eyes fixed on Jesus, feeling or no feeling, and calmly rest on the promises of God.

Not One Promise Has Failed or Will Fail. It is impossible for anyone to comprehend all the richness and greatness in even one of God's promises.

One person sees the beauty and grace of God's promises from one point of view, and someone else, the beauty and grace from another point of view. In His promises God is speaking to us individually, and through these promises He communicates to us His grace and power. To blot out the promises of God from Scripture would be like blotting the sun from the sky, and there would be nothing to gladden our experience. God has placed these promises in the Bible, and through these He draws back the veil from eternity, giving us a glimpse of the glory that awaits us.

Questions: Do you go by feeling to know that God is near? If so, why? If not, what do you go by?

Grow Spiritually by
Reviewing the Life of Christ

Insights From Ellen White's Book *The Desire of Ages*

FEBRUARY 15

"God loved the world so much that he gave his only Son."—John 3:16, NEB

God With Us. A knowledge of God is seen in the face of Jesus Christ. From all eternity He was one with the Father and was the image and outshining of His glory. Jesus came to this world to show us the Father's glory and to reveal His love. Jesus was God's thinking made audible and visible. In the face of Jesus Christ and in the cross of Calvary is seen a love which does not seek its own. This unselfish love is the law of life for heaven and earth. It is the glory of God to give. By love's self-sacrifice, the inhabitants of earth and heaven are bound to their Creator by an indissoluble union of love.

The Fullness of Time. When the time came for Jesus to be born, God sent His Son to be born of the Virgin Mary through the power of the Holy Spirit. Through Jesus a flood of healing grace would be poured on the world, which would never be withdrawn until the plan of salvation was complete. Like every descendant of Adam, He accepted the law of heredity to share our sorrows and temptations, and give us an example of how to live for God.

Questions: Does your mind grasp the reality of the Son of God, who was equal with God, and was willing to become like a human sperm to be implanted by the Holy Spirit in a virgin? Why was He willing to do this?

February 16

"It was not to judge the world that God sent his Son into the world."
—John 3:17, NEB

Jesus as a Child. Jesus lived with Joseph and Mary in a little mountain village. His willing hands were ever ready to serve and help others, showing unselfish courtesy. He would never sacrifice His integrity, and in this He was as firm as a rock. He was constantly on guard to preserve His purity. Neither gain nor pleasure, neither applause nor censure could induce Him to consent to one wrong act. He did not use His physical powers recklessly, but in such a way as to keep them in health and do the best work He could, showing that labor is honorable. He always took time to pray to His heavenly Father and often held communion with heaven by singing, not wanting to lose the blessings He needed.

The Baptism. Jesus and John the Baptist were cousins, but they had no direct acquaintance with each other. John had heard about Jesus' miraculous birth and His sinless life and believed that He was the Messiah, but he had no direct evidence. When John was baptizing people in the River Jordan, Jesus came to be baptized. The very presence of Jesus was holy. Why would He need to be baptized? Finally, John consents, Jesus prays, and heaven seems to open. The Father answers His Son's prayer with a voice from heaven, saying, "This is My beloved Son, in whom I am pleased." And the Holy Spirit appears as a dove fluttering over the head of Christ. John cries out, "Behold the Lamb of God, who takes away the sins of the world!"

Questions: Can you imagine the Father saying, "You are my beloved son, my beloved daughter"? How do we respond to something like this? How do you daily live because of this?

February 17

For it is not as if we had a high priest who was incapable of feeling our weaknesses with us; but we have one who has been tempted in every way that we are, though he is without sin.—Hebrews 4:15, JB

The Temptation. After the baptism, the Holy Spirit led Jesus into the wilderness to prepare for ministry. So He went to the wilderness to be alone, to contemplate His mission and work. While there, He fasted for forty days. Satan brought three temptations to Jesus that we all face: appetite, love of display, and love of the world. Absorbed in communion with the Father, Jesus was soon left alone to face all these temptations. As if in answer to prayer, Satan came disguised as an angel and said, "If you are the Son of God, ease your hunger by using your power to turn these stones into bread." This temptation was for Jesus to use His divine power for His own benefit. It began with a doubt about His being the Son of God, so Jesus knew that this was not an angel from heaven who came to Him. As a human being, Jesus had to control His deep hunger, which He did. He told Satan to go away and leave Him alone, because man must first feed on the Word of God.

Questions: How do you know if Satan is pushing you and tempting you to show others that you belong to God? If you are giving in to the temptation, what changes do you need to make?

FEBRUARY 18

But thanks be to God, who gives us the victory through our Lord Jesus Christ.
—1 Corinthians 15:57, NKJV

The Victory. Then Satan took hold of Jesus, lifted Him up, and carried Him to the top of the temple in Jerusalem. Jesus let him do this. As they both stood there, Satan congratulated Jesus on His steadfast faith. Then he said, "The Word of God says that He will send angels to take care of you so you won't even hurt your foot on a stone. So show your faith in the Word of God by jumping off, and God will take care of You." Jesus answered, "You should not put God's love to the test. That's not faith. That is taking God's love for granted, no matter what you do." When you test God, it shows that you don't trust Him. So Jesus refused to jump. Next, Satan took Jesus to a nearby mountain and caused the beauty of all the kingdoms of the world to pass in panoramic view before Jesus' eyes. Then he tempted Jesus and said, "The world belongs to me, and I'll gladly give it to you if you fall down and worship me." This meant that Jesus would have to give up who He was and bring this world back to God without having to face the horrible future of Calvary. This time divinity flashed through Jesus, and He ordered Satan to depart. Satan could not resist and was forced to obey. Then Jesus fell to the ground, totally exhausted, and was on the verge of dying, so angels quickly came and strengthened Him. Warming back to life, Jesus' heart of love went out in sympathy for humankind, and He went forth to complete the work He had begun.

Questions: Will you be true to God, no matter what advantages are being offered to you? If you have been true to God under such circumstances, are you willing to share your experiences with others?

FEBRUARY 19

"Look! There is the Lamb of God who takes away the world's sin!"
—John 1:29, TLB

We Have Found the Messiah. At the baptism of Jesus, new light was shed on the Messiah's work, which John the Baptist did not fully understand. During the weeks that followed, John studied the prophecies and their teachings with new interest. Before this, he had not understood the difference between the two phases of Christ's work as a suffering Messiah and a conquering King. When Jesus came back from the wilderness and John saw Him among the people, he pointed to Him as the Lamb of God. Then he waited impatiently for Jesus to clarify His mission, but the Savior said nothing.

The next day, two disciples of John, who had seen him point to Jesus as the Lamb of God, went to find Jesus among the crowd. One of them was Andrew, and the other was young John. They asked Jesus where He was staying. Jesus said, "Come and see." So they followed Him. These two were Jesus' first disciples, and they would go and bring others to Him, such as Peter, James, Philip, and Nathanael. These men knew that Jesus was the Messiah and that He had opened the windows of heaven for angels to descend and ascend, taking the prayers of the needy and distressed to the Father and bringing back blessings, hope, courage, help, and life to men and women who follow Christ.

Questions: Are you studying the Scriptures with renewed interest to see what God has there for you? Didn't Jesus say, "Search and you will find"?

FEBRUARY 20

Enjoy life with the wife whom you love.—Ecclesiastes 9:9, NRSV

The Marriage Feast. Jesus began His public ministry by attending a wedding feast to show His love for people. The wedding guests were relatives of His earthly parents, Joseph and Mary. Joseph had died, and Mary had been longing for the past two months to see Jesus. At the wedding feast she saw her dutiful Son, but He didn't look exactly the same—there was evidence of His conflict with Satan in the wilderness. Yet there was a new expression of dignity and power about Him. She was eager to have Him prove to the people that He was the Son of God by working a miracle. Also, she was hoping that He would reveal Himself as the Messiah and take the throne of Israel.

So when she asked Him to help supply the needs of the wedding guests who had run out of wine, Jesus told her that He must do the Father's will above anything else. Mary trusted Jesus and asked the servants to do whatever He asked them to do. Now, by the doorway stood six large stone water jars. Jesus asked the servants to fill them to the top with water. The water had changed into freshly made grape juice that the people called wine. The servants took some to the master of ceremonies, and it tasted better than what the guests had been drinking before. To the mind of Jesus, the gladness of the wedding festivities pointed forward to the rejoicing of that day when He would bring home His bride, the Church, to His Father's house, and the redeemed would sit down with their Redeemer to the marriage supper of the Lamb.

Questions: Are you willing to wait in doing some great and good act so that the credit doesn't go to you but to God? How will you know when to wait and when to go ahead?

FEBRUARY 21

Your new birth was not from any mortal seed but from the everlasting word of the living and eternal God.—1 Peter 1:22, JB

The New Birth. Nicodemus held a high position in the Jewish nation. He was present in the temple courtyard when Jesus drove out the money-changers, and he saw Him working miracles and healing the sick. Nicodemus couldn't help but believe that Jesus was sent from God. Because of his high position, he was not supposed to associate with the common people. So he arranged a secret night meeting with Jesus. Nicodemus said, "Teacher, we know that God sent you here, because no one else could do the miracles that you are doing unless God is with him." Jesus looked at him and said, "You must be born again." This caught Nicodemus by surprise. How could a grown man get back into his mother's womb and be born again? Jesus told him that He was talking about a new spiritual birth through the power of the Holy Spirit. Nicodemus knew the meaning of "new birth," because the change of a convert from heathenism to Judaism was called a new-birth experience. But he didn't feel the need to change.

The Christian life is not simply a modification or improvement of the old life, but a total transformation. This can happen only through the power of the Holy Spirit. How the Holy Spirit works on a person's heart and changes it can't be explained, any more than the wind can be seen. Through the Holy Spirit Christ is constantly working on people's hearts, and suddenly the person surrenders to Jesus. This is called conversion, but it is the result of the constant work of the Holy Spirit on the heart. As the Savior explained to Nicodemus how a new birth takes place, Nicodemus wanted to be changed, and it happened. After Jesus' crucifixion and ascension, Nicodemus came boldly to the front and did all in his power to help the disciples and the newly formed church.

Question: What are you doing to help the church? Is it by teaching, preaching, medical work, visiting those in need, overseas missionary work, helping the hungry and homeless, or helping financially?

FEBRUARY 22

For by one Spirit we were all baptized into one body—whether Jews or Greeks.
—1 Corinthians 12:13, NKJV

At Jacob's Well. One day, on His way to Galilee, Jesus passed through Samaria. It was noon, and being tired from the long trip, He sat down on the little wall of the city well, while the disciples went to buy something to eat. A woman came out of town to draw water. Jesus, being thirsty, asked her for a drink of water. But the woman saw that Jesus was a Jew and said, "Why do you ask me, a Samaritan and a woman, to give you a drink? Jews look down on us." Jesus responded, "If you only knew who is asking you for a drink of water! Go and call your husband so I can talk to him." She said, "I don't have a husband." Jesus said, "You're right—you are not married to the man you're living with, and you have had five husbands."

The woman began to shake, and she asked Jesus, "Are you a prophet?" Jesus appealed to her to give herself fully to God. As He saw her drink in the water of life, His own hunger and thirst were satisfied. When the disciples came back with food, they were surprised to see Him speaking to a Samaritan woman. His face was shining with delight. Meanwhile, the woman went into the city and said to the people, "Come and see a man who told me everything I ever did. Is this the Messiah?" Because she seemed like a radiant new woman, they followed her out to Jacob's well. Jesus looked at the people that were coming, pointed to them, and said to the disciples, "Here is a harvest ready for the reaping."

Question: How do you respond to people of different nationalities or races? Do you accept them, love them, and help them?

FEBRUARY 23

"Ask, and it will be given you; search, and you will find; knock, and the door will be opened for you."—Matthew 7:7, NRSV

"Except You See Signs and Wonders." The Galileans who returned home from the Passover in Jerusalem brought back wonderful reports about Jesus. The news spread throughout Galilee and brought hope to the sick and to the suffering. Now, in Capernaum the news attracted the attention of a military officer whose young son was suffering from an incurable disease, and the physicians had given up on him. It looked as though he wouldn't live long. So the officer went to see Jesus. His faith began to give way when he saw an ordinary, plainly dressed man. He doubted that this could be the Jesus he had heard about. But Jesus knew the officer's concerns and thoughts before the officer had even left home. The officer had decided that he would not receive Jesus as the Messiah unless his request was answered, yet the officer still had a small degree of faith.

Jesus not only wanted to heal the young son but to bring salvation to the whole family. But the officer had to realize his need before he could reach out for the grace of Christ. Too many place their faith in Christ for some special favor, being interested in Him from selfish motives. Jesus said to the officer, "Unless you saw a miracle, you had decided not to believe in Me." The words laid open the officer's heart, and he saw his only motive for coming to Jesus. In deep distress he realized that his selfishness might cost the life of his son. So he pleaded with Jesus, clinging to Him in his great need. The Savior will not draw away from such a one. He said to the officer, "Go your way—your son will live." Not only did the officer believe that his son would be healed, but with strong confidence he trusted in Christ as his Redeemer and Friend.

Question: What is your motive for coming to Jesus? Is it because of a miracle He worked in your life or in the life of others? Is that the only reason?

February 24

"Should you not also have compassion . . . just as I had?"
—Matthew 18:33, NKJV

Bethesda. Jesus went back to Jerusalem, and, walking by the Sheep Gate of the temple in meditation and prayer, He came to the pool that was there and saw sick and suffering people waiting to get into the pool. They believed that when there was a moving in the water, it was from a supernatural power, and the first one into the water would be healed. The Savior saw one case of supreme wretchedness, a man who had been a cripple for thirty-eight years. The Savior looked at him with compassion and asked, "Do you want to be healed?" The man said, "Sir, I have no man to help me into the water when it moves. There is always someone who gets there first." Jesus simply said, "Get up, take your mat, and walk." The man's faith took hold of Jesus' words. Every muscle was filled with new life, and his crippled legs suddenly worked. His muscles responded, and he sprang to his feet a well man.

This same response to Jesus and faith in what He says will bring spiritual healing as well. Of ourselves we are no more capable of living a holy life than the crippled man was capable of walking. Jesus asks us to rise in spiritual health and peace. Do not wait until you feel that you are made whole. Believe His word, and it will be fulfilled. Put your will on the side of Christ, and decide to serve Him. By acting on His word, you will receive strength. Whatever your evil practice or passion, Christ is able to deliver, and He longs to do so. He will forgive you and set you free from what is holding you in sin.

Questions: Do you know that you can direct your will and tell it what to do? You can decide to give it away, let others control it, or give it to Christ. What have you done with it?

FEBRUARY 25

"I was a stranger and you did not take Me in, naked and you did not clothe Me, sick and in prison and you did not visit Me."—Matthew 25:43, NKJV

The Death of John. King Herod, ruler of Galilee, had listened to John the Baptist's preaching and was convicted to repent and change his life. He had taken Herodias, his brother Philip's wife, and he now wanted to be free from her, but she held on to him and convinced him to arrest John and put him in prison. John being locked in prison made him despondent. John's disciples were allowed to visit him, and they kept him updated on the work of Jesus. John was disappointed that Jesus had not set up His kingdom, but he did not give up his faith in Jesus. He would not discuss his concerns with them, but he did long for some word from Jesus Himself. John's disciples went to find Jesus and asked Him, "Are you the One who was to come?" Jesus did not answer right away and let the healing of people be the evidence of His divinity. This is the message they carried back to John, who yielded himself to God for life or death.

On his birthday King Herod held a feast, and the place was filled with guests. Herodias sent her daughter in to dance before the king and his guests. The king was so pleased that he promised to give her anything she asked for. Her mother suggested she ask for the head of John the Baptist. The king was shocked, but he could not go back on his word in front of everyone, and he sent word to the prison. The executioner beheaded John, carried John's head in, and gave it to the girl and her mother. All who follow Christ and sacrifice for Him, with full confidence in God, will one day wear the crown of sacrifice.

Questions: What if God let something like this happen to you? What if you were arrested for being truthful and then put to death just so you would be out of the way?

FEBRUARY 26

"You study the scriptures thoroughly because you think in them you possess eternal life, and it is these same scriptures that testify about me."—John 5:39, NET

The Carpenter's Son. Jesus had grown up in Nazareth. Now He came back to worship there again. There was great excitement, and Jesus was asked to take part in the Sabbath worship service. He was given the scroll of Isaiah to give the Scripture reading. He took the scroll and read: "The Spirit of the Lord is upon Me, because He hath anointed Me to preach the gospel. He hath sent Me to heal the brokenhearted, to preach deliverance to the captives of evil, the recovering of the sight to the blind, to set at liberty those who are bruised, and to preach the acceptable year of the Lord." Then He closed the scroll and handed it back to the attendant, and all eyes were fastened on Him in wonder at how graciously the words came from His mouth. They responded with "Amen, Amen" and praises to God.

But when Jesus added, "This day is the Scripture fulfilled in your hearing," the people were offended, because His mission was different from what they had expected and wanted, so they rejected Him. If they did accept Him, they would have to go contrary to the opinions of their teachers. So they took hold of Him, hurried Him to the edge of a high hill, and with shouts and cursing were ready to push Him over the edge. Suddenly He disappeared! The angels who had been by His side took Him to a place of safety. Through all the ages, angels have been near to Christ's faithful followers. From what dangers we have been preserved through the interventions of angels we will never know, until in eternity we see our angels and are told the providential protections they gave us.

Questions: Do you accept everything the Scripture says? Are you willing to be persecuted for it? From what dangers has God protected you and even worked a miracle to save you?

FEBRUARY 27

Then He said to them, "Follow Me, and I will make you fishers of men."
—Matthew 4:19, NKJV

The Call by the Sea. In the early morning, Jesus went to the Sea of Galilee to get some rest and quiet time from the multitude of people that followed Him. But soon the people found Him. Their numbers increased, and they pressed in around Him. So Jesus decided to get into Peter's boat, and He asked Peter to push a little way from the shore. That way Jesus could be seen and heard by everyone. Peter did so but was a bit discouraged. He thought about John the Baptist, their trip to Jerusalem, and how the priests and rabbis had turned against Jesus. He also thought about how, after fishing all night, he had caught nothing—his nets were empty.

Then Jesus asked him to go out to the deepest part of the lake and let the nets down again. However, fishing is better at night, because that's when the fish come closer to the surface. Even though Peter objected, he did what Jesus told him to do. A miracle took place such as Peter had never seen. When he and his brother Andrew tried to pull up the nets, they were so full of fish that they had to signal to James and John to help them. Both boats were so full that it looked as though they were going to sink. So when the boats came to shore and the nets with the fish were secured, Peter fell at Jesus' feet and said, "Lord, turn away from me—I'm a sinful man. I'm not worthy to be in Your presence." Jesus responded, "Don't be afraid. You will be my disciple—you will fish for men and catch many."

Questions: Do you believe that Jesus can work through you to win others to Him? Can you recall such experiences? If you do, have you praised God for them? If you can't, do you believe that the spiritual seeds you have sown will bring others to heaven?

FEBRUARY 28

"Then you shall call, and the LORD will answer; you shall cry, and He will say, 'Here I am.' "—Isaiah 58:9, NKJV

At Capernaum. Jesus stayed in this city many times, and soon it became known as His city and the center of His ministry. People from many places passed through the city. Here Jesus could meet all kinds of people—all ranks, great or small, rich and poor. He met them on their own ground, as One who was acquainted with challenges and perplexities. His language was pure, refined, and clear. It was like music to those who listened. Jesus taught that the Scriptures were of unquestionable authority, not to be doubted nor hesitatingly accepted. His illustrations made the truths of Scripture plain. He never flattered people, exalted their fancies and imaginations, or praised them. He expressed the truth in the simplest language, and both the educated and uneducated were profited. His kind and sympathetic spirit shone out in His every look and word, and when the people responded, His face lit up with joy.

One day in the synagogue, a man possessed of an evil spirit rushed forward and shouted, "Leave us alone! What do we have to do with you? Have you come to destroy us? I know who You are—You are the Holy One of God!" Confusion filled the synagogue. Jesus rebuked the evil spirit in the man and ordered it to come out and leave the man alone. The evil spirit came out, but when it did, it threw the man to the ground. Then the eyes of the man that had glared with the fire of insanity now beamed with intelligence and with tears of gratefulness. This man's heart had longed for Jesus, but in place of prayer, he could only say what Satan had told him to say. But Jesus had heard the man's heart-cry. No cry from a soul in need will go unheard by the Savior.

Questions: How wonderful that God answers prayer—He is so good. Can you recall answers to prayer? If they were not obvious, were they quiet, providential answers? Have you praised Him for them?

MARCH 1

You Can Make Me Clean. The worst and most hated disease in Jesus' day was leprosy. The Jews regarded leprosy as a judgment of God on account of a man's sin. In the area of Christ's ministry, there were many such sufferers. They heard about the miracles of Jesus, and faith began to spring up in the heart of one of them, but he didn't know how to reach Jesus. Someone took the leper and guided him to Jesus, who was by the lake with crowds of people around Him. The leper saw Jesus healing the sick, the lame, the blind, and the paralyzed. The man's faith got stronger, but as he moved nearer, the other people around him backed away. What a sight—his decaying body was horrible to look at! When he reached Jesus, he threw himself at His feet and cried out, "Lord, if You want, You can heal me!" Jesus looked at him and said, "I will." He laid His hand on the leper and said, "Be clean!" Immediately, the man's body became healthy, the nerves sensitive, and the muscles strong.

But some lepers were not healed, because Jesus knew that they would not use the gift of health as a blessing for others. Then Jesus told the man to go quickly to the priests so that they could pronounce him clean. But the man went directly to his friends to tell them about the Great Healer. This hindered Jesus' ministry, because He was not following the law given to Moses for priests to declare people heathy, and in a short time He had to stop His ministry. The priests who condemned the leper finally certified his cure. In some instances, Jesus did not at once answer the plea for healing and give the blessing that people wanted. When we pray for blessings, the answer to our prayer may be delayed, or the Lord may give us something else in place of what we ask. But this is not so when we ask for deliverance and forgiveness of sin.

Questions: How do you feel if God delays answering your prayers? How about if later you find out that there was a reason for it?

March 2

A man who has friends must himself be friendly.—Proverbs 18:24, NKJV

Levi–Matthew. Matthew was a tax collector for the Romans. He and the other Jews who did this work for the Romans were looked down upon and hated by the people. But Jesus saw in Matthew a heart that was open for the receiving of truth. As Matthew listened to Jesus' teaching, the Holy Spirit convicted him of sin, and he longed for Christ's help. One day, while sitting at his tax-collecting booth, Matthew saw Jesus coming, and to his surprise he heard Jesus say, "Come, follow Me." Matthew turned his booth over to his helpers, left everything, got up, and followed Jesus. Every soul is tested in the same way, whether in their hearts they really follow Jesus or not. The self-sacrifice in Jesus' heart will be seen in their hearts. Wherever He leads, they will be glad to follow.

For Jesus to choose a tax collector as one of His disciples was an offense to many. But a great interest was created among such men, and Matthew longed to bring his former colleagues to Jesus. So Matthew decided to hold a feast at his house, inviting his family, friends, fellow tax collectors, and of course Jesus, who was the honored guest, sitting with the publicans, as they were called. These men were impressed by the Savior's teaching, but some did not accept Him until after His resurrection, when the Holy Spirit was poured out and thousands were converted. Man must be emptied of self before he can be a true believer and a follower of Jesus. The Lord can make man a new creation. The character of Christ will be seen in him who looks to the Author and Finisher of faith.

Questions: Do you depend on your faith in God? Do you realize that Christ through the Holy Spirit gives you the faith you need, if you ask Him?

MARCH 3

"Remember the Sabbath day, to keep it holy."—Exodus 20:8, NKJV

The Sabbath. The Sabbath was blessed and set aside at Creation. It was a memorial of the work of creation and thus a sign of God's power and His love. The work of creation was done by the Son of God, with the Father's blessing. "All things were made by Him, and without Him not anything was made that was made" (John 1:1–3). These are the things that the Sabbath is supposed to keep in our memories. If we fail to accept the righteousness of Christ as our own, the Sabbath loses its significance.

The Sabbath was designed to bring us into communion with God. But when the mind is absorbed with other things, even with religious activities and outward observance only, its significance and meaning is twisted, and it becomes an offense to God. Those who teach that Christ and His disciples did away with the Sabbath forget what Christ Himself said: "I have kept My Father's commandments, and abide in His love" (John 15:10). "Wherefore the Son of Man is Lord of the Sabbath" (Mark 2:28). This makes the Sabbath the Lord's Day. And it is a sign of Christ's power to change us and to make us more like Him.

Questions: What significance does the Sabbath hold for you in addition to remembering that God created everything? Or is it simply a day to rest and worship?

March 4

"The one who loves me will be loved by my Father."—John 14:21, NET

He Ordained Twelve. The Savior knew the character of the men whom He had chosen. All their weaknesses and errors were open to Him. Alone on the mountain, near the Sea of Galilee, He spent the entire night in prayer for them. While Jesus was preparing the disciples for their ordination, one who had not been invited urged that he be one of them. It was Judas, a man who professed to a follower of Christ. Jesus did not reject him, nor did He welcome him as a disciple. With great earnestness Judas said, "Master, I will follow You wherever You go." The other disciples were eager for Judas to be one of them, because he had a commanding appearance and great abilities. They were surprised that Jesus received Judas so coolly. But Judas, instead of walking in the light, was not interested in changing his defects. Soon Satan took control, and Judas became an enemy of Christ.

When Jesus had ended His instruction to the disciples, He gathered them close to Him, and, kneeling in the midst of them, He laid His hands on their heads and offered a prayer, dedicating them to His sacred work. Thus the Lord's disciples were ordained to the gospel ministry. The preaching of the gospel was committed to faulty men rather than to angels. It was to show that the power working through the weakness of humanity was indeed the power of God, and to thus encourage us to believe that this same power can work in us.

Questions: Aren't you amazed at some of the stories you hear about how seemingly insignificant people have done such great things for God? Have you praised and thanked God for working through such people?

MARCH 5

"Happy are those who long to be just and good."—Matthew 5:6, TLB

Sermon on the Mount. Christ seldom gathered His disciples alone to receive His words. It was His work to reach the people. Though the Sermon on the Mount was given especially for the disciples, it was given for the multitude. Christ's first words, as He sat on the hillside, were words of blessing:

"Happy are they," He said, "who recognize their spiritual poverty and feel their need of redemption."

"Happy are the meek." This is a meekness that hides itself in Christ. The difficulties we have are very much lessened by the meekness that hides itself in Christ.

"Happy are those who hunger and thirst after righteousness." The Holy Spirit never leaves unaided the soul who is looking unto Jesus.

"Happy are the peacemakers." As the Psalmist says, "Great peace have they which love Thy law: and nothing will offend them" (Psalm 119:165). Man cannot manufacture peace. The only power that can create and perpetuate peace is the grace of Christ.

"Happy are those who suffer for righteousness' sake." Sometimes Christ's followers are accused of being troublemakers, but such difficulties will add joy to their final triumph when Christ returns.

"Happy are you, for you are the salt of the earth." Salt preserves things and makes them taste better. It is through you that Christ's presence in the world is preserved and brings happiness to people.

"Happy are you, for you are the light of the world." Jesus' salvation seen in you is like sunshine—it will shine everywhere.

Questions: How happy and thankful are you? If you are not happy, why not?

MARCH 6

Faith is confidence in what we hope for and assurance about what we do not see.
—Hebrews 11:1, NIV

The Centurion. Christ marveled at the faith of this nobleman and Roman military officer who came to Him, asking Him to heal his beloved servant. This officer showed kindness to the Jews as they worshiped God, and when he heard about the teachings of Christ, the teachings of the Savior met the needs he felt in his soul. But he felt unworthy to come to Jesus, so he appealed to the Jewish elders to make the request for him, which they did. They went to Capernaum and told Jesus about the desire of the officer and that he was worthy of a response, because he loved the Jewish nation.

Jesus immediately responded and made His way to the officer's home in the city. When the officer heard that Jesus was coming, he sent Him this message: "Lord, don't trouble Yourself to come, because I'm not worthy for you to come to my house." But Jesus just kept coming. So the officer himself went to see Jesus and said, "Lord, I don't feel worthy to come to You. Just speak the word, and my servant will be healed. I tell my soldiers to come or to go, and they do. So all You need to do is to speak, and my servant will be healed." When Jesus heard this, He marveled at the faith of this officer and said, "What faith you have! I haven't found this kind of faith among My own people." Then Jesus said, "As you have believed, so it will be done." That same hour the officer's servant was healed. The officer's heart had been touched by the grace of Christ, so he didn't put trust in himself or in his own kind deeds, but on his great need. He didn't believe in Christ just as a miracle worker, but as the Friend and Savior of mankind.

Questions: Do you believe that Christ is your friend? If so, what for? Why should He be?

MARCH 7

The payoff of sin is death, but the gift of God is eternal life in Christ Jesus our Lord.
—Romans 6:23, NET

Who Are My Brothers? The sons of Joseph from his previous marriage were Jesus' stepbrothers. They heard about Jesus' ministry and were filled with astonishment and concern. They worried that He was wearing Himself out with constant labor, not taking time to eat, and spending entire nights in prayer. Also, they were concerned about His differences with the Pharisees and priests and were hoping that His thinking was not becoming affected by all this. The Pharisees and priests could not stop Him from working miracles, nor could they control His teaching, but they did everything else in their power to misrepresent Him and to twist His words. Still the power of the Holy Spirit followed them and brought conviction to their hearts, but they would not give in.

Jesus said, "Out of what is in the heart, the mouth speaks." Men are influenced by their own words. Uncontrolled expressions affect our thoughts, and soon we believe what we have said, whether it's true or not. Unless we yield ourselves to the control of Christ, we will be dominated by the wicked one. All we have to do is not identify ourselves with the Kingdom of Light, and Satan will take over. The only defense is the indwelling of Christ in the heart and our faith in His forgiveness and righteousness. We need to surrender ourselves to Him every day, or we will be overcome. It is in Him that we are safe.

Questions: Do you surrender yourself to Christ every day? Do you verbalize it and say it to Him? Your body responds to what you hear and deepens what you're thinking.

MARCH 8

*"I have told you these things so that in me you may have peace. In the world you
have trouble and suffering, but have courage—I have conquered the world."*
—John 16:33, NET

The Invitation. Jesus said, "Come unto Me, all you who labor
and are loaded down, and I will give you rest." He spoke these words to
the multitude that followed Him. Whatever your anxieties, worries, and
trials, spread them out before the Lord. Your spirit will be braced for
endurance. The way will be opened for you to stop being embarrassed.
The weaker and more helpless you know yourself to be, the stronger
you will become in the strength Christ gives you.

We are to enter the school of Christ, to learn meekness and
humbleness from Him. Redemption is the process by which we are
trained for heaven. This training involves release from ideas, habits, and
practices that have been learned in the school of the prince of darkness.
The soul is to be delivered from all that is opposed to loyalty to God.
We are afraid to trust ourselves with God, and because we do not make
a complete surrender to Him, we fail to find peace of heart.

Questions: As you grow in Christ, are you becoming more humble and
more dependent on Him?

MARCH 9

"In a moment, in the twinkling of an eye, at the last trumpet, . . . the dead will be raised incorruptible, and we shall be changed."—1 Corinthians 15:52, NKJV

The Touch of Faith. Jesus went to the house of Matthew to meet his tax collector friends. While He was there, a ruler of the Jews came, fell at Jesus' feet, and said, "My little daughter is at the point of death. Please come and lay your hands on her, and she will be healed." At once Jesus set out to go to his home. The disciples were surprised that Jesus would respond to this proud rabbi, but they went with Him. They were still on the way when a messenger pushed through the crowd and told the rabbi that his daughter was dead. Jesus said to the father, "Only believe, and she will live again." Together they hurried to the rabbi's house, which was filled with mourners. Jesus tried to tell them that death was only a sleep, but they would not listen. So He asked them to leave, went into the girl's bedroom, taking the parents and three disciples with Him. Jesus went up to the bed, took the girl's hand, and softly said, "Little girl, get up!" Instantly, the girl's heart started beating, her eyes opened, and she smiled and sat up. Her parents rushed over and took her in their arms, weeping for joy.

On the way to the ruler's house, there was a sick woman in the crowd along the road who had suffered for twelve years. She had spent all her money on doctors, only to be told that her disease was incurable. When she heard about Jesus, she knew in her heart that if she could only touch His robe, she would be healed. But the crowds were big. Suddenly the opportunity came—Jesus was passing right by her! By faith she reached out and touched His robe, and instantly she was healed and in perfect health. It is not enough just to believe *about* Christ; we must believe *in* Him. The woman praised God and tried to quietly slip away. But Jesus stopped and said, "Who touched Me?" Peter said, "Master, people are pushing and shoving! What do You mean, who touched You?" Jesus said, "I felt power go out of Me." Then He looked toward the woman, who came forward and fell on her knees, trembling. Jesus said, "Daughter, be of good comfort—your faith in Me has made you whole. Go in peace."

Questions: Do you wish you had the kind of faith this woman had? Have you asked God for it?

MARCH 10

"Don't hide your light! Let it shine for all; let your good deeds glow for all to see, so that they will praise your heavenly Father."—Matthew 5:15, 16, TLB

The First Evangelists. As Jesus ministered to the multitudes, the disciples were there, ready to assist Him in whatever needed to be done. They watched for interested hearers, explained the Scriptures to them, and in various ways worked for their spiritual benefit. They taught them what they had learned from Jesus. They not only had to work with Jesus but also had to learn to work alone. Often when in conflict with the enemies of the gospel, they repeated Jesus' words, and when they saw the change in people, they greatly rejoiced.

Calling the twelve disciples to Him, Jesus asked them to go out to the towns and villages two by two. No one was sent out alone, but brother with brother. This way they could pray together and encourage each other. They were not to enter into any controversy with the people or priests over who Jesus was, or whether or not He was the Messiah, but to carry on the same work He did, giving hope to the hopeless. Jesus was never rude, but always spoke the truth with love in His heart. He never brought pain to a sensitive soul, and He did not censure human weakness. Even when He had to speak against hypocrisy, unbelief, and sin, there were tears in His voice. When we fix our eyes on Jesus, He will guide us to share the gospel with tact and gentleness, which is more effective than argument.

Questions: Do you correct others with tears in your eyes when they need to be corrected by you? Are you able to do so?

MARCH 11

"Sir, when did we ever see you hungry and feed you? Or thirsty and give you any-thing to drink?" . . . "When you did it to these my brothers you were doing it to me!"
—Matthew 25:37–40, TLB

Give Ye Them to Eat. Christ had gone with His disciples to a secluded place, where it was quiet, in order to get some rest. But it wasn't long before multitudes came looking for Him. As He sat on the hillside, He saw them coming, and His heart was moved with sympathy. Interrupted as He was and robbed of His rest, He was not impatient but was moved with compassion, because the people were like sheep without a shepherd. Leaving the hillside, He found a place where He could best minister to them.

As they listened to Jesus, it seemed like heaven on earth. This went on all day, and Jesus began to look pale from weariness and hunger. The people hadn't eaten anything either. The disciples urged Jesus to dismiss the people so they could go home and buy something to eat on the way. Jesus said, "You feed them." Philip looked at the thousands of people and responded, "Lord, we only have two hundred pennies among us. How can we buy enough bread to feed all these people?" Andrew spoke up. "There is a lad here who has five small pieces of baked bread and two small fish, but what's that for all these people?" Then Jesus asked His disciples to have the people sit down in groups of fifty or a hundred. He took the little boy's lunch, looked up to heaven, blessed it, and told the disciples to feed the people. The food multiplied in their hands, all the people were fed, and twelve baskets of food were left over. Jesus never worked a miracle just for the sake of it. He always worked a miracle to supply a genuine need.

Questions: No matter how few talents you have, do you bring them to Jesus to have them multiplied in His hands?

MARCH 12

It is better to trust in the Lord than to put confidence in man. It is better to trust in the Lord than to put confidence in princes.—Psalm 118:8, 9, NKJV

A Night on the Lake. After people had eaten the food Christ provided for them by working a miracle, the conviction strengthened that Jesus was the long-looked-for Deliverer. They said to themselves, "If He can multiply food to feed thousands, He can turn our country into a paradise. He can break the power of the Roman occupation, heal our wounded soldiers, supply our armies with food, and give Israel the long-sought-after power." In their enthusiasm they were ready to crown Him king. The disciples joined the crowd, saying that their Master was the rightful heir to the throne of David. Jesus knew that those who would exalt Him today would turn against Him tomorrow. So He gave a command for the crowd to disperse and told the disciples to get into the boat and head home. Never before had Jesus given such an irresistible command, and the crowd couldn't ignore it. They dispersed, and the disciples got into their boat. A sudden violent storm came up, and they did all they could to keep the boat from sinking.

In the meantime, Jesus had gone up into the hills to be alone and pray. From a distance He saw the disciples struggling with the storm and the heavy winds on the lake. When their hearts were subdued and they prayed for help, He went to help them. Jesus came down the hill and walked out on the water. When the disciples saw the figure walking on the water, approaching their boat, they were terrified and thought it was a ghost who was coming to get them. Jesus said, "Don't be afraid; I am Jesus, be of good cheer." Peter was almost beside himself with joy when he heard that. He cried out, "Lord, if that's really You, ask me to come to You." Jesus said, "Come." Keeping his eyes on Jesus, Peter got out of the boat and walked on the water toward Jesus. Then he looked back to his companions with self-satisfaction, taking his eyes off Jesus, and he began to sink. Peter quickly turned back and fixed his eyes on Jesus, reached out his hand, and cried out, "Lord, save me!" Jesus took hold of his hand and pulled him up. Then, walking side by side, they stepped into the boat.

Questions: When Jesus works a miracle in your life, does that make you feel proud and become a show-off? How can you tell about the miracle, feel humble, and give Him the glory?

MARCH 13

"He who rejects you rejects Me, and he who rejects Me rejects Him who sent Me."
—Luke 10:16, NKJV

The Crisis in Galilee. After Jesus and His disciples reached the other side of the lake and docked their boat, the news that He was back spread everywhere. The people who had been fed had walked around the lake and wondered how Jesus had gotten back. They had seen the disciples leave in their boat, and they had seen Jesus go up into the hills to pray. They didn't know that He had walked on the water and gotten into the boat. Jesus said to them, "You seek Me because I fed you." So let us not come to Jesus primarily for the earthly benefits He can give us, but first seek for spiritual food that will endure to eternal life. As the news spread that Jesus was back on this side of the lake, people came from everywhere to hear Him, and they brought their sick to be healed.

But the leaders of the people said, "Isn't this the Jesus we all know? We know His parents, the poor family He belonged to, and where He grew up. He's an uneducated carpenter and not worthy of so much attention." Because of His mysterious birth, they insinuated that He was of doubtful parentage and was therefore an embarrassment to Israel. Jesus did not attempt to explain His mysterious birth and did not answer their questions about where He came from. He was willing to be a Man of no reputation and to take on the status of a servant. Anyone who is close to Jesus will understand much of the mystery of a God-filled heart. He will recognize that it is God's mercy that brings reproof of sin, tests the character, and brings to light the purposes of a person's heart.

Questions: How has Jesus tested your character? Do you remember when and how He did it? How did it come out? Did you benefit by it?

March 14

"You have made the commandment of God of no effect by your tradition."
—Matthew 15:6, NKJV

Tradition. The scribes and Pharisees expected Jesus to come to the temple for the celebration of the Passover, so they set a trap for Him. Jesus knew this, so He avoided meeting with them, but they came and looked for Him. Their traditional practices were designed to protect the Ten Commandments, but those practices ended up being more important than the law. The scribes and Pharisees charged Jesus with disobedience, since they said that He was not upholding their traditions. Jesus made no attempt to defend Himself and His disciples. He told the scribes and Pharisees that they were rejecting God's commandments by holding so tightly to their traditions.

The disciples noticed the anger and rage of the scribes and Pharisees and their messengers. Hoping that Jesus would come to some agreement with these leaders, the disciples said to Jesus, "Couldn't You tell that the Pharisees were offended, after you said what You did?" Jesus answered, "Every plant that My Father did not plant will be rooted up." This meant that the customs and traditions that were so highly valued did not come from the Father. Every human invention that is not from heaven and that has been substituted for the commandments of God will be found worthless in the day when God brings every work into judgment to see whether it is good or bad.

Questions: Did you ever have to defend yourself for doing something you knew was scripturally right? How did you go about it? If you didn't have such an experience, how would you go about it if you did?

MARCH 15

For there is no distinction between the Jew and the Greek, for the same Lord is Lord of all, who richly blesses all who call on him.—Romans 10:12, NET

Barriers Broken Down. After His encounter with the Pharisees, Jesus headed west to the hill country bordering on Phoenicia. Just below were the cities of Tyre and Sidon with their heathen temples, magnificent palaces, markets, and harbors filled with shipping. Looking at all this, Jesus wanted to prepare His disciples for their missionary work. Just then a Canaanite woman crossed the border and cried out, "Have mercy on me, Lord—my daughter is terribly bothered by an evil spirit." Inspired by her mother love for her daughter, she came to Him for help. Christ did not immediately answer this woman's request. He first received her as the Jews would, to show His disciples how heartless Jews would treat her. So Jesus walked on as if He hadn't heard her, but she followed Him and continued her pleading. As a Canaanite, she knew she was looked down on as if she were a dog, so she said, "Even dogs are given crumbs from the master's table." For her daughter's sake, she would not give up.

Then Jesus stopped, turned to her, looked at her with pity and love, and said, "O woman, great is your faith! Your request is granted." From that hour her daughter was no longer bothered by the evil spirits, and the woman returned home, happy in the Lord. The reason Jesus came this far was to help the woman and to give to His disciples an example of what it means to be merciful and kind to everyone. In God's sight, all men and women are of equal value, and there are no barriers that faith cannot penetrate.

Questions: How far would you be willing to travel, if you could, to help someone not related to you? If you couldn't drive that far, would you be willing to go with someone who would drive you?

MARCH 16

"Righteous Father, even if the world does not know you, I know you, and these men know that you sent me."—John 17:25, NET

The Foreshadowing of the Cross. Even as the work of Christ on earth was drawing to a close, He knew it all ahead of time. Before He came to earth and took on humanity, He foresaw the whole length of the path He must travel to save that which was lost. Every pain that tore His heart, every insult that was heaped upon His head, and every privation He was called to endure was open to His view before He stepped down from His throne to clothe His divinity with humanity. The path from the manger to Calvary was all in front of His eyes. He knew it all. He was about to tell His disciples what was coming, but first He went to be alone and prayed that their hearts might be prepared to receive what He was going to tell them. But He decided to ask them a question first. "Who do people say that I am?" Peter answered, "You are the Christ, the Son of the living God."

Jesus answered, "Blessed are you, Peter. Flesh and blood did not reveal this to you, but My Father in heaven. Let Me tell you that this revelation of who I am is the Rock on which I will build My church, and the powers of hell will not prevail against it. Let me give you the keys of the kingdom of heaven—they are the words that I speak to you. They can bind and loose things." The Rock of faith is the living presence of Christ in the church. Upon this the weakest may depend, and those who think themselves the strongest will prove to be spiritually the weakest, unless they trust Christ instead of themselves and make Him their strength and efficiency.

Questions: If someone asked you why you believe in Christ, what would you say? Can you give good reasons? Could you give them now?

March 17

As they watched, his appearance changed so that his face shone like the sun.
—Matthew 17:2, TLB

He Was Transfigured. As evening came, Jesus called three disciples to His side—Peter, James, and John—and led them up a rugged path to a lonely mountainside. The disciples did not ask Jesus where He was going but quietly followed Him. Suddenly, Christ stopped and prayed to the Father, with strong crying and tears, to gain strength for what He had to face. Also, He prayed for His disciples, that in the hour of darkness their faith would not fail. Then He prayed for a manifestation of the glory He had with the Father before He came, in order to give these three disciples a glimpse of the kingdom.

Suddenly the heavens opened, a holy radiance surrounded the Savior, and the divinity within Him flashed through His humanity. Christ stood there in godlike majesty, His face shining as the sun, and His garments as white as the light. The disciples were trying to take all this in as they looked at the Savior's glory. Then Moses appeared, representing the resurrected saints; and Elijah appeared, representing those who will be translated. The disciples thought that Moses and Elijah appeared to announce that the kingdom of Christ was about to be set up on the earth. While they were still looking at this amazing scene, a cloud overshadowed them, and a voice spoke from the cloud of glory, saying, "This is My beloved Son, in whom I am well pleased; listen to Him." They fell to the ground, covering their faces. Then Jesus touched them and said, "Get up, and don't be afraid." They opened their eyes, and the heavenly glory had passed away, along with Moses and Elijah. They were alone with Jesus.

Questions: Are you listening to Jesus? The Father told you to. How do you know when you're listening to Jesus and when you're listening to another voice?

MARCH 18

"I believe; help my unbelief!"—Mark 9:24, NET

Ministry. Jesus and His three disciples had been on the mountain the entire night, and as the sun arose, they descended. The three disciples, still silent and awed by what they had seen, came down with Jesus to join the other disciples. A father came up to Jesus and told Him about his son, who had been suffering from demon possession for a long time. Jesus said, "Bring your son here." When the boy was brought, the evil spirit took hold of the boy and threw him to the ground. He began convulsing in agony, foaming at the mouth and filling the air with unearthly shrieks. Jesus looked at the father and said, "If you believe, all things are possible to him who believes." The father cried out, "Lord, I believe, but help my unbelief." Then Jesus turned and said, "You evil spirit, come out of this boy and don't bother him anymore!" There was an agonizing struggle, and the boy lay there, motionless. The people whispered, "He's dead." But Jesus took the boy by the hand, lifted him up, and presented him to his father in perfect health. They praised the Lord together, and the people were amazed at the power of God.

It is faith that connects us with heaven and gives us the strength we need against the powers of darkness, making us able to resist every temptation, no matter how strong. Look not to self but to Christ. He who healed that boy is still the same mighty Redeemer today. Faith comes from the Word of God. If you need help, go to Jesus and cry out, "Lord, I believe! Help my unbelief!" When you do this, you will never perish—never. But faith must be strengthened by prayer, fasting, and humiliation of heart, empty of self. Faith leads to entire dependence on God and unreserved consecration to Him. Only with the help of the Holy Spirit can the darkness of the world and the evil spirits be overcome. The spiritual obstacles that are piled up by Satan across your path will disappear by the demand evoking the power of Christ.

Questions: How do you meet the spiritual obstacles in your way to keep you from growing in Christ? What are these obstacles?

MARCH 19

He asked them, "What were you discussing out on the road?" But they were ashamed
to answer, for they had been arguing about which of them was the greatest!
—Mark 9:33, 34, TLB

Who Is the Greatest? When Jesus returned to Capernaum in Galilee, His purpose was to instruct the disciples in how to work and help the people. Also, He wanted to prepare them for what was coming. So He told them that He would be going to Jerusalem and there be betrayed into the hands of His enemies. Although the disciples were sad to hear this, a spirit of rivalry was still in their hearts about who would be the greatest in the kingdom. Jesus quietly sat there for an hour, waiting for their hearts to calm down and be ready to receive what He would tell them. So Christ went on to Jerusalem, and they followed. The problem was that the disciples did not understand the nature of Christ's kingdom. The strife for the highest place was the same that had activated the problem in heaven. Lucifer had said, "I will be like the Most High." Had he really desired to be like the Most High, he would have had the spirit of the Most High. Lucifer desired God's power but not His character.

Before honor comes humility. The most childlike disciple is the most successful for God. He who feels most deeply the need of divine aid will plead for it. And the Holy Spirit will give him glimpses of Jesus that will strengthen and uplift the soul. From communion with Christ he will try to bring others to Christ. But when men exalt themselves, the Lord loves them but does not need them. The simplicity and love of a child are the qualities that heaven values. These are the characteristics of real greatness. No one who believes in Christ is weak. But don't put anyone else to shame; let all your effort be to lift others up. Sometimes the need to check evil will call for careful sensitivity. Just as we wish Jesus to deal with us, so He asks us to deal with one another.

Questions: Have you experienced a spirit of rivalry or competition in your life that you did not expect? How did you deal with it? If you haven't experienced it, how would you deal with it if you had to?

MARCH 20

If we confess our sins, He is faithful and just to forgive us our sins and to cleanse us from all unrighteousness.—1 John 1:9, NKJV

Among Snares. Three times a year the Jews were asked to come to Jerusalem for religious celebrations. When Jesus got there, the scribes and Pharisees challenged Jesus' teachings. He said, "My teaching is not Mine, but His that sent Me." He knew that the perception of truth depends not so much upon the mind as upon the heart. If truth could be submitted to reason alone, pride would be no hindrance. Truth is received through the work of grace on the heart. Unless the heart is open, it can receive nothing. When the Pharisees and scribes came, dragging a terrified woman with them and pushing her down in front of Jesus, they accused her of committing adultery. They themselves had led her into sin to set a trap for Jesus.

They said to Jesus, "Moses commanded the death of prostitutes. What do You say?" Jesus said nothing, but stooped down and began writing something in the sand. The scribes and Pharisees went over to see what He was writing, and by divine power, each one saw Jesus writing out their own individual sins. When they saw that, they turned and left. Then Jesus looked at the woman and said, "Woman, where are your accusers? No one? Neither do I condemn you; go, and sin no more." At first the woman sat on the ground in fear, not daring to even look at Jesus. When she noticed her accusers leave and heard the forgiving words of Jesus, she began to cry. Her heart melted, and she threw herself at His feet, sobbing her grateful love and, with bitter tears, confessing her sins. This grateful forgiven woman became one of Jesus' most steadfast and faithful followers.

Questions: Are you grateful to the Lord for forgiving you, whether your sins were great or small? Are you willing to forgive others and accept them, whether their sins are small or great? Are you sure?

MARCH 21

Elijah stepped forward and said to the people, "How long will you sit on the fence?
If the Lord is God, follow him."—1 Kings 18:21, NEB

The Light of Life. While in Jerusalem at the temple, Jesus looked at the two large lampstands, and when in the evening they were lit, He said, "I am the light of the world; he who follows Me shall not walk in darkness but in the light of life." In the revelation of God to His people, light has always been a symbol of His presence. In the words of Christ, "I am the light of the world," He showed His oneness with God. To the Pharisees and priests this seemed to be a proud and arrogant thing for an ordinary-looking man to declare; this they could not tolerate. To their question, "Who are You, really?" Jesus replied, "I've told you. I and My Father are one, and I always do those things that please Him." He did not try to prove His claim as the Messiah but simply told them of His unity with the Father. This offended the Pharisees, so they accused Him of blaspheming God and were ready to stone Him. If their minds had been open to God's love, they would have received Jesus. By not receiving Him, they showed that they had no real connection with God, no matter what they said.

There is no compulsion in the plan of God to force men to believe. Man is left free to choose whom he will serve. In the acceptance and surrender to Christ, there is the highest freedom. It is true that we have no power to free ourselves from Satan's control; but when we desire to be set free from sinning and, in our need, cry out for help, we will be given divine energy from the Holy Spirit to obey the will of God. Subjection to Christ is restoration to the true dignity of man. The law of God is the law of liberty. Almost all suffering results from the transgression of God's law. But Satan has perverted this and has led men to believe that suffering is brought on them directly from God, which is not true. "God so loved the world that He gave His only begotten Son, that whosoever believes in Him should not perish, but have eternal life. God did not send His Son into the world to condemn the world, but that the world through Him might be saved" (John 3:16, 17).

Questions: Does your light reflect your oneness with your heavenly Father? What does it reflect? What do you think it reflects? Does it reflect yourself, your own goodness and commitment?

March 22

All we like sheep have gone astray.—Isaiah 53:6, KJV

The Divine Shepherd. Jesus said, "I am the Good Shepherd, and I lay down My life for the sheep." Jesus always used illustrations from life that people were familiar with. So He spoke about sheep and how caring and protective a shepherd is, representing Himself and His hearers. Also, He compared Himself to the gate that opens and closes the sheep pen. He said, "Anyone who climbs over the fence to get into the pen is a thief or robber. The true shepherd goes in through the door. I am the door; if anyone wants to get into heaven and comes through Me, he will have spiritual life more abundantly, and will be saved." The only door to heaven is Christ, and all who have placed something else in place of Christ are like thieves and robbers, taking away people's eternal life.

A shepherd's life becomes one with the sheep, and a strong and tender attachment unites him to the sheep. However large the flock, the shepherd knows each sheep and the name he has given to it, to which it responds when he calls. And if one sheep strays, is lost, and can't find its way back, the shepherd goes after it until he finds it, takes it in his arms, and brings it back. Jesus is the divine Shepherd. He knows His sheep scattered throughout the world. He says, "You are My flock; I have called you by your name; you are Mine. I have carved you on the palms of My hands." Jesus knows us individually; He knows where we live and knows each member of our family. Every soul is as fully known to Jesus as if he were the only one for whom the Savior died. Jesus cares for each one as if there were not another on earth. He knows our sorrows and sees our tears; He also wept and knows what sadness is. He said, "My Father loves Me, and I am endeared to Him even more for giving My life for you."

Questions: Do you have a strong attachment to and love for God's people? No matter how they act?

MARCH 23

"Father, . . . not as I will, but as You will."—Matthew 26:39, NKJV

The Last Journey From Galilee. During the close of His ministry, there was a change in Jesus' way of working for and ministering to people. He had come to Jerusalem for the Feast of Tabernacles, quietly and unobserved, avoiding any excitement and publicity. Then He withdrew quietly. But now, for His final trip to Jerusalem, He traveled in a most public way, taking the longer route and sending messages ahead to announce His coming, which He had never done before. He set His face to go to Jerusalem and would not change His mind, no matter what would confront Him. The one law of His life was to do His Father's will no matter what. He would endure persecution, rejection, condemnation, and death.

It is not part of Christ's mission to compel men to receive Him. He is ever seeking to win by showing His love. He wants only voluntary service and the willing surrender of the heart. Every human being is the property of God. Christ died to redeem them all; they are all the purchase of His blood. Every knock on the door of the heart by the Savior, when it is not opened, becomes less and less sensitive and interested in being opened. Condemnation in the judgment not only results from the fact that we have sinned and have not repented, but also from the fact that we have neglected heaven-sent opportunities to open our hearts to Jesus and receive the power of the Holy Spirit. Not one who in repentance and faith has claimed the protection of Christ will be allowed by the Savior to be controlled by Satan's power. The Savior stands by the side of every soul who is tempted. With His help there is no such thing as failure, impossibility, or defeat. We can do all things through Christ who strengthens us.

Questions: Are you pressuring people, even your friends or family, to accept Christ, or come back to church when you know they need to? How would you go about it?

MARCH 24

"You shall love your neighbor as yourself."—Mark 12:31, NKJV

The Good Samaritan. With the story of the Good Samaritan, Christ illustrated the meaning of true religion. The Jews had no use for the Samaritans—they were considered enemies. Jesus said, "There was a Jewish man who was on his way from Jerusalem to the city of Jericho. He was attacked, robbed, stripped of his clothes, and left half-dead. A priest came by on his way to Jerusalem, saw the man, and went on. Next, a Levite (a priest helper) came by and also did nothing to help the man. Then a Samaritan came along, saw the man, stopped, bandaged the man's wounds, helped him up, and got him on his donkey. Then he covered the man with his own robe, took him to the closest inn, made sure he got something to eat, and made arrangements for both of them to stay overnight. In the morning the Samaritan told the innkeeper to take care of the Jewish man and to make sure he had recovered before letting him go. Also, he promised the innkeeper that he would pay all the expenses for the man when he came back that way.

Jesus forever answered the question that the Jewish lawyer had asked Him, "Whom should I consider to be my neighbor?" Christ showed that our neighbor does not mean just someone in church, but anyone who needs help, no matter what race or color he is, for everyone is the property of God. The spirit we manifest toward others shows our spirit toward God. Also, in this story Jesus gave us a picture of Himself and His mission. Satan has deceived, bruised, robbed, and ruined many of us, leaving us to perish, but the Savior had compassion on us and our helpless condition. He left His glory to come to our rescue. He found us ready to die, took our case into His own hands, healed our wounds, covered us with His robe of righteousness, opened a refuge of safety for us, and paid the cost for it.

Questions: Are you a good and willing Samaritan? Or do you help others because it's expected of you?

MARCH 25

Search me, O God, and know my heart.—Psalm 139:23, NKJV

Not With Outward Show. More than three years had passed since John the Baptist had announced that the kingdom of God was at hand. Many had misinterpreted it to mean that Jesus would set up His kingdom then, but John meant that the kingdom of God begins in the heart, not as an earthly kingdom. The disciples did not fully understand this until their minds were illuminated by the Holy Spirit at Pentecost, ten days after Jesus had gone back to heaven. It is as true now as it was in the days of the apostles, without the illumination of the Holy Spirit. In the religious world today, there are multitudes who believe and who are working for the setting up of Christ's kingdom as an earthly kingdom. They want to see Christ as the Ruler of the whole world, guiding the decisions of councils and courts of justice. But not through the decisions of courts, councils, or legislative assemblies is the kingdom of Christ established, but by the planting of Christ's nature in the hearts of people through the work of the Holy Spirit.

Questions: Has God's kingdom rooted itself in your heart? How loyal are you to His kingdom? Are you as loyal to God's kingdom as a veteran is to his country?

MARCH 26

"Whoever humbles himself as this little child is the greatest
in the kingdom of heaven."—Matthew 18:4, NKJV

Blessing the Children. Jesus loved the little children. The grateful praise from their lips was music to His ears and refreshed His spirit. Wherever He went, His gentle, kindly manner won the love and confidence of the children. But the disciples thought that Jesus' work was too important for Him to stop and bless the children and that the children were too young to benefit from the words of Jesus. One mother left home with her child to find Jesus, and on the way, several other mothers joined her with their children. When the disciples saw them, they were ready to send them away. But Jesus said, "Let them come to Me; don't stop them, for of such is the kingdom of God." He took the children in His arms, laid His hands on them, and blessed them.

If we want our children to have the tender spirit of Jesus, we must encourage generous, loving impulses in them by our example. As you win their confidence, it will be easy to teach them about the great love that Jesus has for all of us. Don't let your unkind character misrepresent Jesus. As the Holy Spirit moves on the hearts of children, cooperate with His work. Nothing can give Jesus greater joy than for children to give themselves to Him in the bloom and freshness of their years. Jesus looks on them with heartfelt longing. His heart is drawn out to them, not only to the best-behaved children, but to those who by inheritance have objectionable traits of character.

Questions: What example are you to children? Would they want to be like you when they grow up? If they do, that is good. If not, why not? What's wrong?

MARCH 27

Jesus wept. Then the Jews said, "See how He loved him!"—John 11:35, 36, NKJV

Lazarus, Come Forth! Visiting the home of Lazarus, Jesus had always found rest. He longed for human tenderness, courtesy, and appreciation, and here He found pure friendship. Lazarus' two sisters, Mary and Martha, loved Jesus. One day, after Jesus had rested, He said goodbye and left the house. It wasn't long afterward that Lazarus was stricken with a sudden illness. His sister quickly sent a message to Jesus, telling Him that Lazarus was sick. But the messenger brought a message from Jesus that this sickness was not unto death. So the sisters clung to the hope that their brother would get well. Two days later, Jesus said to his disciples, "Come, let's go. Lazarus is sleeping, and I want to wake him up." The disciples said, "If he's sleeping, he's doing better. So why go?" But Lazarus had died. When Martha heard that Jesus was coming, she hurried to meet Him and said, "Lord, if You had been here, my brother would not have died." Jesus looked into her sorrowful eyes and said, "Your brother will live again." She said, "I know—he will be raised at the resurrection in the last days." Jesus responded, "I am the resurrection. Do you believe that?" Then Martha left and quickly got Mary. When Jesus saw the two sisters weeping, He wept and groaned in sorrow.

Then He asked them to show Him where Lazarus was buried. When they got there, Jesus asked the men to roll away the huge stone from the opening of the cave. Martha said, "Lord, don't do that. Our brother has been dead for four days, and his body already stinks." Jesus insisted, "Roll away the stone!" Then He looked up to heaven and said, "Father, I thank You that You always hear Me." He said this so that the people there would understand that it was by faith and prayer, in cooperation with His Father, that He worked His miracles. Then Jesus spoke loudly, His voice penetrating the ears of the dead, "Lazarus, come out!" There was a movement in the tomb, and out came Lazarus, his eyes beaming with intelligence. They untied him, and he threw himself at Jesus' feet. And while family and friends were rejoicing, Jesus quietly withdrew.

Questions: Have you thought of what it will be like to see your loved ones, family members, and friends raised from the dead? How is this possible? Can you explain it to someone? Are you sure the reason you give is the right one for them?

MARCH 28

"Blessed are you when people insult you . . . and say all kinds of evil things about you falsely on account of me."—Matthew 5:11, NET

Priestly Plottings. Bethany, where Lazarus lived, was not too far from Jerusalem, and the news of his resurrection spread everywhere. The Jewish leaders soon had the facts from those who had been there. So they immediately called a meeting to decide what to do. Even though the Sadducees were not favorable toward Christ, they were not full of hatred for Him as the Pharisees were. Still, they too were alarmed, because they did not believe in the resurrection of the dead. They scientifically reasoned that it would be impossible for a dead body to be brought back to life. But after the resurrection of Lazarus, they decided that Christ should be put to death. Now, the Pharisees did believe in the resurrection, but they wanted to get back at Jesus for not approving their religious practices and for condemning them for their religious pride. So at this meeting they passed a law that anyone who professes faith in Jesus should be expelled from worships at the synagogue. Previously, Nicodemus and Joseph of Arimathea had prevented a condemnation of Jesus, so they were not invited to this meeting.

The high priest, who was in charge of the meeting, said that even if Jesus were innocent of all the accusations, He needed to be put out of the way because He was a troublemaker. Jesus was weakening the authority of the priests and rulers and standing in the way of their relationship to the Romans, which would affect the well-being of the nation. It is better that one man be killed than the whole nation suffer, he said. The council received the words of Caiaphas, the high priest, as the words of God, and they decided to put Christ to death at the first chance they had. They regarded themselves as patriots, upholding and defending their country. Jesus knew that this was not yet the time for Him to die, so He quietly withdrew from Jerusalem, taking His disciples with Him.

Questions: Have you ever been called a troublemaker? Why? How would you feel if you were accused of being a troublemaker when you know that you haven't been one?

March 29

For whom the Lord loves He corrects, just as a father the son in whom he delights.
—Proverbs 3:12, NKJV

The Law of the New Kingdom. Soon it was time for the Passover, and Jesus returned to Jerusalem with His disciples. In His heart was the peace of perfect oneness with the Father as He pressed toward the place of sacrifice. The disciples were amazed at their Master's courage, but they were afraid of what might happen. He gathered them together and opened to them the betrayal and suffering that awaited Him. He told them that He would be turned over to the Romans, mocked, spit on, scourged, and crucified, but that on the third day He would rise from the grave. As the disciples listened, they could not understand all this and were afraid. With patience and love He taught them and calmed their fears.

John and his brother, James, loved Jesus very much and wanted to be closest to Him in His kingdom. Their mother was a devoted follower of Christ and had ministered to Him. With a mother's love for her sons, she wanted Jesus to give them an honored place in the new kingdom. Jesus dealt tenderly with them, not rebuking their ambition to be above the other disciples, for He read their hearts. He knew that their love for Him was not just human love but was an outflowing of His own redeeming love for them. He would not rebuke them but would purify their hearts still more.

Questions: When you show your love to people, is it a natural outflowing of your heart for people, or is it the outflowing of the love of Jesus in your heart? How can you know the difference?

MARCH 30

"Bear fruits worthy of repentance."—Matthew 3:8, NKJV

Zacchaeus. On His way to Jerusalem, Jesus passed through the busy city of Jericho, with a population of many different people, including Roman officials, soldiers, and tax and customs collectors. Many caravans were also on their way to the Passover celebrations at this time. The people had heard about the raising of Lazarus and were eager to see Jesus. One of the chief tax and customs collectors was Zacchaeus, a Jew, who was hated by his countrymen. His wealth came from injustice and the misuse of his authority. Yet this wealthy customs official was not the hardened man he seemed to be. He had heard about Jesus and wanted to see Him. Zacchaeus had also heard about John the Baptist and his call to repentance. He knew the Scriptures and was convicted that his dishonesty was wrong. But hope bloomed in his heart, because, had not Matthew, one of Jesus' disciples, also been a tax collector?

The streets were crowded, so Zacchaeus, a small man, climbed up into a tree near where Jesus would be passing. He kept looking with eager eyes to see Him. Suddenly the crowd stopped below the tree, and Jesus looked up at Zacchaeus, who could hardly believe it, and said, "Zacchaeus, come down. I want to go to your house today." Zacchaeus was overwhelmed, but he got down and guided Jesus to his house. Before this, the Holy Spirit had already been working on his heart. In the house he promised Jesus that he would make things right and give back to people what he had overcharged them in taxes. No repentance is genuine without a reformation in action. Believing in Christ is not a cover-up of unconfessed sins and a continued sinful life. Zacchaeus accepted Jesus not only as a passing guest in his home but as One to permanently abide in his soul.

Questions: How honest are you when you pay your taxes? Or, if you've made a mistake in calculating them, how do you rectify it? Isn't being honest with the government being honest with God?

MARCH 31

"Why are you criticizing her?"—Matthew 26:10, TLB

The Feast at Simon's House. Simon was one of the few Pharisees who had openly become one of Christ's followers. He accepted Jesus as a teacher and hoped that He might be the promised Messiah, but he had not accepted Jesus as his Savior. Simon had been healed of leprosy by Jesus, so in gratitude he invited Him and His disciples to his home, including Lazarus. People expected Lazarus to tell them what it was like to die and be raised to life again. They were surprised that he told them nothing. Martha, the sister of Lazarus, was there serving the people, and Mary was sitting at the feet of Jesus, listening to everything He said. She heard Him talking about His approaching death, and she wanted to honor Him while He was still alive. So she knelt down by Jesus, poured the expensive ointment on His feet, mixed it with the dropping of her tears, and then wiped them with her long, flowing hair. The room was filled with the smell of the sweet ointment.

Judas was upset with all this. He thought it was a waste of money to use such expensive ointment on Jesus' feet. He said to himself, "That ointment could have been sold and the money kept to help the poor." However, as treasurer of the money people gave to the disciples for the poor, Judas would keep some of it for himself. The disciples didn't know about this, and they trusted Judas. Then Jesus spoke up for everyone to hear and said, "Mary has done a good thing. She has anointed My body for burial. You can always feed the poor." As Jesus continued talking to His disciples, Judas was convinced that Jesus knew about his planned betrayal. As the disciples listened to Jesus, they could tell that His heart was grieved over their lack of gratitude for all He had already done for them.

Questions: Do you realize God's heart is sad when you don't express your gratitude to Him for what He has done? How would you feel after you did a lot to help someone and they didn't even thank you?

APRIL 1

I saw heaven opened, and . . . He has on His robe and on His thigh a name written:
KING OF KINGS AND LORD OF LORDS.
—Revelation 19:11,16, NKJV

The King Cometh. Five hundred years before Christ, the prophet Zechariah had foretold the coming of the King to Israel. Planning to ride into Jerusalem on a young donkey, as the kings of Israel did when they first came to the throne, Jesus sent His disciples to find a mother donkey and its colt and to ask the owner to lend it. At His birth, Jesus in the manger was dependent on the hospitality of strangers who lent a stall as a resting place for Him and Mary. Now He was again dependent on a stranger's kindness, this time for an animal to ride on. As He rode into Jerusalem as did the kings of old, multitudes greeted Him with happy hearts and singing. Unable to welcome Him with costly gifts, they spread their outer robes as a carpet for Him to ride on. It was His purpose to publicly present Himself as their Redeemer and call their attention to His sacrifice that was to crown His mission to a fallen world.

Before Him was Jerusalem with the gleaming temple, which was then one of the wonders of the world. Jesus stopped and looked at the temple, and the crowd got quiet. As they looked at Jesus, His face seemed sad, His eyes were filled with tears, and a cry of anguish burst from His quivering lips as if from a broken heart. Israel's King was in tears. In the distance He saw the hill called Calvary on which He was to be crucified. No wonder the Savior wept in agony, not only because of Calvary but also over the doomed city. One soul is of more value than worlds in space, but here was a whole nation to be lost. No wonder Jesus cried. As He rode down from the Mount of Olives toward the city, there was no welcome for Him there, and the rulers came out to disperse the crowd. But the ride of Christ into Jerusalem was only a shadow of what His second coming will be, surrounded by angels and being welcomed by His rejoicing people.

Questions: Would you want to miss that day, the day to see Jesus coming surrounded by angels? What can you do to make sure you're there? Christ has a part, and so do you. What is your part?

APRIL 2

Obey God because you are his children; don't slip back into your old ways.
—1 Peter 1:14, TLB

The Temple Cleansed Again. At the beginning of His ministry, Christ had driven out of the temple those who were defiling it. Now at the close of His ministry, He had to do it again, because things had gotten worse. There was buying and selling, exchanging of money, dishonesty, and corruption. Jesus knew that He had to act. Divinity flashed through His humanity, which had never been seen in Him before. Every sound was hushed, and there was such a deep silence that it seemed almost unbearable. Jesus spoke with power and said, "My house is called a house of prayer, but you turned it into a marketplace full of thieves. Get out of here, and take your things with you!"

The rulers spoke up and asked Him, "By what authority do you claim to do this?" Jesus answered with a question of His own: "By what authority did John the Baptist preach, his own or by the authority of God?" If they said, "By his own," the people would turn against them. If they said, "By God's authority," then Jesus would say, "Why didn't you listen to him?" So they said, "We can't answer Your question." Jesus said, "Then I'm not going to answer your question. But let me ask you another question. A certain man had two sons. He asked the first son to go and work in the vineyard. The son said, 'I don't want to.' Afterwards, he repented and went. Then the man asked his second son to go and work in the vineyard. This son said, 'Sure, I'll go,' but he didn't. Which one of these two sons did what their father wanted them to do?" The rulers said, "The first one, of course." Jesus responded, "Why don't you listen to God and do what He says?"

Questions: How do you feel about the church? Is it primarily a place of worship and prayer for you or primarily a place of fellowship and socializing?

APRIL 3

For the Lord's sake, obey every law of your government.—1 Peter 2:13, TLB

Controversy. The priests and rulers could not refute what Christ had said. They were only more determined to trap Him. So they sent some young Pharisees to talk to Him, whom they thought Jesus would not identify as being Pharisees. They started by saying, "Master, we know that what you teach is right. What do you think? Should we pay taxes to Caesar?" They expected either a yes or no answer. Jesus responded, "Show me a coin." They did, and He said, "Whose image is on the coin?"

They said, "Caesar's." Jesus said, "Give to Caesar what belongs to Caesar, and give to God the obedience and respect that belongs to Him."

Then the Sadducees raised the question of the resurrection. They reasoned that if there is a resurrection and we take the same bodies to heaven, then all the earthly things would continue there as they are here. That's why they denied that there is a resurrection. Next, a lawyer came to Jesus and asked, "Which is the greatest commandment of all that God gave us?" Christ said, "The first one is that we love God with all our heart and soul, and the second one is that we love our neighbor as ourselves." By saying this, Jesus summarized all of the Ten Commandments. The first four have to do with our relationship with God, and the last six have to do with our relationship to man. All ten together make one whole.

Questions: Every orderly family has to have rules such as: "If you drop it, pick it up; if you dirty it, you need to wash it." God's family throughout the universe also has ten rules. Do you consider yourself a member of God's family?

APRIL 4

Let them praise Your great and awesome name—He is holy.
—Psalm 99:3, NKJV

Woe on the Pharisees. It was the last day of Christ's teaching in the temple, and He warned the priests and Pharisees what would happen if they persisted in their evil ways. The people were charmed by Jesus' teaching, but they were also greatly perplexed by what He said to the priests and Pharisees, because they respected and looked up to them. The people also marveled that these men would not believe in Jesus when His teachings were so plain and simple. The priests and Pharisees loved to be called "Rabbi" or "Master." Jesus told the people that they were not to give any man such a title, indicating his control of their conscience or faith. This applies to us today when we call a man "Reverend," as if he is spiritually over us. Jesus said, "Only one is your spiritual Master, and that is Christ." The Scripture, speaking about God, says, "Holy and reverend is His name" (Psalm 111:9, KJ21).

The Pharisees respected the graves and tombs of the prophets and said to each other, "If we had lived back then, we would not have killed the prophets; they were God's servants." This should show us the power of Satan to deceive, for these same men were making plans to kill Jesus. By their rejection of the Savior and their turning Him over to Pilate, demanding His crucifixion, they would soon reap the hatred that they sowed, the destruction of the temple and the city of Jerusalem by the Romans.

Questions: Titles are needed for identification of responsibilities. If you've earned one or have been given one, does it make you feel proud, or does it humble you and make you more dependent on God?

APRIL 5

"Everyone who asks receives, and he who seeks finds, and to him who knocks it will be opened."—Luke 11:10, NKJV

In the Outer Court. There were some Greek men who came to Jerusalem to worship, and they said to Philip, "Sir, we would like to meet Jesus." Philip went and told Andrew, and together they went and told Jesus. When the Savior heard the request of the Greeks, His face lit up. He could sense the hunger of their hearts for salvation. The Greeks had heard about Christ's triumphal entry into Jerusalem and His supposed taking of the throne of Israel. They wanted to know the truth about all this. So Jesus went to the outer court of the temple where the non-Jews worshiped, met the Greeks, and had a personal interview with them. This was Thursday, and He knew they would soon see Him convicted as a criminal and nailed to the cross. But through the cross the dividing line between Jews and non-Jews would be broken down, and people from all over the world could be saved through Him.

As Jesus sat and talked to the Greeks, the work of redemption passed through His mind, from the time it was first laid out in heaven to what was soon to happen, that He would have to die. He said, "Unless a grain of wheat falls into the ground and dies, it cannot produce grain. He who loves his current selfish way of life and doesn't want to change will lose it. But he who dies to self will spring up with a new life that will be eternal. If anyone wants to serve Me, let Him follow Me, and wherever I am, there he will be, and My Father will honor him."

Questions: In God's sight there is no dividing line between people, and none are of more value than others. Is there such a dividing line in your mind? If so, what can you do to erase it?

APRIL 6

"But the person who endures to the end will be saved."—Matthew 24:13, NET

On the Mount of Olives. As Jesus left the temple, He said to the priests and rulers, "Your temple will be left to you desolate." This struck terror in their hearts. The disciples heard it and pointed out to Jesus the beauty and strength of the temple, its massive stones and huge walls, which could never be destroyed. Jesus said with sadness, "I see it all; the temple is indeed beautiful and strong, but the day will come when not one stone will be left sitting on another." Then Jesus led the way up to the Mount of Olives, and when the disciples were alone with Him, Peter, John, James, and Andrew came to Him and asked, "When will these things happen to the temple? Will this be a sign of Your coming and the end of the world?" Jesus didn't group together the destruction of the temple with the end of the world, but left the disciples to study out the meaning for themselves of what He was about to say to them.

What Jesus taught them that day was not only for the disciples but for everyone. Before answering the disciples' question, the first thing that Jesus said was, "Don't be deceived. Many false teachers will appear and deceive many. They will work miracles and lead many astray. You will hear of wars and rumors of wars, but don't be troubled; these things must happen, but the end is not yet. Nation will fight against nation; there will be famines, pestilences, and earthquakes in various places, but the end is not yet. Many will stumble, fall, and leave the faith they once had." These are some of the warnings He gave about the dangers that will precede His second coming. The final crisis is gradually stealing upon us, and the hour of probation to decide for Christ is fast closing.

Questions: How will you respond when you see miracles? Do they convince you that the person doing them can be trusted? How do you test such things?

April 7

*May the Lord direct your hearts into the love of God and into
the patience of Christ.*—2 Thessalonians 3:5, NKJV

The Least of These My Brethren. When Jesus returns in glory, and all the angels with Him, He will separate those who are His from those who are not and will gather His people together to be with Him. Angels are sent to help His people. They are passing through the whole earth to comfort the sorrowing, to protect those in danger, and to win the hearts of men to Christ. Not one is neglected or passed by. God has equal care for all the souls He has created. We don't have to go to the Holy Land to visit the places where Jesus lived to walk in His footsteps. By doing what Jesus did and living as He did, we are walking in His steps. Love to our fellow man, no matter how educated or uneducated, no matter how rich or poor, is demonstrating the love of God to them. It was to implant this love, to make us children of one family, that the King of glory came to be with us. His parting words were, "Love one another as I have loved you." When we love others as He loves us, then His purpose is accomplished, and we are fitted for heaven, for we have heaven in our hearts.

Questions: Can you love others as Jesus loves you? If not, how can you get to be that way? What do you have to do?

APRIL 8

"I too, am a servant of Jesus as you are, and as your brothers."
—Revelation 22:9, TLB

A Servant of Servants. The whole life of Christ was one of unselfish service. He came not to be served, but to serve. It was the time of the Passover celebration, and in the evening, Jesus wanted to be alone with His disciples. This would be the last Passover evening meal He would share with them. Previous Passovers were always times of calm joy, highly valued by the disciples. But this time Jesus was troubled, for He knew that it would only be a matter of hours before He was arrested and that the disciples would desert Him. He knew that after His arrest, He would have to go through the most humiliating process that a criminal has to go through, and He was aware of the cruelty of those He had come to save. However, this evening He was not thinking about Himself, but His disciples. Jesus looked into their faces, and there were moments of silence; He appeared to be waiting. They were still hoping that Christ would assert His power and were also thinking about who would be the greatest in His kingdom. If there was to be a highest place, Judas was determined to have it.

The custom at the Passover was for people to wash the dirt and dust of their feet before worship. The pitcher of water and basin were there for them to use. But no servant was present to do the washing, and the disciples, giving in to pride, each refused to humble himself to do the job of a servant. So Jesus did the job. He got up, took the towel, the water, and the basin and then got down to wash the disciples' feet, even the feet of Judas. Jesus' last act for them was to be their servant. When Jesus came to wash Peter's feet, Peter refused and offered to wash Jesus' feet. Jesus said, "If you don't let Me wash your feet and make you clean, you can have no part with Me." Peter said, "Lord, if that's the case, wash my head and hands too." Jesus said, "That's not necessary." Now Judas, seeing Jesus humble Himself like this, was offended. So he decided that nothing would be gained by being one of Jesus' disciples, and he made up his mind that he would betray his Master.

Questions: Can you imagine washing the dirty feet of the person you know will have a part in having you falsely arrested and executed? How much would it take to do it? Would you do it?

APRIL 9

I remember thee upon my bed, and meditate on thee in the night watches.
—Psalm 63:6, KJV

In Remembrance of Me. It was time to eat the Passover meal and to remember Israel's deliverance and freedom from captivity in Egypt. As Jesus ate the Passover meal with His disciples, He instituted in its place the communion service as a remembrance of His great sacrifice to deliver people from the captivity of Satan. It is to be observed by His followers everywhere until He comes the second time in power and glory. As they ate in silence, Jesus said, "This night one of you will betray Me." This amazed everyone. Who would betray the Savior? Fear and distrust came over them. They didn't trust their own hearts, so one after another asked Jesus, "Lord, is it I?" Judas asked no questions and said nothing. His silence made all the others look at him. Finally, he asked, "Lord, is it I?" Jesus answered, "You said it." Surprised at his exposure, Judas got up and hurriedly left the room. This was his last chance to repent, but when his plan was exposed, he became even more determined to carry it out.

The communion service is not to be a time of sorrow, with people thinking about their sins and their past experiences. They are not to call to mind the differences between them and others. All these things were to be made right during the time of the footwashing. Now it was time not to stand in the shadow of the cross, but in its saving light. When our duties seem hard and our burdens heavy, remember that Jesus endured the cross for you, because He loves you and wants to save you. We are never to forget what Jesus did for us. His sacrifice is the center of our hope; on this we must fix our faith. We owe not only our spiritual life, but our earthly life to the death of Jesus. Every loaf of bread is stamped with the love of Christ, and every meal we have is because of His willingness to give us life, that one day we should live forever.

Questions: Do you see your meals as a gift from heaven paid for by Calvary? When you bless the food, do you bless Him for it as well?

APRIL 10

For all the promises of God in him are yea, and in him Amen,
unto the glory of God.—2 Corinthians 1:20, KJV

Let Not Your Heart Be Troubled. Judas had left the room, and Jesus was alone with the eleven remaining disciples. He was ready to talk to them about His death, but He decided to first talk to them about His mission. It was His joy to know that all His humiliation and suffering would glorify His Father. The Savior's words were full of hope. He said, "Let not your hearts be troubled. You believe in God, believe also in Me. In My Father's house there are many mansions; if it were not so, I would have told you. I will go to prepare a place for you, and I will come back to take you home to be with Me, where I will be." While He was gone, they were to build characters fit for those heavenly mansions. There are not many ways to heaven—there is only one way, through Christ, and He would not forsake them.

Every humble prayer is heard by Jesus in heaven. It may not be beautifully expressed, but if the heart is in it, it will reach the heart of Jesus, and He will present it to the Father without one awkward, stammering word. He knows that the path of sincerity and honesty is not free from difficulty, but each difficulty is a call to prayer. Christ's followers are of great value to Him. He is disappointed when they place a low value on themselves. On the other hand, He is pleased when they make the highest demands on Him to help them obey and glorify His name. There are many who believe and talk about Christ and about the Holy Spirit, yet they receive no benefit from it. They do not surrender their hearts to the Holy Spirit. They want to use the Holy Spirit's power to do what they want to do or to have things done for them, instead of letting the Holy Spirit guide and direct things.

Questions: Do you want to use the Holy Spirit to do great things for God, or are you willing to submit to the Holy Spirit and let Him direct you to do things for God, great or small? Are you praying for that willingness?

APRIL 11

"Greater love has no one than this, than to lay down one's life for his friends."
—John 15:13, NKJV

Gethsemane. In company with His disciples, Jesus slowly made his way to the Garden of Gethsemane. His body swayed as He walked, and twice He would have fallen, had they not supported Him. At the entrance of the garden, Jesus asked his disciples to stay there and pray for Him. Then He took Peter, James, and John, went a little distance to a more secluded area, and told them to stay there and pray for Him. He went a little farther, threw Himself on the ground and prayed, "O, My Father, if possible, take this cup of pain away from Me; nevertheless, not My will but Your will be done." He staggered back to the three disciples and found them sleeping. This happened three times. The mighty angel who stands in the presence of God came down to strengthen Him, and Jesus went back to the three disciples and said, "You can sleep now if you want; they are on their way to arrest Me."

This woke all the disciples up, and they followed Him to meet the mob. No marks of His agony were on His face as He stepped forward. He asked them whom they were looking for; they said, "Jesus of Nazareth." He said, "I am the one, so you can let the others go." As He said this, the angel moved between Jesus and the soldiers, and they all fell down. When they got back on their feet, Judas walked up to Jesus and kissed Him on both cheeks. Jesus looked at Judas and said, "Are you betraying Me with a kiss?" Then the soldiers, stepped forward, and tied the hands of Jesus. When Peter saw this, he drew his short sword and swung it at the high priest's servant. The man ducked, but the sword sliced off his ear. Then Jesus said to the soldiers, "Just a minute." He released His hands, reached out, touched the man's head, healed the wound, and gave him a new ear. Then Christ looked at the priests and elders who were there, and said to them, "You could have arrested Me when I was teaching in the Temple. Why did you have to come out here at night to secretly arrest Me?" The disciples wondered why Jesus didn't use His power to save Himself. But when they saw that He did not resist His arrest, they all left Him and ran.

Questions: When things don't go as you would like them to go, do you stop praying, go your own way, and do your own thing that you see is best for you?

APRIL 12

It is impossible for God to lie. . . . [It's] an anchor to the soul,
both sure and steadfast.—Hebrews 6:18, 19, NKJV

Before Annas and the Court of Caiaphas. The soldiers hurried Jesus past the olive groves and through the streets of the sleeping city to the court of Annas, the retired high priest and head of the priestly family. He was the one who had to see Jesus first, and then Jesus would have to be seen by Caiaphas, the high priest in office, before being tried by the Sanhedrin, the Jewish Supreme Court. But only Pilate, the Roman governor, could pronounce the death sentence. The first hearing with Annas was called at night to show that Jesus had been secretly undermining the nation. Christ denied these accusations. It seemed to one of the officers that Jesus was being disrespectful to the high priest, and he slapped Him across the face, followed by abuse and insults. By now it was morning, and Annas ordered Jesus to be taken to the court of Caiaphas.

As Caiaphas questioned Jesus, the thought came to him that Jesus might be the true Messiah, but he quickly banished the thought and proceeded with the trial. The Supreme Court was divided, and finally Caiaphas called in false witnesses, which he had bribed, to accuse Jesus of wanting to destroy the Temple which the Romans had built. Finally, Caiaphas said, "In the name of God, I ask You whether You are the Son of God." To this Jesus could not keep silent, because it called into question His relationship to the Father. So He said, "One day you will see the Son of Man sitting next to God." When Caiaphas heard that, he stood up and tore his robe as a sign of condemnation, followed by another wave of abuse and mockery. Even the priests and rulers forgot their dignity and abused Jesus with foul language. Those in the courtroom shouted, "He is guilty; put Him to death!" So early in the morning, He was taken to Pilate for final review and the death sentence.

Questions: How much abuse are you willing to take for Christ? Jesus could have stopped it, but didn't. He took this pre-crucifixion abuse for you because He loves you, didn't He?

APRIL 13

For there will be no prospect for the evil man;
the lamp of the wicked will be put out.—Proverbs 24:20, NKJV

Judas. The history of Judas presents the sad ending of a life that might have been honored by God. His character was laid open to the world for what he had done to betray Jesus. Judas was an intelligent man but naturally had a strong love for money, which overbalanced his love for Christ. He sold his Lord for thirty pieces of silver, the price of a slave, and he became a slave to his own desires. Judas felt in his own heart the evidence of Christ's love for him. He was drawn to the Savior and had in his heart a desire to be changed. The Lord gave him a place among the twelve, trusted him to do the work of an evangelist, and gave him power to heal the sick. Judas never came to the point of surrendering himself fully to Christ and coming under the divine molding. He retained his own judgment and opinions, and held on to his disposition to criticize and accuse. In his own estimation, he was an honor to the cause of Christ.

The turning point came when Judas realized that Christ was talking to the people in the Temple about spiritual food, not promising them prosperity and an abundance of worldly goods. From that time on, he expressed doubts about the Savior's mission. He repeated the arguments of the priests and Pharisees against Jesus and introduced texts of Scripture that had no connection with the truths that Christ was presenting. All this was done in such a way as to make it appear that he was being conscientious and supportive. His purpose was to teach Christ a lesson and force Him to show His power and deliver Himself, then Judas would get the credit for having placed Christ on the throne of Israel. In amazement, he saw that Christ made no attempt to deliver Himself. Judas could not endure the torture of his guilty conscience any longer. In the courtroom he threw himself at the feet of Jesus, confessed his sin, and pleaded with Jesus to deliver Himself. But Jesus knew that Judas was not really repenting or wanting to change, just being outwardly sorry for what he did. Then Judas rushed from the courtroom, shouting, "Too late! Too late!" And he went out and hanged himself.

Questions: Are you willing to do anything to uplift Christ, even if it means lying a little sometimes? Do you enjoy being in the limelight when speaking for Christ?

APRIL 14

Just then, as he was presiding over the court, Pilate's wife sent him this message: "Leave that good man alone; for I had a terrible nightmare concerning him last night."
—Matthew 27:19, TLB

In Pilate's Judgment Hall. Pilate, the Roman governor, was called out of bed early in the morning to settle this demonstration of the Jews, demanding justice. When the Roman soldiers brought Jesus into the judgment hall, Pilate looked at Him with unfriendly eyes. He determined to treat this prisoner with severity and settle this case as quickly as possible. But when Pilate carefully looked at Jesus, he had never seen a prisoner that had such goodness and nobility. This made a favorable impression on Pilate, who had heard about the miracles that Jesus had done. He demanded of the Jews what accusation they had against this Prisoner. The Jewish leaders knew that Jesus had to be accused as a political offender in order for Pilate to try Him. So they accused Jesus of telling the people not to pay taxes to Caesar, because He was the new King of Israel. Pilate turned to Jesus and asked, "Are you the King of the Jews?" Jesus replied, "You said it." When Pilate learned that Jesus was from Galilee, Pilate sent Him to Herod to be tried. Herod questioned Jesus, let his soldiers abuse Him, and then sent Him back to Pilate.

Then the Jewish rulers demanded that Pilate do something, so he decided to have Jesus scourged and then let Him go. The soldiers took Jesus away, stripped Him naked, abused Him, scourged Him, and took Him back to Pilate covered with blood. When the Jewish rulers saw Jesus, it did not create any sympathy in them, and they demanded His crucifixion. Then Pilate tried another way to release Jesus and said, "I'll give you a choice: Do you want me to release Barabbas or Jesus?" Now, Barabbas had been arrested by the Romans and given the death sentence, because he had stirred up a rebellion against Rome and presented himself as the Messiah, with plans to set himself up as ruler. But the Jewish leaders and the people did the unbelievable—they shouted for the release of Barabbas and the crucifixion of Jesus. So Pilate turned to Jesus and said, "Forgive me; I tried, but I cannot save You." Then he ordered Jesus to be scourged again and crucified.

Questions: Have you ever stood before a judge in all innocence waiting for his decision which could go against you and end in your execution? Oh, my, what Jesus went through for you, for us!

APRIL 15

I have been crucified with Christ, and it is no longer I who live,
but Christ lives in me.—Galatians 2:20, NET

The Crucifixion. The news of Christ's condemnation had spread throughout Jerusalem, and people from all levels of society made their way to Calvary. Now the heavy wooden cross that was meant for Barabbas was placed on the bleeding shoulders and back of Jesus. Because of the several times that Jesus had been scourged, He had lost so much blood and was so weak that He could not carry the heavy cross and fell fainting to the ground. The Roman soldiers had to find someone to help Jesus. There was a Jew named Simon had come to Jerusalem just as Jesus was being taken to Calvary, and the Roman soldiers ordered him to carry the cross. Arriving at Calvary, Jesus and the two followers of Barabbas were tied and nailed to the crosses. The crosses were lifted up and allowed to fall into the holes prepared for them. The jolt was agonizing. At the top of Jesus' cross, Pilate ordered a sign to read, "Jesus of Nazareth, King of the Jews." The priests and rulers complained, because they cried out, "We have no king but Caesar." Pilate said, "What I have written, I have written."

During a crucifixion, it was permitted to let each prisoner have a drug for pain. Jesus was allowed the same, but when He tasted it, He spit it out, for He realized that it would deaden His mind. Now, of the two men who were crucified with Jesus, one cursed Jesus, but the other gave His heart to Christ and asked to be saved and taken into His kingdom, which Jesus promised to do. As Jesus looked below the cross, he saw His mother and the disciple John and said to them, "Mother, from now on, John is your son. And John, please take care of my mother," which John gladly agreed to do. Jesus felt the terrible weight of sin being placed on Him as the Father withdrew Himself from His Son. This broke His heart. In the thick darkness that covered Calvary, Jesus cried out, "Father, Father, why have You forsaken Me?" Suddenly the darkness surrounding the cross lifted, and in a trumpet-like voice, Jesus cried out, "It is finished! Father, into Your hands I place My life!" Then He bowed His head and died.

Questions: Do you praise the Lord that your salvation has been paid for? How often? Do you do it daily or just once in a while? Don't ever forget that you have been set free from Satan's enslavement.

APRIL 16

For you are bought with a price; therefore glorify God in your body and in your spirit, which are God's.—1 Corinthians 6:20, NKJV

It Is Finished. All heaven triumphed because of the death of Christ and the defeat of Satan. It was for us, as well as for the angels and the unfallen worlds, that the great work of redemption was accomplished. The cross tore away Satan's disguise, and he could no longer tempt the angels, for the last link between them had been broken. But Satan was not then destroyed, because the angels and the unfallen worlds still did not fully understand all that was involved in the great controversy between good and evil. God's principles of governing the universe had to be more fully revealed, so for their sake and ours, Satan's existence had to be continued.

God did not change His law, but gave His Son to die to uphold the law. If the law could have been changed, then the Son of God would not have needed to die. God's love is expressed in His justice, as well as in His mercy. True justice always upholds what is right, for it is the foundation of God's throne. Satan tries to convince people that mercy does away with God's law, which is not true. God's character never changes; He is the same yesterday, today, and forever. This is what gives us confidence in Him, and we know that we can trust Him. If God made one change in the law and set us free to do what we wanted, there would be chaos in the universe. Everyone will be tested; obedience or disobedience is the question to be decided. The end will come, Christ will return, and God will vindicate His law. He will deliver His people, and the universe will be made eternally secure and clean forever.

Questions: Are you glorifying God by taking care of your body as you should? Don't defile it, keep it pure. Are you keeping it as healthy as you can? Remember, it belongs to Him.

APRIL 17

"Therefore My father loves Me, because I lay down My life that I may take it again."
—John 10:17, NKJV

In Joseph's Tomb. The long day of shame and torture was over, and at last Jesus was at rest. He had been crucified on Friday, and now He was resting on the Sabbath. There was joy in heaven. The work of redemption for man had been accomplished, and through God's promise a great future lay ahead. On the day of Christ's death, three men had declared their faith in Him as the Son of God: the commander of the Roman guard, the man who carried the cross for Jesus, and the criminal who gave his heart to Jesus and died on the cross next to Him. Pilate and the priests and rulers did not want Jesus to hang on the cross during the Passover. So Pilate ordered the soldiers to break the legs of those crucified to hasten their death, but they found that Jesus was already dead and would be buried where all the other criminals were buried. But Joseph of Arimathaea and Nicodemus went to Pilate and asked for Christ's body. Pilate granted their request, and the two men returned, took the body of Jesus down from the cross, carefully wrapped it in a burial sheet, and carried it to Joseph's tomb, which he had prepared for his own death.

That weekend many were going over the Scriptures in their minds, trying to understand things. Some went to the priests, asking for an explanation of the prophecies of the Old Testament about the coming Messiah, which they couldn't explain, so they tried to come up with some false interpretations. Then the priests and rulers went to Pilate and requested that he place a Roman seal on the stone that covered the opening of the tomb to make sure that the disciples would not roll it away, take the body, and say that Jesus had been resurrected. Pilate agreed, and he also stationed one hundred soldiers at the tomb and around the area to make sure nothing like that would happen.

Questions: How would you feel if Jesus were caught in the grips of death forever? No Jesus? Wouldn't that be terrible? That would make our lives hopeless, wouldn't it? Are you grateful to God that Jesus is alive? Have you told Him so?

APRIL 18

If Christ is not risen, your faith is futile; you are still in your sins!
—1 Corinthians 15:17, NKJV

The Lord Is Risen! Angels surrounded the tomb and were guarding it, ready to welcome the Prince of Life. Suddenly, there was a great earthquake, and the mightiest angel from the heavenly courts was descending. Gabriel rolled away the large stone from the opening of the tomb as if it were a pebble. Then he called out, "Son of God, Your Father is calling You!" Christ came out of the tomb, and the angels bowed before Him and welcomed Him with songs of praise. At the sight of the angels and the risen Savior, the Roman guards fainted and lay there as dead men. When the angels disappeared, they staggered to their feet. On their way to Pilate, they were telling everyone what they had seen happen. When the priests and rulers heard about it, they asked to see the soldiers, who tremblingly told what they had seen. When Caiaphas heard this, he was speechless. Then he asked the soldiers not to tell anyone what had happened but to tell the people that during the night, they had fallen asleep and the disciples had come and stolen the body of Jesus. The soldiers were stunned; to say that would mean their execution. Caiaphas and the priests went to see Pilate and urged him to overlook the fact that the guards had fallen asleep. Pilate questioned the guards privately. They told him everything, and he did not pursue the issue.

When Jesus had been placed in the tomb, Satan triumphed. But he was angry with his angels, who were supposed to be watching the tomb but ran from the angel Gabriel. And when Satan saw Christ come forth from the tomb, he knew that his power would come to an end and that he would finally die. When Christ came out of the tomb in response to His Father's call, He came out by the power He had in Himself, and in a strong voice He proclaimed, "I am the resurrection and the life!" An earthquake had opened other graves, and those who had worked with Him but had died were given life and were witnesses for Him that He had risen from the dead. When Christ ascended, they ascended with Him as living trophies of His victory over death. Life that was lost through the sin of Adam was restored, and immortality is promised to the believer.

Questions: Are you so engrossed in this life that you keep forgetting the future that awaits you? How often do you think of the life that awaits you?

APRIL 19

"You are looking for Jesus . . . , who has been crucified. He has risen; He is not here."
—Mark 16:6, NASB

Why Weepest Thou? The women who had stood by the cross came to the tomb, weeping, not knowing about the resurrection of Christ. Mary Magdalene was the first to get there, and seeing that the stone had been rolled away, she raced to the disciples to tell them. Meanwhile, the other women came to the tomb and wondered who had rolled away the stone. Suddenly, a man in shining garments appeared, sitting on the stone that he had rolled away. He said, "Don't be afraid. Are you looking for the body of Jesus? He's not here—He has risen. Come and see for yourself." The women got excited. The Savior was not dead, but living. They ran to tell the good news to the disciples. Then Peter and John ran to the tomb. John got there first, looked inside, and sure enough, it was empty. But he saw that the grave clothes were not carelessly thrown aside as if someone had stolen the body, but neatly folded, which thieves would not have done. One of the angels had gone inside, untied the wrappings of the body of Christ, and Jesus Himself had folded the grave clothes and placed them to one side. Everything that Jesus does, He does with care and in an orderly way.

By this time, Mary had come back to the tomb, crying, not knowing what had happened. She looked inside the tomb and saw two men sitting there. She thought that these men were involved in taking away the body of Jesus. Then she heard a voice behind her, saying, "Why are you crying?" Mary turned and thought the man she saw was the caretaker. With her head bent over in tears, she said, "Tell me where you've taken the body, so I can care for it." Then Jesus called Mary by her name, as tenderly as only He could. She recognized His voice, fell at His feet, and was ready to hold and kiss His feet. Then Jesus raised His hand and said, "No, don't touch Me and hold Me back. I have not yet gone to say hello to My Father and your Father." When Jesus came back, He appeared to the other women, and told them to tell the disciples, especially Peter, who had sorrowed so much, that He would meet them by the lake in Galilee. He wanted to show them that He was a living Savior and that He cared for them as much as He had before.

Questions: Just think, the day of weeping will turn into joy. Aren't you excited about that? You can share that joy with others. How do you do it?

APRIL 20

Wait on the Lord: be of good courage, and he shall strengthen thine heart.
—Psalm 27:14, KJV

The Walk to Emmaus. Late in the afternoon on the day of Christ's resurrection, two followers of Christ were on their way to the small town of Emmaus. As they slowly walked along, they talked about the trial and execution of Jesus, and they were utterly discouraged. Soon they were joined by a stranger, who came up behind them and asked them why they were so sad. It was Jesus, who understood their grief and wanted to comfort them and wipe away their tears. With quivering lips, Cleopas told this Stranger how disappointed they were because their Master, who was so mighty in deeds, was condemned by the rulers and priests and put to death, and all their hopes were gone. They had forgotten that He had told them it would happen and that He would rise again. He said to them, "O, how slow you are to believe all that the prophets have written!" Then, beginning with what Moses said, He explained to them from the Scriptures all that had been said about Him, and He told them that on these prophecies their faith must rest.

As the sun was setting, they continued along the mountain road. Soon it was dark, and when they got to a place to rest, they decided to stay there overnight. The Stranger seemed to want to go on, so they urged Him to stay with them. Had these men not urged Jesus to stay with them, they never would have known who this Stranger was. Jesus never forces His presence on anyone. He is interested in and stays only with those who need Him. As they sat down to eat and their Companion folded His hands to pray, the two men saw the nail marks in His hands and excitedly said, "This is Jesus! He has risen from the dead!" They got up, ready to throw themselves at His feet and worship Him, but He had disappeared. Then they turned to each other and said, "Didn't our hearts burn within us when He talked with us on the way and opened the Scriptures to us? Let's go tell the disciples what happened." So they took off, stumbled along in the darkness, and ran as fast as they could to get to Jerusalem.

Questions: How well acquainted are you with Scripture and the promises of God? Should you be more acquainted with them than you are?

APRIL 21

Always be thankful, for this is God's will for you who belong to Christ Jesus. Do not smother the Holy Spirit.—1 Thessalonians 5:18, 19, TLB

Peace Be Unto You. When the two men reached Jerusalem, it was still dark, but the moon was bright as they found their way to where the disciples were staying. All was quiet. They knocked and gave their names, the door opened, and Another went inside with them. Then the door was closed and locked. The two men found great excitement among the disciples, who said, "The Lord has risen from the dead; He really has, and Peter has talked to Him." Suddenly, they saw another Person standing in the room, and they wondered how He had gotten in since the door was locked. Then Jesus spoke up and said, "Why are you afraid? Look at My hands and feet. Come and touch Me—a spirit doesn't have body and bones." When they saw His wounded hands and feet and recognized His voice, they could hardly believe it. Jesus took a deep breath, breathed out, and said, "Receive the Holy Spirit." He did this because the Holy Spirit gives power to every soul who takes Jesus as his Savior. Christ also made it clear to the disciples not to judge the spiritual life of others. That is God's responsibility. He is faithful and just to forgive all who come to Him and repent.

Thomas was not there with the disciples that day. When he heard that Christ had risen, he didn't believe it. Why would Jesus appear to all the disciples and not to him? Besides, as he understood it, the Messiah was supposed to come and set up an earthly kingdom. Yet deep in his heart he had a faint hope that Jesus' resurrection was true, because he loved Him so. One evening Thomas decided to go to the disciples and meet with them. Suddenly, Jesus stood there, yet the doors had been locked. He looked at Thomas and said, "Don't be so faithless; come here and look at My hands and feet and touch them." Thomas needed no other proof. He threw himself at the feet of Jesus, and cried out, "You are my Lord and my God!" Many, like Thomas, wait for something they can see before they believe. Others believe even if they don't see what they would like to see. Jesus did not condemn Thomas for his hesitation to believe, but used this experience with him to show us His understanding and His love.

Questions: Are you a doubting Thomas? How much evidence do you need before you believe? What is the evidence that is available to you?

APRIL 22

Those who . . . measuring themselves by themselves, and comparing themselves among themselves, are not wise.—2 Corinthians 10:12, NKJV

By the Sea Once More. After His resurrection, Jesus had said that He would meet the disciples by the Sea of Galilee. They decided to wait until after the Passover weekend so that their absence would not look suspicious. Then seven of them went home to Galilee, where much of Christ's ministry had taken place. They had learned a lot during those three years. When they got there, the evening was pleasant, and Peter still had his old love for boats and fishing. Besides, they needed food and clothes, which a night of fishing would give them. They fished all night but without success. In the morning as they came near the shore, they noticed someone standing there. The man called out, "Did you catch anything?" They shouted back, "No, we didn't." The stranger shouted, "Throw your net out on the right side of the boat!" They did, and their net was so full that they could hardly pull it to shore. John recognized the stranger and said to Peter, "It's the Lord!" When Peter heard that, he jumped out of the boat and made his way to the shore to stand next to Jesus. Then the other disciples came to shore, dragging the net full of fish with them. They noticed a small fire with fish on it and bread nearby. They couldn't believe it. Jesus said, "Also bring some of the fish you caught," which they did. They stood there in awe.

Then Jesus spoke to Peter, who at the judgment hall had denied being His disciple three times. Now Jesus wanted to restore the disciples' confidence in Jesus. Open sin has to be confessed openly. So he asked Peter three times, "Do you really love Me?" Peter answered, "Yes, Lord. You know everything. You know all about me and that in my heart I really do love You." Peter's old self-confidence was gone, and he humbly depended on Jesus to help him. As they were walking along the shore, Peter saw John behind him and asked Jesus, "Lord, You asked me to take care of the new believers, for they are Your sheep. What will John do?" Jesus said, "What does that matter to you? Keep your eyes on Me." Peter did that the rest of his life.

Questions: Are you concerned about what God has asked others to do, or are you keeping your focus on what God has asked you to do? Do you know what that is?

APRIL 23

"This gospel of the kingdom will be preached in all the world as a witness to all nations, and then the end will come."—Matthew 24:14, NKJV

Go Teach All Nations. Before Jesus ascended to heaven, He said to His disciples, "All power in heaven and on earth has been given to Me; now go and take the good news of salvation to all nations. And I'll be with My people, even to the end of the world." Then Jesus called together all the believers who could come to Galilee, and soon about five hundred believers were assembled there in little groups on the mountainside. Christ told them that His sacrifice on behalf of humanity was full and complete. The conditions of the atonement had been fulfilled, and the work for which He had come had been accomplished.

To His disciples He said that His mission for this world was not yet complete. They needed to preach the gospel to all nations and create one united church. But they and those who would accept Him as their Savior would be persecuted by men, thinking they were doing the will of God. The disciples' ministry would include more than just preaching. It would include helping the needy, relieving the sick and suffering, and strengthening those of little faith. The Holy Spirit would be given to them and would be their Helper.

Questions: Would you like to be a foreign missionary, and if so, where would you like to go if you could? Are you willing to pray about it? Are you willing to help others financially so they could go?

APRIL 24

"He who has seen Me has seen the Father."—John 14:9, NKJV

To My Father and Your Father. The time had now come for Christ to ascend to His Father. So Jesus made His way to the Mount of Olives, overlooking Jerusalem. It was from here that He would go back to heaven. The disciples didn't know that this was their last meeting with Jesus. When they got to the top of the Mount of Olives, Jesus stopped, the disciples gathered around Him, and as He lifted up His arms and blessed them, He was lifted up. A cloud of glory surrounded Him, and He was hidden from their sight. But His words came back to them: "Lo, I am with you, even to the end of the world," and the sweetest and most joyous music they had ever heard came floating down to them from the angel choir.

Then the two most exalted angels stayed behind and said, "Why are you standing here looking up to heaven? This same Jesus who gave His life for you will come again to establish His kingdom of glory." The disciples themselves had seen Jesus ascend.

All heaven was waiting to receive the King of Glory. As they neared the Holy City, the escorting angels called out, "Open up, you gates, and let the King of Glory come in!" The angels by the gates responded, "Who is this King of Glory?" They knew who He was, but they wanted to hear His praise. The escorting angels answered, "The Lord, strong and mighty! The Lord has been mighty in battle against evil. Open up, and let the King of Glory come in!" The gates of the city opened, and Jesus with the escorting angels went through the gates with a burst of praise and music. In the city the heavenly council and the representatives of the unfallen worlds were assembled to welcome the Redeemer, eager to celebrate His triumph and glorify Him. But He waved at them to hold their praise until He had seen the Father. As He approached the Father, the arms of the Father encircled His Son and they shook hands—their compact to save humankind had been fully carried out. Then the Father gave the word: "Let all the angels worship Him!" and praise filled all of heaven.

Questions: Have you noticed how the Father welcomed His Son? Can you imagine the Father welcoming you like that? How will you feel when He pulls you close and puts His arms around you?

Steps to Christ

Insights Into God's Love and How to Come to Christ
From the Teachings in Ellen White's Book *Steps to Christ*

APRIL 25

"He who has seen Me has seen the Father."—John 14:9, NKJV

God's Love for Man. Nature and revelations from the Bible tell us of God's love. Our Father in heaven is the source of life. God made man perfect, but he sinned. God's plan is to lift man up from the ruin that sin has brought. God's love is written in every flower. It reveals His character, and so does the Bible. God wants His children to be happy. Satan has pictured Him to be watching for every sin and mistake that we make in order to punish us. To remove this misconception, Jesus came to live here. He came to show us what the Father is really like.

Jesus was never rude, never condemned human weakness, and always spoke the truth in kindness and love. When He denounced pretense and iniquity, He did so with tears in His voice. He wept over Jerusalem, the city He loved. Such was the character of Christ, which is the character of God. Christ's great sacrifice was not made in order to force the Father to love us, but because the Father *did* love us. God so loved us that He gave His Son to come and die to save us, not to condemn us (John 3:16,17). God suffered with His Son on Calvary. With His heart the Father paid the price for our redemption also.

Questions: Are you rude at times? Are you rude to others, to family, to friends, to church members?

APRIL 26

Grace, mercy, and peace from God the Father and the Lord Jesus Christ our Savior.
—Titus 1:4, NKJV

The Sinner's Need of Christ. Originally, man was created perfect. He had a well-balanced mind and noble powers, but through disobedience he became a captive of Satan, his nature was changed, and selfishness took over. He would have remained that way if God had not stepped in to rescue him. It's impossible for us to change ourselves and escape from sin. We can't change our hearts just by education, self-development, will power, and proper behavior. The change must come from the Holy Spirit working inside of us. Only the grace of Christ can give us a new life. Also, it is not enough just to know that God is a loving, caring God and to see the importance of His law. We need a Savior. Let us appreciate Him and thank Him for what He did for us and is doing for us. Let us place ourselves in a right relationship to Him and by His power be transformed into fellowship with Him. It is only through Christ that we can be brought into harmony with God.

Questions: Is your relationship with Christ the most important relationship to you? How about your relationship with family?

APRIL 27

"Repent therefore and be converted, that your sins may be blotted out."
—Acts 3:19, NKJV

Repentance. Repentance means to be sorry for sin and to turn away from it with our whole heart. There are many who do not understand this. They are sorry that they have sinned, and they outwardly change because they're afraid of what else will happen to them, but that is not repentance in the Bible sense. There must be a hatred of sin and a longing for a pure heart. As David said, "Create in me a clean heart, O God; and renew a right spirit within me" (Psalm 51:1–14). This kind of repentance is beyond our own power. Many think that they can't come to Christ unless they first repent, but repentance should not stand in the way of coming to Christ. We must come to Him as we are and ask for repentance. It is the Savior who gives us genuine repentance (Acts 5:31). He is the only one who can implant in the heart a hatred of sin. Christ is drawing to Himself whoever has a sincere desire to do right.

God does not regard all sins as equal. There are degrees of guilt, but there is no sin that is small. All sin not covered by Christ excludes a person from heaven, but some sins are more offensive to God than others. While drinking and drugging are sins, pride and selfishness are even more offensive to Him, because they close the heart and are contrary to His character. If you see your sinfulness, don't wait to make yourself better before you come to Christ or for better opportunities to do so. Come to Christ just as you are—God will not push you away. He loves you, and as you submit yourself to Him, He will make you better. So be honest with yourself, and when the evil one comes and tells you what a great sinner you are, tell him that Christ came to save sinners and that you belong to Him.

Questions: Do you realize that you inherited a sinful nature, which places you in the category of sinners? How can that be changed and the cancer of sin eradicated?

APRIL 28

If we confess our sins, He is faithful and just to forgive us our sins.
—1 John 1:9, NKJV

Confession. The conditions for receiving forgiveness from God are simple, just, and reasonable. The Lord does not ask us to do hard things to receive forgiveness. The men and women who confess their sins and forsake them will have mercy. Confess your sins only to God, who will forgive them, and simply admit your faults to your loved ones and friends. True confession always has to be specific, not just general. Some add an excuse for their sins or blame circumstances for what they did. This kind of self-justification added to confession is not prompted by the Holy Spirit and will not be acceptable to God. True repentance and confession will lead a man to accept his responsibility and acknowledge his sins. The broken and humble heart will see sin in the light of the cost of Calvary to pay for it. So as a young son confesses his wrongs to a loving father, so will the truly repentant man confess his sins to his loving heavenly Father.

Questions: Can sins be forgiven just by accepting the forgiveness that Christ offers to the world? Or do known sins have to be admitted and confessed?

APRIL 29

Humble yourselves in the sight of the Lord, and He will lift you up.
—James 4:10, NKJV

Consecration. The whole heart must be given to God, or a change can never take place. God wants to heal us and set us free from the power of the evil one. The warfare against self is the greatest battle that is ever fought. The giving in and surrendering everything to God requires a struggle—it is not easy. This is not blind, unreasonable submission as Satan would have us believe. God says, "Come now, and let us reason together" (Isaiah 1:18). God never forces anyone to submit, because that would prevent all development, and man would become a machine. It is for us to choose to be set free from sin. Now, some choose to do what God asks them to do so they can get to heaven, but such religion is worth nothing. We do what God asks us to do because we love Him.

Many are asking, "How do I surrender myself to God?" There's always the feeling that God cannot accept them because of their broken promises and past failings. What we need to understand is the power of the will, the power of decision. Everything depends on this. Decide to give Him your will, do so again and again, and He will work in you to bring about change. Having a desire to be good is fine, but this is not enough. Many are hoping and desiring to be changed, but they don't choose to yield and give their will to Christ. If we do this, strength will be given to us through a constant surrender to God.

Questions: Can God forgive sins that are repeated? What are the conditions?

APRIL 30

Without faith it is impossible to please Him.—Hebrews 11:6, NKJV

Faith and Acceptance. It is peace of heart that you need, heaven's forgiveness and love in the soul. Money can't buy it, education can't produce it, and your efforts can't make it happen. God offers it to you as a gift. It's yours if you reach out and take it. God promised to give you a new heart and a new spirit, and He will do this, for God does not lie. Believe His promise, confess your sins, give your heart to Him, and determine to serve Him. As surely as you do this, He will fulfill His promise. Believe that you are forgiven and made clean, and God will supply the fact. Don't wait until you feel that you are made new, but say, "I believe it, not because I feel it, but because God said so." However, there is a condition, that we pray according to His will, ask for His blessings, believe, and thank Him that we have received them.

Now that you have given yourself to Jesus, don't draw back, but say every day, "I am Christ's, for I have given myself to Him and will live for Him." Some think that they must first be placed on probation and prove to the Lord that they have changed. Here is where thousands fail. They do not take God at His word that pardon is freely extended to them. Satan is ready to steal away all assurance that God offers. Say to Satan, "Jesus died for me, loves me, and wants to give me eternal life. I have a compassionate heavenly Father, and even though I have turned against Him, He will take me back because He loves me and cares about me."

Questions: How do you build assurance in Christ? How do you build love for your heavenly Father?

MAY 1

"Love the Lord your God with all your heart, with all your soul, and with all your mind . . . [and] love your neighbor as yourself."—Matthew 22:37–39, NKJV

The Test of Discipleship. A man may not be able to tell the exact time or place, or remember all the chain of events in the process of his conversion, but this doesn't mean he is not converted. The work of the Holy Spirit is silent, but His regenerating power gives birth to a new life and starts the process of creating a new man in the image of God. A person's character is not determined by his occasional good deeds or bad deeds but by the habits of his words and actions. Some people have a well-ordered life because they're worried about their reputation and want to be thought of as good people, but they may do this for selfish reasons. The question is: Who has our heart? Do we have Jesus in our thoughts? Does He have our love and affection? Do we want to please Him in everything we do?

There are two errors against which we must especially guard. The first is looking to ourselves and what we can do under our own power to bring us into harmony with God, which is impossible. The second error is also dangerous, thinking that once we accept the grace of Christ, we don't have to keep His law, as though the way we live has nothing to do with our redemption. Obedience shows respect and is a true sign of discipleship. Christ's grace helps us to obey. If you give yourself to Christ and accept Him as your Savior, no matter how sinful you have been, His character is credited to you, and God accepts you as if you had never sinned. So keep up your connection with Christ by daily surrendering your heart and will to Him. Do not become discouraged because of your shortcomings and mistakes. The Father loves you and cares about you. The closer we get to Jesus, the more of our mistakes we will see and the more we will feel our need of Him. This is what it means to be growing in grace.

Questions: Have you ever thought about the two great errors that Christians make? Which error do you have a tendency to make? Is there another one in addition to the two mentioned?

MAY 2

To You I will pray . . . in the morning I will direct it to You, and I will look up.
—Psalm 5:2, 3, NKJV

Growing Up Into Christ. Becoming the sons and daughters of God is like being born, and is like a seed that is put into the ground, dies, and then comes up with new life. These illustrations give us a better understanding of the beginning of spiritual life. And as it is with new life, so it is with growth. It is God's power that gives birth and makes the seeds grow. They don't grow on their own, and we can't grow spiritually on our own. The whole world is surrounded by God's grace, like the air we breathe, and as we breathe in God's grace, we really begin to live. Many have the idea that they must do some of the spiritual work alone. They went to Christ for forgiveness, which was given to them, and now they try to live right by their own efforts, but every such effort will fail. Everything depends on our continued union with Christ. He is the Author and Finisher of our faith, and He is with us not only at the beginning of our relationship with Him but at every step along the way. By faith you became a Christian, and by faith you continue to grow with Him.

Consecrate yourself to God first thing in the morning; make this first before anything else. Surrender yourself to God, and place your life into His hands. This new life in Christ may not give you an excited feeling, but there will be a steady and peaceful trust. Your hope is not in yourself; it is in Christ. You are tied to His strength and might. So you are not to look to yourself but to Christ. Let your mind dwell on His love and character. Depending totally on Him, you are being slowly transformed to become more and more like Him. When we think about ourselves all the time, we lose sight of our Savior and give Satan a chance to take hold of our thoughts and turn us away from Christ. We should never make ourselves the center of our thinking. Rest your heart and soul with God, and leave yourself in His hands.

Questions: Do you surrender yourself to Christ daily? If not, why not? Do you tell Him in your thoughts or do so quietly as if speaking to Him directly?

MAY 3

*By the grace of God . . . I labored . . . not I, but the grace of God
which was with me.*—1 Corinthians 15:10, NKJV

The Work and the Life. God is the source of life, and when He is in our hearts, His light will shine out to others. When the love of Jesus is in our hearts, we will want to be a blessing and help others in whatever needs they have. The Savior's life was not a life of just thinking about Himself. He came to make the world a better place. When we do what we can to bless and help others, it will be a blessing to ourselves. This way we become more and more like Jesus, and our love for Him grows stronger. God could have used angels to do all this work, but He wanted to give us the privilege of working with Him. Every act of sacrifice for the good of others strengthens the spirit of kindness in us, and we grow closer to Jesus. Just as strength comes from exercise, and without it we become weaker, so it is in our spiritual life.

The Lord looks at the kind of attitude and spirit we have in doing things. We don't have to be great missionaries to please Him. We can perform the humblest duties and please the Lord. It's the spirit in your daily life that matters most of all to Him. The humblest followers of Jesus can be a blessing. Just by quietly and faithfully doing your work, your life is not useless. You are being fitted up for the great and selfless immortal life that is to come.

Questions: How do you become more and more like Jesus? What do you need to do, and what should you pray about?

MAY 4

Wait on the LORD; be of good courage, and He shall strengthen your heart.
—Psalm 27:14, NKJV

A Knowledge of God. There are many ways by which God is trying to make Himself known to people. Nature, with its sunshine and rain and the rich harvest of food, is one way. The green fields, the trees, and the beautiful flowers are another way. It is through these that He speaks to our hearts. God is the lover of what is beautiful, and that includes beautiful characters. If we would listen and look at nature, we would find lessons of obedience there. We also see lessons in the stars and the small atoms; they all obey the Creator. God cares for everything and keeps everything going. So it is with people. When we get up in the morning to go to work, when we pray, when we go to bed at night, each one of us is watched over by our heavenly Father. There is no smile that He does not notice, nor is there a tear that is shed that He does not see.

We also find lessons in the circumstances that surround us. The Holy Spirit speaks to our hearts and opens to us, through the Bible, the history of His people who struggled like we do. Sometimes they fell, took courage, got up again, and gained the victory through the power of the grace of God. The Bible was not written just for the scholar but for everyone. So we shouldn't just take what people say about God but also what the Bible says. There is nothing better to strengthen our thinking than reading and studying the Bible. One text or passage studied until we understand it in relation to Christ and salvation is of more value than casually reading many chapters. Some passages in Scripture are very plain, while others go deeper and need more concentration and study. Always compare Scripture with Scripture, and let the Bible interpret itself. But always begin your study with prayer, asking the Holy Spirit to guide you. He was appointed by God to be our Teacher, and He brings us closer and closer to Christ, giving us the strength we need.

Questions: How appreciative are you of the Holy Spirit? Do you pray to Him and thank Him for what He has done for you and will do?

MAY 5

Pour out your heart before Him.—Psalm 62:8, NKJV

The Privilege of Prayer. Nature and Scripture teach us about God, and the Holy Spirit speaks to us and guides us, but all this is not enough without prayer. We must talk to God and open our hearts to Him. We may think about God, His works, love, mercy, and blessings, but that is not enough. We should talk to Him as we would to a trusted friend and tell Him something about ourselves and our daily life. Prayer brings us up to God—it doesn't just bring God down to us. Why do we pray so little? Prayer is the key in the hand of faith that unlocks the blessings of heaven. There is no time or place in which it is inappropriate to pray to God. We can always lift our hearts up to God, even in crowds of people and even if the atmosphere around us is not good. So keep your wants, joys, sorrows, cares, and fears before God. You can't burden Him or tire Him out. Take everything to Him. Nothing that disturbs our peace of mind is too small for Him to notice. There are no chapters in our life that He can't read or issues that are so complex that He can't unravel.

Praying in the name of Jesus is more than just mentioning His name at the beginning and ending of our prayers. It means that we should pray in the spirit that Jesus had. And it's beneficial to pray together with others, whenever possible; if we don't, we lose much. But as beneficial as praying with others is, this should not take the place of private, personal prayer. Our God is a tender, loving heavenly Father. He is your best Friend. We should keep every blessing we receive from God in our thoughts and express our gratitude to Him, which is like a melody of praise to His heart.

Questions: What spirit do you have when you pray privately, and what spirit do you have when you pray publicly? Are you praying in the spirit of Jesus?

MAY 6

He who comes to God must believe that He is, and that He is a rewarder of those who diligently seek Him.—Hebrews 11:6, NKJV

What to Do With Doubt. Those who are new Christians sometimes doubt. God never asks us to believe without giving us evidence on which to base our faith, which appeals to sound thinking. We can't always understand everything, but we have no reason to doubt what God has said in Scripture. The more we read and study the Bible, the deeper is the conviction that it truly is the Word of God. Satan loves to create doubt or to produce pride in what we know from the Bible. The Scripture must always hold a higher position of authority for us than purely human reason. In order to arrive at truth, we must have a deep desire to know it and a willingness to obey it. Jesus said, "If any man wants to do God's will, he will know that what I say is true" (John 7:17). If someone asks you why you believe in Jesus, tell them it is because He is your Savior. If they ask why you believe in the Bible, tell them it is because it is the voice of God to your soul. Yes, you may have the witness in yourself that Jesus is the Son of God and that the Bible is true. This has been true throughout the history of the church, and it will be so in your experience too.

Questions: Do you have doubts about your experience with Christ? Doubts about what you believe? Doubts about the Bible?

MAY 7

Rejoicing in the Lord. Jesus showed us the true character of the Father, and He wants us to show it to others. We don't represent Christ or the Father as they really are if we are always despondent and complain in anger. Christ wants us to be thankful for His love and redemption. But Satan is the one who would like us to be down and make Christianity look gloomy and sad. It's not smart to keep thinking about all the unpleasant and bad things in our past life. That will discourage us and fill the soul with darkness, keeping out the light of God and discouraging others. Let us thank God for the bright pictures of redemption and salvation that He has given us. Group together the blessed assurances of His love, and place your faith in His Son. When we doubt God's love for us and don't trust what He says, we dishonor Him and make the Holy Spirit sad. By doing this we are hurting ourselves, for every expression of doubt makes doubt stronger. So let's talk about things that will give us hope and spiritual strength. Don't tell your friends all your troubles, telling them your doubts and discouragements, but take everything to God in prayer.

Questions: What things do you focus on in your past life? Unpleasant experiences, or blessings? What do you focus on presently?

MAY 8

Even so, come, Lord Jesus.—Revelation 22:20, KJV

Come, You Blessed. Jesus was deeply serious about what He came to do for us, but He was never gloomy. Let's hold on to our confidence in our Savior and serve God the best we can. As Christians, we are not walking in uncertain paths—we know where we're going. Let us look at what the Lord has done for us, the tears and disappointments that He has taken away, and the hope that He has given us. The troubles we have will not be stronger than the strength we have from God. Look at the promises of God, who promised us that one day the gates of heaven will be opened to admit His children into the Holy City. From the lips of Jesus, the King of Glory, we will hear His rich musical voice say, "Come, you blessed of My Father, inherit the kingdom I have prepared for you."

Questions: Has the hope you have in Jesus Christ increased your confidence in the promised future? Are you holding on to that hope? How?

How to Live for Christ

Insights From Ellen White's Book *The Sanctified Life*

MAY 9

For to me, to live is Christ.—Philippians 1:21, NKJV

The Meaning of Such a Life. As we see in Scripture, sanctification, meaning entire consecration, has to do with our entire being—body, soul, and spirit. There is a theory of sanctification which is false and dangerous. The entire consecration of such believers consists of talk, while they make their own wants and will supreme. The greater their distance between them and their Savior, the more righteous they appear in their own eyes. They set up their own opinion and depend on their own feelings of what is right and wrong. Their lives may represent the truth of the gospel, but if they would look more closely and their minds would dwell on the character of Christ, the more they would feel their own defects and their need of Christ. They would not make false claims about their own righteousness, but would exalt Jesus. There is no such thing as instant holiness or sanctification. True sanctification, meaning entire consecration, is a daily work, continuing as long as we live, and throughout eternity we will be learning and growing in our love for Christ.

Questions: Are you growing daily in your love for Christ? Are you sure? How do you know?

MAY 10

Be strong in the Lord.—Ephesians 6:10, NKJV

Trust and Dependence. Those who are truly walking with Christ will not put their trust in themselves but will in humbleness depend on Christ. In their lives will be seen self-denial, self-sacrifice, kindness, love, patience, meekness, and fortitude, both in prosperity and in adversity. They gain the necessary strength through prayer, and their watchfulness will increase so as not to be trapped by the evil one. It is sad to see professed Christians led astray. But the testing time of the gold of pure faith and love will come. Many who for years thought they were secure in their faith will be without foundation. But the humble in heart, who have daily stood on the Rock of their salvation, will stand during the end time.

Questions: If you are a courageous person, do you depend on your courage alone to accomplish something? Where does God come in?

MAY 11

"Every good tree bears good fruit."—Matthew 7:17, NKJV

Fruit-Bearing. A truly righteous man is unconscious of his piety and goodness. Biblical principles have become the spring of his life, and it is just as natural for him to bear the fruit of the Spirit as for a fig tree to bear figs or for a rosebush to grow roses. His life is hid in Christ, and he does not boast of it. Meekness is the fruit of the Spirit and the result of sanctification, entire consecration and submission to the will of God. Meekness subdues the heart and gives the mind a fitness to have the Word of God engrafted. God considers meekness as valuable as gold and pearls, for it connects man with Himself. "Behold what manner of love the Father has bestowed on us, that we should be called the sons and daughters of God" (1 John 3:1).

Questions: Has everything you've done in life had good results? If so, praise the Lord. If not, how can you correct the bad results? If you can't, what is it that you *can* do?

MAY 12

He knelt down on his knees three times that day, and prayed and gave thanks before his God, as was his custom since early days.—Daniel 6:10, NKJV

Life Principles. Daniel is a bright example of what men and women may become when they unite with the God of wisdom. Daniel's life is on record for our encouragement. Taken as a captive to Babylon, he was brought to a severe test to see if he would follow the teachings of Scripture by physical and intellectual discipline or if he would listen to the king and be honored by receiving great advantages and promotions. But Daniel did not hesitate in making his decision. He would obey God and follow the Scriptures, no matter what the cost. There are many today who would do the opposite, deciding that Daniel was too narrow-minded. But Daniel did not dare trust his own judgment and moral power. He was subjected to the severest temptations that assail the youth of today. Prayer to him was a necessity, and he made God his strength in all transactions of life, resisting temptation and, in the grace of meekness, standing for the right. To him, the approval of God was dearer than life itself.

The life of Daniel is an inspired illustration of what constitutes sanctification and total commitment. It presents an important lesson, especially for the young. In order to reach the highest standard of moral and intellectual attainment, it is necessary to seek wisdom and strength from God, and to do so with strict temperance and balance in all the habits of life, as Daniel and his companions did. What if they had compromised and yielded to the pressure of the heathen officers? If they had made a single departure from what was right and indulged their appetite by eating a Babylonian diet, it would have weakened their physical strength, intellect, and spiritual power. One wrong step would have led to others, until their connection with heaven was broken. But Daniel clung to God, and the gift of prophecy was given him to interpret current happenings in his day and to write on future events to the end of time.

Questions: Do you have good judgment? If so, are you thankful for it? How far do you go in depending on and trusting your own judgment? Where does God come in?

MAY 13

"I have redeemed you; I have called you by your name; you are Mine."
—Isaiah 43:1, NKJV

Health and Natural Law. Let no one regard with indifference the health of the body and think that it will not affect their spirituality. Wrong habits of eating and drinking do not promote health, and they lead to errors in thought and degrade the nobler faculties. Paul wrote, "May the God of peace sanctify you wholly. Don't you know that your body is the temple of the Holy Spirit and that you are not the owner? God has bought you with a price. So glorify God in your body and spirit" (1 Thessalonians 5:23; and 1 Corinthians 6:19, 20). We are warned against using stimulants, alcohol, narcotics, morphine, drugs, and tobacco, which are harmful to the body. Everything that conflicts with natural law creates a diseased condition of both body and soul. As Christians, we need to regulate our habits in order to preserve the full vigor of every faculty for serving Christ. The money spent for things that are harmful to the body ought to be placed into the Lord's treasury for helping the poor and the saving of souls.

Questions: Are you careful what you spend your money on? What things can you do without in order to give donations through the church or other organizations to feed the hungry and help the poor? Have you thought about this?

MAY 14

"Whoever is ashamed of Me . . . of him the Son of Man also will be ashamed."
—Mark 8:38, NKJV

Three Young Men. In the same year that Daniel and his companions successfully passed their final exam and were taken by the king of Babylon into government service, events happened that severely tested their integrity. When King Nebuchadnezzar wondered about the future of his country, the Lord gave him a remarkable dream. God gave Daniel the same dream. So Daniel went to the king and told him the dream. Nebuchadnezzar was happy to learn about the dream that he had forgotten, but he overlooked the succeeding kingdoms that would come, and he set up a huge golden statue to represent Babylon. Then he called all the officials together for the dedication and asked them to bow down before the golden statue at the sound of the music. If they didn't, they would be thrown into the burning furnace nearby. Daniel was absent, taking care of urgent government business, but his three friends were there. They refused to bow down and were thrown into the fire, but they were not consumed, for Jesus was standing beside them to keep them safe. Nebuchadnezzar was shocked by what he saw. He asked the three men to come out, and they did.

These three Hebrews possessed genuine consecration, for they did not stop to weigh the consequences of their decision. They did not ask themselves, What will people think of us if we refuse to obey the king, or how will this affect our reputation and prosperity? The most intense longing of a person truly committed to God is the desire to know what God would have him do to glorify Him. These three men enjoyed the highest intellectual culture and positions of honor. But none of this led them to forget God, nor did they turn aside from God because of threats. During any future time of trouble, God's people will stand unmoved, and Christ's presence will comfort and strengthen them.

Questions: When you need to stand publicly for God, are you able to do it? What if you were, suddenly and unexpectedly, publicly tested? How can you prepare for this?

MAY 15

"Be faithful unto death, and I will give you the crown of life."
—Revelation 2:10, NKJV

Daniel's Life Saved. When the Medes and Persians took over Babylon and Darius became king, he reorganized the government. He divided it into 120 provinces, put a prince in charge of each one, and then placed three presidents over all of them—and the top one was Daniel. The presidents and princes didn't like that, and they tried to find a way to get rid of Daniel. While Daniel made no claim to sanctification, he lived a life of faithfulness and consecration to God. It was his faithfulness to God's law and his habit of unashamedly praying three times a day that gave his enemies the accusation they were looking for. They persuaded Darius to make a law that no one should pray to any god or ask any man for a favor except from the king. If they did, they were to be killed. This was to honor the king, and Darius agreed. When Daniel heard about it, he turned to God more than ever, for he knew what this meant for him.

The king was sad when the princes and presidents accused Daniel of breaking the law, and with deep sorrow Darius allowed them to throw Daniel into the den of lions. As the king watched, he said to Daniel, "Your God will deliver you." Early the next morning the king went to the lions' den and called to Daniel, who answered, "The God I serve sent an angel who shut the mouths of the lions so they would not hurt me." The king was so happy that Daniel was still alive that he ordered Daniel to be taken out of the den and his accusers to be thrown in, and they were immediately killed. The trap that Daniel's enemies had set for him proved to be their own ruin.

Questions: Has God worked miracles in your life to save you? Can you share your experiences with others without becoming proud of what God did? Have you forgotten that it's all about Him and not about you?

MAY 16

"They shall be My people, and I will be their God."—Ezekiel 11:20, NKJV

Daniel's Prayers. As the time was near when the captivity of the children of Israel would end, Daniel carefully studied the prophecies of Jeremiah and thought this meant that God would prolong their captivity. So he humbled himself and, with fasting and prayer, turned to God on behalf of his people. Daniel does not use his own faithfulness as an argument for God to answer his prayer, but he identifies himself with the sins of his people and, with tears, pleads with God not to extend the time of captivity. He was given evidence that his prayers were heard. If we as a people would humble ourselves and pray as Daniel did, we would be given evidence that our prayers are being heard. Those who claim to be sanctified and committed to God often have no desire to search the Scriptures and to pray in order to understand more clearly what true sanctification means.

As Daniel was praying, the angel Gabriel was sent from heaven to help him understand the prophecies and the future of God's people. Not long afterward, Daniel wanted to learn more from Gabriel on what he had said earlier. Daniel fasted and prayed for three weeks, and one day as he was praying, he looked up and saw a man clothed in fine linen like gold. The man's face had the appearance of lightning, and his eyes looked like flames of fire. This was the same description of Christ that the apostle John had centuries later. It was the Son of God who appeared to Daniel, who by now was an old man, and the Majesty of Heaven gave him light for those who would live in the last days. Daniel was a devoted servant of God and had been so all his life. His purity of character and unwavering fidelity to God is an inspired illustration of true sanctification.

Questions: How do you feel about the prophecies for the last days? Do you fully believe what will happen? Have you ever taken time to fast and pray? How long? Would you be willing to miss a meal or even fast for one day or several days?

MAY 17

"As the Father loved Me, I also have loved you; abide in My love."
—John 15:10, NKJV

The Character of John. The apostle John, while he had some serious defects of character such as being proud, ambitious, and quick to resent slight or injury, was never cowardly or vacillating but had a warm and loving heart. Jesus loved him dearly, and the Savior's affection was returned by John with all the strength and devotion that John could muster. This was more than human friendship, but the love and gratitude of a saved sinner. John esteemed it the highest honor to work and suffer in the service of his Lord, and the love in his heart led him to put forth all the effort he could in helping others, especially those in the church. The depth of John's love for his Master was not the *cause* of Christ's love for him, but the *result* of His love. John wanted to become like Jesus, and under the influence of the Savior's love, he became meek and lowly of heart, for self was hidden in Jesus.

There may be marked defects in our character, but when we become true disciples of Jesus, grace changes us, and sanctifies us, and we become living representatives of Christ in disposition and character. Those who possess the spirit of Christ will have no ambition to have a position above their brothers, but are small in their own eyes. Those who overlook duties right in front of them and who neglect mercy, kindness, courtesy, and love are neglecting to be like Christ. He is full of love, grace, and blessings and is ready to bestow them on us. Do we urge Jesus to take up His abode in our hearts and in our homes? John constantly sought to bring his life in harmony with the Divine Pattern and was fighting against his own faults, trying to be more like Christ, for he knew that meekness, humility, and love were essential for growth in grace.

Questions: Is Jesus your pattern to live by? Is He your model for living? If so, do you recall the changes, whether great or small, that have taken place in your life because you followed the divine pattern?

May 18

Nevertheless the solid foundation of God stands.—2 Timothy 2:19, NKJV

The Ministry of John. John grew up in the society of uneducated fisherman and did not enjoy the privilege of going to school, but by associating with Christ, he received the highest education an ordinary man can receive. After the ascension of Christ, John stood out as a faithful worker for the Lord, and when threatened with imprisonment and death, he would not be intimidated. He spoke for his Lord whenever he could. There were some perilous times for the church, because Satan's delusions through deceptive doctrines and skepticism were everywhere. Some pretended to be true to the cause of God but were deceivers. John was filled with sadness as he saw errors come into the church. Some claimed that Christ had released them from obedience and from keeping the law of God, while many others taught that the law and the traditions of the Pharisees should be kept rigorously. John saw the danger in these two extremes, and he met them with promptness and decision. These are similar to the dangers that we face today.

John enjoyed true sanctification and commitment, but he did not claim to be perfect and sinless. He pointed out: "He who claims to know God and doesn't live according to His commandments is a liar, and the truth is not in him" (1 John 2:4). In this age of liberality, those who believe what John said and who keep God's commandments are accused of being intolerant. John points out that we should be courteous and kind, but we are to call sin for what it is and not compromise our faith. There is no sanctification without obeying all the commandments, including the fourth one, which instructs us to keep the Sabbath. Some excuse themselves by saying that there are many good people who don't keep the Sabbath, and should they keep the Sabbath, it would make them different from others. But God's character and His commandments have not changed.

Questions: How important is the Sabbath to you? What spiritual significance do you see in keeping it? Could you share this with others?

May 19

"Blessed are those who are persecuted for righteousness' sake, for theirs is the kingdom of heaven."—Matthew 5:10, NKJV

John in Exile. The success that attended the preaching of the gospel stirred up the enemies of Christ. The Roman emperor took a stand against Christians, and a terrible persecution began. By now John was an old man, the last survivor of the apostles, but he continued to preach with great success, which encouraged his brothers and sisters. Finally, the hatred for Christians focused on John for his unwavering fidelity to Christ, and he was arrested and taken to Rome to stand trial. False witnesses accused him of subverting the nation, and even though he defended himself with clarity and simplicity, which had a powerful effect on those in the courtroom, it stirred up even greater hatred in their hearts. The emperor was filled with rage because he couldn't undermine John's reasoning. So he banished John to the rocky island of Patmos, where criminals were kept. But John was not shut away from Christ.

John kept the Lord's Day, the Sabbath, the same day that God blessed and on which He rested at Creation. The disciple remembered how the Divine Legislator stood on Mount Sinai and wrote the law on tablets of stone. And how God could give His Son to die for rebellious humanity at such tremendous pain to His own heart of love was a mystery that was hard for John to understand. As he recalled the wonderful life of Christ, the Savior suddenly appeared to him, not as a Man of sorrow and grief but transformed, with no marks of humiliation, with eyes as little flames of fire, a shining face like the sun, feet glowing as brass, and a deep musical voice like a great waterfall. John fell at the feet of the Son of God as dead. As wonderful a disciple as John was, his character appeared exceedingly defective in comparison to Christ's glory. Such will ever be the feeling of those who best know their Savior and Lord.

Questions: How would you feel if you were put in prison for your faith? Have you ever thought about this? How dear would Jesus be to you? How dear to you is He now?

MAY 20

Be thankful to Him, and bless His name. For the LORD is good.
—Psalm 100:4, 5, NKJV

Christian Character. The character of a Christian is best seen by a person's daily life. The law of God is the only standard of moral maturity. Jesus lived by His Father's commandments, and He is our pattern. What He would not do, we should not do, and God's grace will help us. A child who loves its godly parents will show it by being obedient. We, too, will listen to and obey our loving heavenly Father, and that obedience will produce the "fruit of the Spirit, which is love, joy, peace, longsuffering, gentleness, goodness, faith, meekness, temperance" (Galatians 5:22, 23). The peace of God will rule our hearts, and we will be thankful. This is sanctification as taught in the Bible.

Questions: What are the evidences in your life that you are keeping God's commandments from the right motive? Are you sure? How do you know your motive is right?

MAY 21

Teaching the things which concern the Lord Jesus Christ with all confidence.
—Acts 28:31, NKJV

The Christian's Privilege. Many who are seeking for holiness of heart and purity of life are perplexed and discouraged, because they are constantly looking to themselves for the answers. They mistake feeling for faith. They need to look away from self and not even put faith in their faith, but look at the love of God and put their faith in what He has promised. Sometimes discouragements and doubts will come and threaten to take away our confidence. When that happens, we need to keep our eyes on Jesus, feeling or no feeling, and not try to heighten our emotions and think that this is a sign of our sanctification. Instead, let the eye of faith see Jesus with His wounded hands standing before the Father on our behalf. This is where our strength comes, from what Jesus has done for us.

Daily prayer is essential for sanctification and growth in grace. If your mind wanders during prayer, bring it back to the presence of Jesus. Our relationship to Christ is the greatest business of life. Everything else must be subordinate to this. Let us not withhold our affections and gratitude from Him. Our Savior claims all of each of us, just as He gave all of Himself for us. Paul says, "Who shall separate us from the love of Christ, and will troubles, famines, wars, and persecutions? No, not present or future things, not even death and angels" (Romans 8:35–39). Our only safety is to daily surrender ourselves to Jesus, and to constantly grow in grace and in the knowledge of the truth; this is sanctification.

Questions: Do you begin your prayers with gratitude to God before you tell Him your needs? What has He done for you?

Sermon on the Mount

Insights From Ellen White's Book *Thoughts From the Mount of Blessings*

MAY 22

Now faith is the substance of things hoped for.—Hebrews 11:1, KJV

On the Mountainside

Years before Jesus was born, the Israelites would gather in a valley. From the mountains on either side, one group would proclaim the blessings of God and the other group, the disciplines of God. When Jesus was here, He went to an unnamed mountain in Galilee, and from there He spoke to His disciples and the people about the blessings of God. Let's go back there in our imaginations, sit with the disciples on the mountainside, and listen to Jesus, and think about what His words meant to the people who were there. The true devotion to God had been lost by the people, who focused on tradition and ceremonies, and the leaders expected the promised Messiah to come and set up His kingdom, bringing all nations under His rule. So they would not accept this humble and lowly Teacher from Nazareth.

On the mountain by the Sea of Galilee, Jesus had spent the whole night in prayer for His disciples. In the morning He called them together, laid His hands on them, and set them apart to the work of the gospel. As the people sat on the mountainside, their hearts were filled with thoughts of earthly glory and the end of the Roman occupation. They looked forward to the end of a life of hard work, little food, rough clothes, and only a thin blanket at night. Christ's blessings gave them hope for a change from poverty.

Questions: How do you bring and give hope to people who have none? Can you think of ways to do it?

May 23

"Pride goes before destruction. . . . Better to be of a humble spirit."
—Proverbs 16:18,19, NKJV

The Beatitudes

Part 1. "Blessed are the humble in heart and spirit, for the kingdom of heaven belongs to them." There is something about this new Teacher that holds their attention. Love seems to flow from His very presence. They open their hearts to Him and listen, and the Holy Spirit opens to them the meaning of Jesus' teaching that people in all ages need to hear. Pride does not feel a need for spiritual help. It leads people to think of themselves as reasonably good, and they become content with themselves. But Christ first makes penitent those whom He pardons. They begin to see nothing good in themselves and realize that what they did was mingled with self. They don't feel worthy, and they ask God to be merciful to them.

Whatever may have been your past, if you come to Jesus just as you are, spiritually weak and helpless, our loving and compassionate Savior will greet you, throw His arms of love around you and clothe you with and His robe of righteousness around you, and present you to the Father as sinless and pure. You will be able to say, "Father, it is in Your Son that I have righteousness and strength."

Questions: How much of what you do is mingled with self? Have you considered others, such as your family and friends? What do you do when someone calls you selfish, only thinking about yourself? If this is true, what can you do to change?

May 24

"Repent therefore and be converted."—Acts 3:19, NKJV

Part 2. "Blessed are those who mourn, for they will be comforted." The mourning Jesus talks about here is true sorrow for sin. The Savior said, "If I be lifted up, I will draw all men unto Me." As a person is drawn to Jesus uplifted on the cross, he sees the sinfulness of his own humanity. He sees that he has been loved with unspeakable love but that his life has been a life of ingratitude for what Jesus, his best Friend, has done for him. When we come to Jesus, we shall be comforted and be set free from slavery to sin. To remove the roughness from our characters, the polishing may be hard and even painful, but the Lord does careful work. He will do this for all who put their trust in Him. In such mourning there is no false motive and thought of self. It is about Jesus and how we hurt Him, and yet how much He loved us and is ready to forgive us.

Questions: When you repent, do you name specific sins or just make a general statement? Which is an indication of true repentance?

May 25

Seek the Lord, all you meek of the earth, . . . seek righteousness, seek humility.
—Zephaniah 2:3, NKJV

Part 3. "Blessed are the meek, for such will inherit the new earth." Such a person has felt his need of Christ, has come to Him, been sorry for his sins and has mourned, and now he learns to be patient, gentle, and meek, even under wrong treatment. This characteristic is one of the first qualifications of Christ's kingdom. Jesus humbled Himself, emptied Himself in all that He did, and submitted Himself to the will of the Father. He says, "Learn of Me, for I am meek and lowly of heart." A true disciple of Christ is empty of self, pride, and love of supremacy, and there is silence and peace in the soul. Everything he or she does is done in the spirit of Christ, and does not take slights and insults to heart and answer with anger. The kingdom is promised to the humble and kind. Through self-surrender we inherit what Jesus did for us, a kingdom where there will be no disappointment, no pain, sickness, sorrow, weeping, death, partings, and broken hearts. Jesus will be there to lead us to fountains of living water.

Questions: How often do you think of the wonderful future that awaits you because of Christ? When have these thoughts cheered you along the way? Can you be specific?

MAY 26

For the eyes of the Lord are on the righteous, and His ears are open to their prayers.
—1 Peter 3:12, NKJV

Part 4. "Blessed are those who hunger for righteousness, for their hearts will be filled." Righteousness means right-doing and reflecting the love of God to others. The righteousness of God and His love is seen in Jesus Christ. No human being can satisfy the hunger and thirst of the soul as Christ can. Just as we need food to keep up our physical strength, we need Christ, who is the Bread from heaven, to sustain our spiritual life. To have spiritual life and strength we must pray to Christ, submit to Him, and depend on Him. When we do this, we will be changed and become new men and women. It is impossible to do for ourselves what Christ can do for us. The Holy Spirit will be given to every follower of Christ when the whole heart is surrendered to Jesus. God has poured out His love to us in Christ on Calvary, and His grace will sustain us, "for by grace we are saved and that not of ourselves. Amen."

Questions: Where could you go to buy the grace that you need to be saved? What do you do when you are given such a gift as God gives you free of charge? What do you do to express your gratitude?

MAY 27

Love suffers long and is kind.—1 Corinthians 13:4, NKJV

Part 5. "Blessed are the merciful, for they shall receive mercy." By nature the heart of man is unloving, but when Jesus is in our hearts, we love and forgive others, for God has loved and forgiven us. Were we worthy of love and forgiveness? No. So let's not condemn others, but show love and forgiveness to them. The question we should ask is not "Are they worthy?" but "How can I benefit them?" There are many whose life situation is a struggle. Easy words, expressions of appreciation and sympathy, are like a cup of cold water to a thirsty traveler. There is peace in the soul of those who are compassionate in spirit, and there is blessed satisfaction in the heart of self-forgetfulness for the good of others. The Holy Spirit in the soul will soften hard hearts and awaken concern for the sake of others.

Questions: Do you feel that the Holy Spirit is leading you when you're doing good things for others? How often do you thank the Holy Spirit personally for helping and guiding you?

MAY 28

"He who has seen Me has seen the Father."—John 14:9, NKJV

Part 6. "Blessed are the pure in heart, for they shall see God." All who are to enter God's kingdom will develop a growing distaste for careless manners, bad language, and coarse thinking. When Christ is in the heart, there will be improvement of thought and manners, pure motives, freedom from pride and self-seeking, but humbleness and unselfishness. For hearts that have been purified by the indwelling of the Holy Spirit, all is changed. They see God in a new and endearing relationship. They see Him as wanting to embrace each one of His spiritually reborn children. They want to be like their Father. The spiritually pure in heart live as if the heavenly Father is present. No matter how long they live on this earth, in the future they will see Him face to face.

Questions: Do you think that your heavenly Father would have given His life for you and suffered everything for you that Jesus did? Have you ever thought of the emotional pain the Father suffered, having to stand by and watch His Son being mistreated when He could have stopped it? He didn't stop it because of His love for you. How much do you appreciate your Father? How often do you tell Him so?

MAY 29

Depart from evil and do good; seek peace and pursue it.—Psalm 34:14, NKJV

Part 7. "Blessed are the peacemakers, for they shall be called the children of God." Christ came as the Prince of Peace. It was His mission to restore the peace that was broken by Adam and Eve. Whoever repents, renounces sin, and opens his heart to Christ will have part of this heavenly peace. Christ in your heart will remove hatred, anger, and fighting. Whoever leads someone else to Christ and helps him to stay with Christ is considered by heaven as a peacemaker.

Questions: How many have you brought to Christ either directly or indirectly? Do you know? If not specifically, have you sown and are sowing heavenly seed that will bring a harvest to be known by you when you get to heaven?

May 30

For if we live, we live to the Lord; and if we die, we die to the Lord. Therefore, whether we live or die, we are the Lord's.—Romans 14:8, NKJV

Part 8. "Blessed are those who are persecuted for Christ, for theirs is the kingdom of heaven." Jesus does not present to His followers the hope of having a life free from trial. Rejection and even persecution could come to those who are in Christ. This may change according to the circumstances. The Lord has not promised a walk with Christ free from trials and tests of faith. But He has promised, "My grace is all you need, for My strength will help your weakness." Jesus will be by your side. Satan can persecute and even kill the body, but he cannot kill the faith and spirit. Those who die for Christ are actually conquerors, and the glory and character of God is revealed through them. When Christ comes, these victorious ones will be with Him and sing about the glory and goodness of God and the love of Christ, who gave His life for them. They will praise His name forever and ever.

Questions: When trials and tests of faith come to you, how do you relate to them? Have you had such experiences? If so, what were they or what are they? How are you handling them, coping with them?

MAY 31

"If you then, being evil, know how to give good gifts to your children, how much more will your heavenly Father give the Holy Spirit to those who ask Him!"
—Luke 11:13, NKJV

Part 9. "You are the salt of the earth." Salt is a preservative, and Christ calls His followers salt, because through His grace they become His helpers in saving and stabilizing the faith of others. Like salt that must be mixed with other things, we must mingle with others to help them. We are not saved in groups but as individuals. Personal influence is needed, so we must come close to others if we want to help others. The love of Jesus in the heart will radiate out to others, and when received, it will give them moral power. This is not the power of man himself, but the power of the Holy Spirit that does the transforming work.

Jesus said, "If salt loses its saltiness, what is it good for?" When the grace and power of God are gone, believers become cold and are soon without Christ. Without a living relationship with Christ and faith in Him as a personal Savior, it is impossible for our influence for good to be felt by others. Unless the Holy Spirit can use us to communicate Jesus to others, we are like tasteless salt and useless. When the love of Christ fills the heart, it will flow out to others. It is this, and only this, that makes us the salt of the earth that Jesus talked about.

Questions: Are you like salt in people's lives to preserve their faith, or are you being salty in your disposition? If salty, what will you do to change your saltiness to preserving salt?

JUNE 1

"No one, when he has lit a lamp, covers it . . . but sets it on a lampstand."
—Luke 8:16, NKJV

Part 10. "You are the light of the world." When Jesus taught the people, He made His lessons interesting and held the attention of the people by illustrations from nature. They had come together to hear the Lord in the morning just as the sun was coming up. As the new day was beginning and the birds were singing, Jesus looked at His disciples and the people and said, "You are the light of the world." His followers were to shed the light of heaven into the lives of others who were still walking in the darkness of the night of ignorance and sin. Jesus added, "Let your light so shine that others will see the good in you, and glorify your Father in heaven, who is also their Father."

Jesus did not say, "Work to make your light shine, but let it shine." If Christ is in your heart, it will shine out to others. Through you the Father's mercy, goodness, kindness, and love will be made evident to others through the Holy Spirit. There is no prejudice or nationality in the heart of God. The Father loves everyone and wants them to be saved. His deep and unfathomable love for us is seen in the cross of Calvary, as the Father allowed His Son to be mistreated and crucified. What heart and emotional pain the Father must have suffered as He watched His Son being mistreated, spit on, beaten, and nailed to a piece of wood, when He could have stopped it. But He didn't! Why? Because of His love for us. That is beyond comprehension. Talk it, share it, and sing it in your heart. This is the light that needs to shine out to others and to the world.

Questions: Are you sure you have no prejudice in your heart toward people of another race, nationality, or religion? If not, praise the Lord. If so, what will you do about it, and how will you do it?

JUNE 2

Then the LORD said to Moses, "Come up to Me on the mountain . . . and I will give you . . . the law and commandments which I have written."—Exodus 24:12, NKJV

The Spirituality of the Law

Jesus said, "I did not come to do away with the law, but to carry it out." It was the Son of God in His glory during the Old Testament who proclaimed the Ten Commandment law from Mount Sinai. Then when He became one of us and sat on the hillside teaching the people, He unfolded the principles of the law He had given at Sinai, which are the principles of His kingdom. The words of Christ that He spoke to the people that day were spoken calmly and in love, but with power and earnestness that stirred the listeners' hearts. The Savior's divine love and tender voice drew the hearts of the people to Him. The majesty, purity, and beauty of the truth, with its deep and gentle influence, was taking firm hold upon many minds. But Jesus was closely watched by spies, and the rulers and leaders whispered to the people that what Jesus taught was not in harmony with the writings of Moses as they interpreted them.

Questions: How do you respond to people who interpret the Scriptures differently from you? Are you patient and kind, or do you avoid them? What's the best way for you to relate to them? Do you know?

JUNE 3

"If you love Me, keep My commandments."—John 14:15, NKJV

Part 1. "Whosoever breaks one of the commandments, and helps others to do so, is looked on as least by the kingdom of heaven. But whoever keeps the commandments and helps others to do so, is looked on as great by the kingdom of heaven." There is not one commandment that is not for the good and happiness of man, both in this life and in the life to come. On this earth, the Ten Commandments are like a protection around us, to keep us from obeying Satan. To disobey in one point opens the door to disobeying and breaking the other commandments. Everyone who does this is working out his own unhappiness and eventual ruin.

Questions: Do you think we'll need the Ten Commandments in heaven? Why? If not, will everyone be allowed to do what he or she wants? How would that work? If we will need them there, why?

JUNE 4

"I have kept My Father's commandments."—John 15:10, NKJV

Part 2. "Unless your right-doing exceeds the claim of the right-doing of the Pharisees and rulers, you cannot enter God's kingdom." The Pharisees and scribes not only accused Jesus of not living up to the laws of Moses but also accused His disciples, who were often troubled by these accusations from the religious teachers. Jesus came to the rescue of His disciples, showing them that what the Pharisees and scribes said didn't mean much, as they were not in a saving relationship with God, but only following rules and regulations without the true faith which purifies the soul and transforms a person's character. They were keeping the law according to their own ideas and for their own reputation as being men of God. Jesus showed the people what it means to keep the commandments of God by the way He lived, by what He did and did not do.

Questions: Are you keeping God's commandments because you were brought up that way, or are you keeping them of your own free choice? Or is it both? Are you sure it's from your heart? If so, when did you make that decision?

JUNE 5

Do not let yourself become quickly provoked, for anger resides in the lap of fools.
—Ecclesiastes 7:9, NET

Part 3. "Everyone who is angry with his brother is in danger of God's judgment." Those who angrily condemn others for their sins also are guilty, because they are full of hatred. In a nearby region there were places for men to hide who were committing robberies and murder. People denounced them as being evil men. Yet at the same time they had evil in their hearts, hating all those who didn't agree with them. They especially hated the Roman occupation troops. The spirit of hatred originated with Satan, who did not hesitate to put the Son of God to death.

God places a high value on every human being. Every soul is His property. Even the most degraded person is to be treated with respect. If not, God will hold us accountable for speaking contemptuously about others. As Jesus said, "Who are you to judge another person?" Whoever condemns someone else for turning against God shows that he himself is worthy of condemnation. Accusations are the weapons of Satan, the evil one. Jesus does not want us to use Satan's weapons against others, but to follow His example of relating to others. As He said, "Be reconciled to your brother."

Questions: How much do you value yourself? Why? Are you sure it's for the right reason and not just because you're focusing on yourself? How do you make sure it's for the right reason?

JUNE 6

Turn away my eyes from all that is vile.—Psalm 119:37, NEB

Part 4. "Whoever looks at a woman and lusts after her has already committed adultery in his heart." With the presence of the Roman occupation troops, all kinds of heathen customs with lust and drinking had come into Palestine. The Romans with their girlfriend lovers would be seen everywhere, on the parade grounds and on the lake in their pleasure boats. But Jesus did not focus on the pagan Romans as expected, but on the evil and secret thoughts of His people. He pointed to their secret thoughts, their evil desires, and their lustful hearts. When one falls into sin, that particular sin was not created at that moment but is the result of what was hidden in the heart and dwelt upon. As a man thinks, so is he.

Questions: What are you doing to protect your thinking? Are you watching too much television, or the wrong kind, no matter what means you're using? If you are, how can you change? What are you doing to change?

JUNE 7

"My Father, . . . not as I will, but as You will."—Matthew 26:39, NKJV

Part 5. "If your right hand causes you to sin, cut it off." From a physical standpoint, that's what is done to an arm or a leg that is full of cancer, to keep it from spreading through the whole body. How much more should we be willing to give up whatever would spread evil in the soul! God is not only willing to deliver us from physical suffering and death but from spiritual corruption and spiritual death. Eternity alone will reveal the glorious destiny that we have when restored to God's image. So that which causes our soul to stumble must be given up and sacrificed. The surrender of our self to God, especially the surrender of our will to Him, is illustrated by the cutting off of an arm or leg or the removing of an eye.

It may seem that surrendering our will to God will cripple us, but this is the only way to overcome evil. If you cling to self and refuse to surrender to God, you are choosing eternal death. Yes, it will require a sacrifice to surrender yourself to God, but you are surrendering the lower life for a higher life. God does not want to destroy you by asking you to surrender your will to Him. Our will is to be given to Him, so that we can receive it again, purified and refined. However hard this surrender may be, it is very profitable for our spiritual health and well-being.

Questions: Can you trust God with your will? Are you hesitant because God might force you to do what you don't want to do? Do you think that God would do that? Or, by guiding your will, won't He help you to do what really matters? Have you surrendered your will to Him and told Him so?

JUNE 8

Male and female created he them; and blessed them, and called their name Adam.
—Genesis 5:2, KJV

Part 6. "Is it lawful for a man to divorce his wife?" Among the Jews at the time, a man was allowed to divorce his wife for the smallest thing, and she was not allowed to remarry. On the mountainside, Jesus taught the people that the only reason for allowing divorce is if a man's wife or a woman's husband has been unfaithful and committed adultery. Marriage is a gift from God, instituted by Him at the time of Creation, but marriage has been perverted by sin, so it is the purpose of the gospel to restore its purity and beauty. Marriage represents the sacred union that exists between Christ and the redeemed ones whom He has purchased at the cost of Calvary.

In the New Testament, Paul, writing to the Ephesian Christians, points out that the Lord considers the husband to be the "house-band," the protector of the wife and the home. "Husband, love your wife, even as Christ loves the church and gave Himself for her." God's grace alone can make marriage as He planned that it should be, a blessing for everyone and a representation of the togetherness of God's larger family in heaven. Even for those who have found bitterness and disappointment in marriage, Christ through the Holy Spirit offers to sweeten the bitter lot. Through the surrender to God, His love and grace can accomplish what human power and wisdom fails to do.

Questions: How is your marriage? How kind, courteous, and helpful are you to your husband or wife? If your marriage needs changing, what should change? Should you change, or your husband or wife, or both of you? What are the two of you doing to help make the necessary changes? Where does Jesus come in?

JUNE 9

"The devil . . . is a liar and the father of it."—John 8:44, NKJV

Part 7. "Take not an oath by heaven or God's throne." Jesus condemned this practice of swearing by God to make it look like what you said was true when it wasn't. But Jesus did not condemn taking the regular judicial oath. Jesus Himself, at His trial before the Jewish high court, did not refuse to testify under oath that He was the Son of God. There are many who swear by God that what they're saying is true when they're lying and bearing false witness. God can read our hearts, and He knows whether we're telling the truth or not. We can not only lie by our words but also by a look and the tone of our voices, and give a false impression. Such things are deceptions of Satan, and those who do this are being used by the wicked one. Our words, as followers of Christ, should not only be truthful but also pure, without cursing to emphasize that what we are saying is true. What pleases God is for us to be honest in all things and in all ways.

Questions: Do people believe what you say because they know you to be an honest person, or do you have to confirm what you're saying by taking an oath to prove it? How about the purity of your language? Is it punctuated with cursing and swearing? If so, how do you intend to change that?

JUNE 10

"The Lord is my helper; I will not fear. What can man do to me?"
—Hebrews 13:6, NKJV

Part 8. "Don't resist someone who doesn't treat you right; don't fight back." There was constant irritation between the Jews and the Roman occupation troops, who would force them to do things. The Jews would see the soldiers stand in formation around the Roman flag and commit themselves to that symbol of power. Often the Romans would take a Jewish peasant from the field and make him carry their load up the mountainside. So the people looked to Christ as the longed-for Messiah and hoped that He would humble the pride of Rome. As Jesus looked at the upturned faces of the people with the spirit of revenge written all over them and saw how they longed for power to crush the Romans, that's when Jesus said what He did. Jesus wanted to reach the hearts of His enemies. Even on the cross, He prayed for them.

When the Roman soldiers made the Jewish peasants carry their equipment one mile, Jesus told them to be willing to carry it two miles. In other words, Jesus told His followers not to resist the Roman occupation troops and their authority, but to do even more than what was expected. And if they were taken to court, they should not resist the decision of the Roman court, for it would only make things worse for them. Jesus talked about doing what we can to help each other, especially the poor among us. However, we know that we need to be careful not to give indiscriminately to anyone who comes up to us asking for money.

Questions: Can you imagine what it would be like to live under occupation troops? Some church members have. They were willing to obey the foreign troops, but when they were asked to give up their faith, they refused and suffered for it, even died because of it. Are you sure you would be loyal to Christ under those circumstances? Think about it—don't just give a quick answer.

June 11

But God demonstrates His own love toward us, in that while we were yet sinners,
Christ died for us.—Romans 5:8, NKJV

Part 9. "Love your enemies by praying for them. Be the children of your Father which is in heaven." Jesus pointed His hearers to the Ruler of the universe under a new name, "Father." He would have them understand how tenderly the heart of the Father longs for them and that He cares for every soul. Such a concept of God as Father has never been given to the world by any religion except by the religion of the Bible. The Jewish priests believed that God loved those who served Him, according to their ideas, and that all the rest of the world was under His frown and curse. Not so, according to Jesus—the whole world was under the sunshine of His love. Accepting Him as our tender, loving Father, we will become like Him and not only be kind to those who please us but to everyone. It is only the Holy Spirit who can help us to extend kindness to everyone, even to those who hurt us. To do so is the insignia of the royalty of heaven.

Questions: Do you love God, or are you afraid of Him? Do you see Him as a loving heavenly Father? What is your relationship to Him as a loving Father? Do you express your gratitude to Him every day for what He has done for you and for His love for you?

JUNE 12

And though I . . . understand all mysteries and all knowledge, and though I have all faith, . . . but have not love, I am nothing.—1 Corinthians 13:2, NKJV

Part 10. "Be therefore perfect as your heavenly Father which is in heaven is perfect." This means to be fully grown and mature and reflect your heavenly Father. The "therefore" means a conclusion to everything that Jesus said before. He came to help us to become like our Father in character. This is a standard that, with the help of the Holy Spirit, we can attain, because everything that God asks us to do is a promise by Him that He will help us achieve what He wants us to be. With untold love the Father loves us, and this awakens love in our hearts for Him. God does not compel us to do this, but He uses love as the means to change us. It is God's nature to give. He tells us who He is, and He wants to help us reflect His goodness, because we are His children and were born again by the Holy Spirit to take part of His nature and be like Him. This last beatitude ended Jesus' sermon on the mount.

Questions: What do you think about Jesus' sermon on the mount? Have you looked at it as if He were speaking directly to you? As if you were there sitting at His feet, listening to Him? Put yourself there in your imagination. How do you apply what Jesus said to your own life? Can you explain?

JUNE 13

This requires the steadfast endurance of the saints—those who obey God's command-ments and hold to their faith in Jesus.—Revelation 14:12, NET

The True Motive in Service

Part 1. "Don't show off your goodness to others to be admired by them." While the priests and Pharisees claimed to be jealous for the honor of God's law, self-glory was the real object that they were after. Christ made it clear to them that the lover of self is a transgressor of the law. The problem with human nature is that self is the center of our lives, unless we are born again and transformed by the Holy Spirit. Even when we uphold God's law, we need to be careful not to think that we are earning our way to heaven. Our acts of charity and good works should not be done to bring glory to ourselves. The kind of character that the grace of Christ develops in the soul is the opposite of selfishness. His followers are to bring glory to God, not to themselves. When Christ is in the heart, our prayers, our performance of duty, our benevolence, and our self-denial will not be the subjects of our conversation. Jesus will be magnified. Sincerity and purity of motives are what heaven values. We are not to think of reward but of service. Our deeds of kindness may have been done in secret, but the Father sees what we do, knows our hearts, and will one day reward us.

Questions: Can you explain how you plan to magnify the Lord in what you're doing? How does the Lord come through so that others will recognize the Lord in all of it?

JUNE 14

"Our Father, . . . Your kingdom come. Your will be done."
—Matthew 6:9, 10, NKJV

Part 2. "When you pray, don't be like the Pharisees in what they do." They had set times for prayer, and even if they were in the street and that time came, they would stop and, with a loud voice, say their prayers. All this was done for self-glorification. Jesus taught His disciples that private prayer is not to be made public. He wanted them to have a place for secret prayer, where they could have communion with God. Yes, we need to confess our sins to God, but He also watches for some return of gratitude, as a mother watches for a smile from her grateful child. To those who seek God in secret, telling Him their needs and asking for help, their requests will not be useless. God will answer their prayers in a way that is best for their eternal good.

Questions: Do you believe that God hears and answers every prayer of yours and answers it for your eternal good? What if His answers are delayed and not presently evident? How do you handle delays or no immediate answers?

JUNE 15

Building yourselves up on your most holy faith, praying in the Holy Spirit.
—Jude 20, NKJV

Part 3. "When you pray, don't keep repeating yourself as some people do." Some see long and repetitious prayers as having merit to do away with their sins, and they rejoice that they have power in themselves to do this. The Pharisees had adopted this idea of prayer from systems of false religion. This idea still exists in our day. Prayers, even the most eloquent prayers, do not have merit and power in themselves to take care of sin. God does not look for our ceremonial prayers but for the cry of broken and subdued hearts with a sense of weakness needing help. These are the prayers that find their way to the merciful and kind heavenly Father, to His forgiveness of sin and the spiritual blessings of grace.

Questions: When are repetitions of prayer needed and acceptable, and when are repetitions just a routine? Some people use prayer beads. Should you help these people to realize that such prayer repetitions do not make prayers more powerful? If so, how could you do it without discouraging them?

JUNE 16

I will greatly rejoice in the Lord, . . . for He has clothed me with the garments of salvation, He has covered me with the robe of righteousness.—Isaiah 61:10, NKJV

Part 4. "When you fast and pray, don't be like the hypocrites." Fasting is more than refusing food and wearing mourning clothes. Those who fast because of sorrow for sin never put on a display. The point of a fast that God has in mind is not to punish the body for sin but to help us have a clearer insight into the awfulness of sinning. When we humble our hearts before Him, we receive His pardoning grace and strength to carry on. Repentance is a turning away from self to Christ so that He can live His life through us. There is nothing gloomy about the religion of Jesus. If we have a mournful attitude as we live for Him, we misrepresent Him. And though in words we may claim God as our Father, if we are gloomy, we act as if we are orphans. Christ wants us to make His service appear attractive, as it really is. Leave your burdens at the foot of the cross, and go on you way rejoicing in His love for you.

Questions: What can you do to make the service of God look attractive? How would you do that?

JUNE 17

If riches increase, do not set your heart on them.—Psalm 62:10, NKJV

Part 5. "Don't accumulate for yourself treasures here on earth." Thieves can steal what you have, and disasters can come and take away what you have. Make heavenly treasure first, because where your heart is, that's where you thoughts will be. Money has been the ruling passion of human beings throughout the ages, and it still is today. Lay away spiritual treasures up in heaven. No one can steal them there, nor can disasters sweep them away. These alone of all you possess are forever yours. Forming a Christlike character is what Christ values more than anything else that you have or that you can give Him. Christ sees this as a spiritual treasure and as a reward to Him for what He has done for you.

In every effort to help and benefit others, we are living the life of Christ. When we give time or money toward spreading the gospel, we ourselves are being changed to reflect the love of Christ. And at the final day, when the things of earth will perish, we will see what living for Jesus here on earth has gained in the souls that have been saved because of us. We will meet them with joy and, together with them, sing the praises of our Savior and our heavenly Father.

Questions: Can you imagine what it will be like when people you don't know come up to you in heaven and thank you for what you did to bring them to Christ, directly or indirectly? You and they will praise the Lord forever.

June 18

You are my hope, O Lord God; you are my trust from my youth.
—Psalm 71:5, NKJV

Part 6. "Let your eye be single to the glory of God, and your whole body will be full of light." Singleness of purpose and wholehearted devotion to God is what Jesus pointed us to. Real life begins when all compromise with sin is at an end. As Paul said, "This one thing I do, I forget those things that are behind, and press toward the mark of the high calling in Christ." Temptation begins by permitting the mind to waver and holding back from giving ourselves fully to Christ, which opens the door to sin. Even a sinful desire held on to strengthens the soul not to give itself to God. Here we see the same law in the spiritual realm that operates in nature: what we plant and sow, we reap. By holding on to evil desires and not responding to the pleadings of divine love, we lose that love for good, the desire for God, and the heart capacity to receive the light of heaven. No one is ever deserted by God and given up to his or her own ways, as long as there is hope for their salvation.

Questions: What would you do without the hope you have in Jesus Christ? How do people live without such hope, and how can you help them?

JUNE 19

There is . . . one Lord, one faith, one baptism; one God and Father of all.
—Ephesians 4:4–6, NKJV

Part 7. "No man can serve two masters." Christ did not say that a man will not serve two masters but that he cannot. The interests of God and the interests of the world have no union. On one side of the line is the self-centeredness of the world, and on the other side is the self-denying follower of Christ. The Christian cannot stand with one foot on each side of the line, and no one can take a neutral position. He who does not give himself totally to God ends up under the control of another power. The enemy is constantly working to steal away the hearts of Christ's soldiers. As the apostle John says, "Love not the world; if any man loves the world, the love of the Father is not in him."

Questions: Are you having difficulty making Christ your only Master? Why? How can you change that?

JUNE 20

*Do not be conformed to this world, but be transformed by
the renewing of your mind.*—Romans 12:2, NKJV

Part 8. "Be not anxious and worry as the world does." There are times when we need to be concerned about the needs of our family, but we also need to remember that God loves us. He is not unmindful of our needs and concerns. Jesus pointed the people to the birds and the flowers that God had made to cheer us along the way. There is no little bird that the Father does not care about and sees when it falls. If the Father cares so much about little birds, will He not care that much more about us, His own children? On the flower petals, God has written His message of love. Why has He given us the singing birds and the fragrant flowers? God was not satisfied just to help you with your existence, but He filled the earth and the sky with glimpses of beauty to tell you of His loving thoughts toward you.

Just as the flowers spring up from the cold earth and even from the muddy river bed, they sprout up and unfold their beauty. The same way God will help you by His grace to spiritually sprout up and blossom with a life that is beautiful. Recommend God's love to others by your kindness, and they will also sprout up and blossom for Him. He will become their daily companion and familiar Friend, and their lives will be transformed into His image.

Questions: If your heavenly Father cares for the little birds, do you believe that He cares for you? Have you had evidence of such care in your life? Do you sense His care for you today? Are you willing to tell others of recent evidences of such care?

JUNE 21

I [John] saw a new heaven and a new earth. . . . There shall be no more death, nor sorrow, nor crying. There shall be no more pain.—Revelation 21:1–4, NKJV

Part 9. "Seek first the kingdom of God." The people listening to Jesus were still hoping for some announcement that He would set up the expected earthly kingdom. Jesus told them that this is what the people of the world are looking and hoping for, but God's kingdom is a spiritual kingdom. So you need to first give yourself to God's service and then look after the necessities of life. God wants to work out His righteousness in your life and character. Jesus submitted everything He did to the will of His Father. God's everlasting arm encircles everyone who turns to Him for help. The world will pass away, but the City of God will open its golden gates to receive those who, while on earth, learned to depend on God for guidance, wisdom, comfort, and hope in good times and hard times. The angels will welcome them into the City of God with songs of joy.

Questions: Can you imagine what it will be like when the angels see you coming through the gates of heaven and burst into song? Can you share such faith and hope with others by telling them what will happen when they walk through the gates of heaven?

JUNE 22

Your faith and hope are in God.—1 Peter 1:21, NKJV

Part 10. "Don't worry about tomorrow and the future; there is enough to be concerned about one day at a time." The events of tomorrow are open to the eyes of God, and we are not to take on the responsibility of God to set everything right. When we believe that God loves us and intends to do us good, we will stop worrying about the future. He gives His grace to us every day for the needs of that day. One day alone is ours, and each day we are to place our hands in the hand of Christ, casting all our cares and worries on Him, for He cares about us. If we give ourselves to Him every day and be converted anew every day, we will be joyous and happy in the Lord.

Questions: What do you think about the words of a song that say, "One day at a time, sweet Jesus, that's all I need from You. Just show me the way that I should go, one day at a time"? Do you really need to know the whole future of your life, or is knowing Jesus each day sufficient for you?

JUNE 23

Oh, give thanks to the LORD, for He is good! For His mercy endures forever.
—Psalm 107:1, NKJV

The Lord's Prayer

Part 1. "This is the way you should pray. Say, 'Our Father.' " Jesus gave the Lord's Prayer twice, first to the people in the Sermon on the Mount, and some months later to His disciples alone. One day the disciples found Him absorbed in prayer. Unaware of their presence, He prayed to the Father aloud. His face was shining with light, and He seemed to be in the very presence of God. As the disciples listened to Jesus' prayer, their hearts were awed and humbled. The Savior is not telling us to restrict our prayers to the exact words in the Lord's Prayer but to their significance and meaning. He taught us to begin with gratitude, then make our wants and needs known to God and claim His mercy and promise.

Jesus wants us to call His Father our Father. These are the very first words we are to use in approaching God. We have a divine relationship with Him. We are the sons and daughters of God. We are His children. We should rejoice that we are the recipients of such amazing love. In Him we are one family. God is our Father. He hears every word that we speak, listens to every prayer, feels our sorrows and disappointments, and notices how we treat our father, mother, sister, brother, friend, and neighbor. His plan for us is to uphold His honor, His character, and to be part of His spiritual family. Jesus wants us to look to God as our own Father, who is in heaven.

Questions: How do you treat each of your family members and neighbors? How do you relate to them? What can you do to make that relationship even better?

JUNE 24

I will praise the name of God with song.—Psalm 69:30, NASB

Part 2. "Holy and reverend is Your name. Your kingdom come." We are never to treat the name or titles of God lightly. By prayer we come into the audience chamber of God. When the angels come into His presence, they veil their faces and approach His throne with deep reverence. We are to honor His name by the way we live. God is our Father. The interests of His kingdom should be our first interests. We should pray for God's kingdom to come. In God's time it will surely come. But before His coming, Jesus said that we should take the gospel, the good news of His grace, to the whole world. For this purpose we should give ourselves to God and help others to come to Him, that they may receive forgiveness and the inheritance that God has in mind for them.

Questions: The interest in God's kingdom should be uppermost in our minds. Is it in yours? What are you doing for His kingdom, and what are you doing to hasten it?

JUNE 25

"To obey is better than sacrifice."—1 Samuel 15:22, NKJV

Part 3. "Thy will be done on earth, as it is in heaven." The will of God for us is expressed in the Ten Commandments. These ten principles are the principles of heaven. The angels consider doing God's will as the highest service of love. This service is not done in the spirit of legalism, as Satan made it out to be. When he opposed God's law and accused God of being arbitrary and dictatorial, that the law even existed came as a surprise to the angels, for their service had always been done out of love for God. Obedience to them was not a burden, something they had to do, but it was a joy for them to obey God and serve Him. As Christ said, "I delight to do Your will, my Father. Your law is in my heart."

Questions: How is God's will being done in heaven? How is it being carried out in your life? Could you tell others how you do it so they understand and are willing to carry out His will in their lives?

June 26

These were more noble-minded . . . examining the Scriptures daily.
—Acts 17:11, NASB

Part 4. "Give us this day our daily bread." In the first half of the Lord's Prayer, Jesus taught us about the sacredness of the Father's name and His kingdom. He taught us that we are the sons and daughters of God. We are part of His kingdom, and Christ is holding our place for us. But every day we should pray for what we need, both spiritually and physically, even for our daily food, and then thank Him for what we have. If God gave His Son for us because He loved us, will He not be concerned about our other needs? Also, when we pray for our needs, we should also pray for the needs of others, the hungry and destitute, and do what we can to help them. The prayer for daily food includes not only physical food but spiritual food as well. We receive Christ through the Scriptures, and the Holy Spirit is given to us as we read the Word of God. Every day we need to open the Bible and pray, and it will strengthen us for the day's needs and responsibilities. God has a purpose in all this, for He wants us to depend on Him and realize His constant care for us.

Questions: Are you noble-minded by searching daily? The Scriptures should be our daily spiritual food. How are you doing with your daily personal devotions? How do you feel when you miss a day? Does it bother you or doesn't it? If it doesn't, what's the problem? How can you correct it?

JUNE 27

In Him we have redemption through His blood, the forgiveness of sins, according to the riches of His grace.—Ephesians 1:7, NKJV

Part 5. "Forgive us our sins, as we forgive others their sins." Jesus is teaching us that we can receive forgiveness from Him only as we forgive others. He who has an unforgiving spirit cuts off the channel through which he can receive continued mercy from God. We should not think that we have to wait until the one who has injured us confesses his wrongs, or that we are justified in withholding our forgiveness until then. We should not feel sorry for ourselves to the point that we cannot have forgiveness in our hearts before there is a confession on the part of those who have injured us.

The one thing essential for us to be able to forgive is to hold on to the love that God has for us. Satan would love to lead us to think that because of our mistakes and sins, the Lord will not hear our prayers and forgive us. Even while we are praying, Satan whispers to us that there is no use to pray, since our prayers are blocked because of who we are and what we did. When we feel ashamed of what we did and think that we cannot pray because of it; that is the time to pray. Forgiveness and reconciliation come from God, not as a reward for what we did but as a gift to us through the righteousness of Christ. "If we confess our sins, God is faithful and just to forgive us our sins and cleanse us from all unrighteousness" (1 John 1:9).

Questions: How easy or hard is it for you to forgive others, especially those who have hurt you? Can you just tell yourself to forget it? Forgiveness is the only way for the memory of it to stop hurting. How do you get Jesus to give you the grace to forgive those who hurt you so the hurt will stop?

June 28

You have been my help; do not leave me nor forsake me.—Psalm 27:9, NKJV

Part 6. "Let us not be overtaken by temptation, but deliver us from the evil one." Temptation is an enticement to do what is not right. Satan tempts us to do evil so he can claim us as his own. In the symbolic prophecy of Zechariah, Satan is seen accusing Joshua, the high priest representing God's people, and he points to their filthy garments of sin. But the Lord says to Satan, "I have saved Joshua, forgiven his sins. He is mine. I have taken away his filthy garments and clothed him with my robe of righteousness" (Zechariah 3:1–4).

We should pray that God will not let us be drawn away from Him by our desires. We should surrender our lives to His guidance every day, asking Him to lead us in safe paths. We can't offer this kind of prayer and then go about our duties doing what we want to do. It's never safe to even think about the advantages of giving in to Satan's suggestions, no matter how flattering. The only safeguard is having Christ in our hearts and faith in His righteousness and love for us. Christ will never abandon one soul for whom He has died and who has given his heart to Him. Live in contact with Christ, place your hand in His, and He will firmly hold your hand and never let go.

Questions: Do you like flatteries, or can you handle them in the proper way so God will be glorified? How do you go about doing that?

JUNE 29

"Call upon Me in the day of trouble; I will deliver you, and you shall glorify Me."
—Psalm 50:15, NKJV

Part 7. "Thine is the kingdom, and the power, and the glory. Amen." This last sentence in the Lord's Prayer is like the first one, pointing to our heavenly Father. As nation fights nation, kingdom fights kingdom, and there are famines, earthquakes, and troubles, we are not to think that our hope is lost or that God has forsaken the earth. In Him we have hope, no matter what happens. God is our Father and everlasting Friend.

There is a crisis ahead of us such as the world has never before seen, but the coming events are in the hands of our Maker. His divine power will not leave us. He who never slumbers nor sleeps is continuously watching over His people. He who rules in the heavens is our Savior. Though the faith of His people will be tested, He is watching over them, and their destiny is safe in His hands.

Questions: How often do you praise the Lord for the assurance you have that He will see you through the difficulties of the end time? Can you give this assurance to others when you talk to them about the difficulties of the last days?

JUNE 30

The righteous God tests the hearts and minds.—Psalm 7:9, NKJV

Not Judging but Doing

Part 1. "Judge not, that you be not judged." The determination to earn our own salvation by what we do will lead us to set up all kinds of our own rules as a protection against sin. But this will lead us to focus on ourselves and become self-centered critics of others. This is what the Pharisees did, and they came from worship not humbled, not grateful for what had done for them, but with spiritual pride, thinking of their own attainments and critical of others. This led other people to do the same thing. We are not to set ourselves up as the standard by which to judge others or to make our opinions or interpretations of Scripture criteria for others. We are not qualified to sit in judgment of others. By doing so, we are condemning ourselves. To the Lord alone, who knows the hearts of people and who deals tenderly and compassionately with them, is given the right to decide the case of each one of us.

Questions: Do you believe that God is a just Judge, One who never makes a mistake? Are you tempted to believe that God is unfair by not taking some seemingly good people that you know to heaven? How do you handle this?

July 1

But they, measuring themselves by themselves, and comparing themselves among themselves, are not wise.—2 Corinthians 10:12, NKJV

Part 2. "Why focus on the little speck in your brother's eye and overlook the large piece of wood in your own eye?" Jesus is here talking about one who is quick to detect a character flaw in someone else and is zealous in trying to point it out. In doing this he shows that he lacks the spirit of Christian love and patience, and he misrepresents the gentle and courteous spirit of the gospel. He who sets himself up as a standard for others and presumes to judge their motives is putting himself in the place of Christ.

We must be good before we can do good and spiritually help others. We cannot exert an influence that will help others to want to do better until our own heart is humble and made tender by the grace of Christ. If Christ is in us, we will have no disposition to accuse and condemn, but to bless, help, and save others. Not until we are ready to sacrifice our own pride and self-dignity, and even be willing to lay down our life to save an erring brother, can we really touch his heart deep down. We need to let Christ be seen in our lives for Him to reveal His gentle spirit though us and create a new life in the lives of others.

Questions: Do you measure your spirituality by others? How do you know if you're doing that? And if you are, how do you correct it?

JULY 2

Blessed be God, who has not turned away my prayer.—Psalm 66:20, NKJV

Part 3. "Ask, and it shall be given to you; seek, and you will find; knock, and it will be opened to you." This is a thrice-given promise. By saying this, Jesus outlines no conditions except that we hunger for the Lord's mercy, desire His counsel, and long for His love. To ask shows that we realize our need. To seek shows that we not only long for His blessings but long for Him to fill us with His presence. God is seeking us, and we need to yield to the drawing of His Spirit. To knock means that we come to God at His invitation and are admitted into the closest intimacy with Him. So knock and wait at the door of mercy with firm assurance, for He will open the door and gladly receive you in.

He makes us understand His longing for us by comparing it to parents who love their children and are willing to do good to them. Would a loving parent turn away from a hungry child? But how much more does our heavenly Father love us, and He is willing to give the Holy Spirit to us when we ask Him. Should anyone dishonor God by imagining that He would not respond to the appeals of His children? With what wonderful tenderness Jesus has described the Father's love for us! Let us not forget that when we come to God as our Father, we acknowledge our relationship to Him as His child. We trust His goodness and yield to His will. His love for us is carved in the palms of the hands of His Son.

Questions: Can you imagine that when you see Jesus, you will see the scars in His hands and some on His head? Do you mean that Jesus will be scarred for eternity because of His love for you? Would you like to go to heaven with scars and have such for eternity? How does this make you feel about Jesus?

July 3

Create for me a pure heart, O God! Renew a resolute spirit within me!
—Psalm 51:10, NET

Part 4. "Therefore, however you want people to treat you, treat them the same way." Christ teaches that we should not be so concerned about how we should be treated, but how we should treat others. As we associate with others, we should put ourselves in their place. Enter into their feelings, their difficulties, disappointments, joys, and sorrows. We should identify ourselves with them. This "golden rule" is the principle of true courtesy. This is illustrated in the daily life of our Savior as it flowed out to others. The love of God leads us to open our hearts and to let Jesus come in, and the influence of the Savior and His grace will soften and purify our actions toward others. This is the truth as it is in Jesus.

Questions: Are you able to put yourself in the place of others and their trials? Do you think this is possible? How do you do that?

JULY 4

When [Barnabas] came and had seen the grace of God, he was glad, and encouraged them all that with purpose of heart they should continue with the Lord.
—Acts 11:23, NKJV

Part 5. "Small is the gate and narrow is the way which leads to life everlasting." In the time of Christ, people lived in walled cities, mostly situated on hills or small mountains. At sunset, just before night came, the gates were closed. If someone wanted to get home before dark, he had to hurry and follow the narrow road up the hill; if he delayed, he would be left outside. If he lived in an open village in the lowlands, one without walls or gates, the road would be wide, and there was no hurry to get home. But such villages had no protection, no security.

What Jesus said was familiar to everyone, and He applied it to our spiritual journey and the destination that we have in mind. There is plenty of room when traveling on the wide road to follow our inclinations and do whatever our self-love tells us to do. There is selfishness, pride, immorality, false doctrines, and no need to look for the road; it's right in front of you and easy to follow, but it ends in death. Our own ways, our own will, and our own self-centered ambitions must be given up. We cannot follow the world's standards and expect to arrive at our heavenly home in the City of God.

"Keep your eye on the small gate. Many will try to get in but never will." The traveler wanting to get into the city before the gates were closed had one purpose in mind. Jesus said that this same earnest purpose must be part of the Christian life. We should not conclude that the Christian road is necessarily an easy one. The greatest personal battles ever fought are against hereditary tendencies and habits, and so are the repeated challenges to surrender to the will of God, yielding to the sovereignty of His love. Every act of obedience and trial endured for Christ's sake is a step upward. If we take Christ as our guide, He will lead us safely home.

Questions: What size gate is your eye on as you approach the various-sized gates leading into heaven? Wouldn't it naturally be the big one, easy to get in? Why does Jesus suggest the small, narrow gate? What do you think?

JULY 5

The Lord is my rock and my fortress and my deliverer.—Psalm 18:2, NKJV

Part 6. "The house did not fall, because it was built on solid rock." The people who were listening to Christ were deeply moved. His words struck at the root of their ideas and opinions, and they knew that to accept His teachings would require a change in their habits of thinking and action. Jesus ended His teaching on the mount of blessing with an illustration about the whole structure of faith that the Pharisees and rabbis had built. The peasants who had built their houses in the valleys or on the grassy slopes were often swept away by heavy unexpected storms. But those who had built their houses on solid rock in the hills withstood the storms. Jesus said that if people would accept what He said and receive those teachings in their hearts, it would be like building a house on solid rock. His words will never be swept away. He is the Rock of Ages.

We build our spiritual house on Christ by obeying His word. It is not he who merely enjoys Jesus who is righteous, but he who does righteousness, who surrenders all to God and is doing the will of our heavenly Father. Doing the words of Christ is not earning God's favor; He already loves us, and we have received His love as a gift. Those whose hearts have been changed by the Holy Spirit—not those who now and then yield to His power, but those who are daily led by the Holy Spirit—are the sons and daughters of God. Follow the light you have. Set your heart to obey what you know, and the Holy Spirit will lead you closer to Jesus and give you power to obey. God promised, "I will strengthen you. I will help you. I will uphold you with My right hand."

Questions: How are you coming along with building your spiritual house? What materials are you using? Can you tell others?

Jesus as a Human

Insights From Ellen White's Book *The Desire of Ages*

JULY 6

For this is the way God loved the world: He gave [sent] his one and only Son.
—John 3:16, NET

"God With Us." *From the days of eternity Jesus was one with the Father, one with Him, for there never was a time when Jesus was not.* He was the image of God's greatness and majesty, the outshining of His glory. To make the Father's glory known, He came to this world. Jesus was to reveal God to men and angels, to make God's thinking and His amazing grace and love audible. We behold God in Jesus. He could have remained at the Father's side and retained the glory of heaven, but He chose to give the scepter back to the Father and step down from the throne of the universe. The Savior took on human nature and became one of us, a tie never to be broken, forever to retain His human nature. God permitted Jesus to face the life that is common to every man and fight the battle as every human has to fight, at the risk of failure and loss.

Questions: Would you be willing to take on a lower nature? Forever?

JULY 7

"God did not send his Son into the world to condemn it, but to save it."
—John 3:17, TLB

The Commitment. *Jesus' love for us was stronger than His pain and death on Calvary, and it was also a reflection of the Father's love, who died for us in His Son.* Satan presented God as selfish and oppressive. Having undertaken our redemption, God spared nothing, however dear, that is necessary for our salvation. The Father gives all the resources of infinite power into the hands of Christ for the sake of humanity, to convince us that there is no greater love in heaven or earth than God's love.

Questions: What would you do if you were given infinite power? How would you use it to save everyone? If you would not, why not?

July 8

"Blessed are the poor in spirit."—Matthew 5:3, NET

"We Have Seen His Star." *Baby Jesus and His parents were so poor that they had to be sustained with gifts from the wise men from the East directed to Bethlehem by God.* When they saw Him, they recognized the presence of divinity. They gave their hearts to Him as their Savior and gave Him gifts of gold and other treasures. Through these gifts the Father supplied the means for Joseph and Mary to go to Egypt to avoid the massacre of the male babies by Herod. This was the Savior's reception when He came to this world. God could not trust His beloved Son with men, even though He had come for their salvation.

Questions: What would you do if men from other countries came to honor you? How would you respond? What if they gave you presents of gold and silver?

July 9

Every scripture is inspired by God and useful for teaching [others].
—2 Timothy 3:16, NET

As a Child. *Jesus' mother watched with deep interest the purity of His character.* Through the Holy Spirit she received wisdom to cooperate with heaven in the development of Jesus. His mother was His first human teacher. From her lips and from the scrolls of the prophets He learned of heavenly things. Since He gained knowledge as we do, His intimate acquaintance with Scripture shows how diligently His early years were given to the study of God's Word. From the first dawning of intelligence, He was growing in spiritual grace and the knowledge of God. Yet, it was necessary for Him to be constantly on guard in order to preserve His purity.

Jesus lived in a peasant's home, and He faithfully and cheerfully acted His part in bearing the burdens of the household. He was a willing servant, a loving, obedient son working with His own hands in the old carpenter shop, wearing the simple garb of a common laborer. He carried cheerfulness and tact into His labor. Often He expressed the gladness of His heart by singing. He whose word of power upheld the worlds even stooped to relieve a wounded bird.

Questions: Are you willing to preserve your purity at any cost? How far would you go with a commitment like that?

JULY 10

"Blessed are the peacemakers, for they will be called the children of God."
—Matthew 5:9, NET

Days of Conflict. Jesus did not ignore His responsibilities to His earthly parents, and He faithfully performed the duties of a son, a brother, a friend, and a fellow citizen. He was not exclusive. In a gentle and submissive way, Jesus tried to please those on all levels of society with whom He came in contact. He was gentle and unobtrusive, but He maintained His stand on Scripture. Even in His youth He had to learn the hard lesson of patient endurance and silence. Because of His obedience to the law of God, He was called stubborn.

Jesus relieved every case of suffering that He saw. He had no money to give, but He often denied Himself food in order to help those more needy than He. When His brothers spoke harshly to the poor, Jesus afterward went to those poor, spoke words of encouragement, and quietly placed His own meal in their hands. All this displeased His older brothers, and they accused Him of thinking Himself superior to them. But He loved them and treated them with unfailing kindness.

Poverty marked His life at every step. He did not strive for recognition, and even in the lowliest position He was content. The one thing that Jesus hated was sin. He could not witness a wrong act without pain that was impossible to hide. Jesus never defended His own rights. As a result, His work became hard, because He was so willing and uncomplaining. Yet He never became discouraged, because He lived above all those difficulties. He never retaliated when roughly treated, bearing all insults patiently. He was always concerned about others and passed no human being by as worthless, but sought to inspire every soul with hope, no matter how rough and unpromising their situation.

Questions: What would you do if you were living in poverty? What would you do if you had power to change it?

JULY 11

"What should we do (before we go)?"... "Be baptized in the name of Jesus Christ."
—Acts 2:37, 38, NET

The Baptism. *Jesus responded to the call of God to begin His public ministry when John the Baptist was preaching. He* recognized that His time had come to turn from His daily toil to ministry. So he said goodbye to His mother and went to the Jordan River to be baptized by John. Coming out of the water, Jesus bowed in prayer, and a new and important responsibility was opened to Him. As one with us, He must now bear the burden of our guilt. Every sin, every discord, every defiling lust that transgression had brought was torture to His spirit. Yet He must tread this path, for He had laid off His glory and accepted the weakness of being human for the salvation of man. Never before have angels listened to such a prayer. The Father Himself answered the petition of His Son, and a voice from heaven said, "This is My beloved Son, in whom I am well pleased." God spoke to Jesus as our representative. Despite all our sins and weaknesses, we are not cast aside as worthless.

Questions: Are you willing to be baptized, even a second time? Why?

July 12

Resist the devil and he will flee from you.—James 4:7, NET

The Victory. *After Jesus was baptized, He went into the hills to be alone with God and prepare for His ministry; while there, He was severely tempted by the devil.* Jesus manifested perfect trust in His heavenly Father and gave us an example of submission and trust. Satan appeared as an angel of light, saying that he had a message from heaven. He tempted Jesus, asking Him to prove to him that He was the Son of God. Christ refused, because to prove His divinity would bring doubt on what the Father had said at His baptism, and He would give in to Satan. Jesus gained the victory over Satan's angelic appearance by submission and faith in God, and by holding to Scripture.

Questions: Are you willing to stand by Scripture at any cost? Are you sure?

July 13

"Teacher, I will follow you wherever you go."—Matthew 8:19, NET

"We Have Found the Messiah." *When Jesus returned from His preparation for ministry, He quietly mingled with the followers of John the Baptist without drawing attention to Himself.* When the people did look at Him, they saw a face full of divine compassion and power, yet every glance of the eye and feature of the face were marked with humility and love. His manners were gentle and unassuming. Jesus came to us in poverty and humiliation. By taking on humanity, Jesus united His interests with us and became the means of men and women communicating more deeply with God and God with us.

Two disciples of John the Baptist decided to follow Jesus. They were John, the brother of James, and Andrew, the brother of Peter. These were the first fruits of His ministry, and there was joy in the heart of the divine Teacher as these men responded to His love and grace.

Questions: Can you stay humble even when you're being admired? Are you sure?

July 14

At the Marriage Feast. Jesus did not begin His public ministry by doing some great work, but ministered to people's happiness at a wedding in a little Galilean village. Every act of Christ's life on earth was in fulfillment of the plan that had existed from the days of eternity. Before He came to earth, the plan was laid out before Him in all its details, and He did not back away. When He came to live among us, He was guided step by step by the Father, and with submission He waited until He was told when to act. After the miracle at the wedding, He withdrew so quietly that the disciples didn't even notice it. To the mind of Jesus, the gladness at the wedding festivities pointed forward to the rejoicing of that day when He will bring home His bride to the Father's house.

Jesus reached the hearts of people by going among them as one who desired their good. He met them at their daily work and manifested an interest in what they did. The example of Christ in linking Himself with the interests of people should be followed by all who receive the gospel of grace, meeting others where they are. If our eyes are fixed on Jesus, we will see a compassionate Redeemer and will catch His spirit and compassion.

Questions: Are you willing to visit people at their daily work? No matter what kind of work they do?

July 15

Do you not know that you are God's temple and that God's Spirit lives in you?
—1 Corinthians 3:16, NET

In His Temple. *When the celebration of the Passover came, Jesus decided to mingle unnoticed with the people on their way to Jerusalem.* Many came who were sick, blind, lame, and deaf, who had to be brought there on litters. Some were too poor to buy food or to give the smallest offering. When Jesus came into the temple, He took in the whole scene, and His heart of pity ached when no one seemed to take pity on the poor and sick. Indignation, authority, and power were seen in His face. Soon the attention of the people was riveted on Him. The confusion hushed, and the deep silence was painfully felt. Looking at Christ, they see divinity flashing through humanity. Jesus seems to be standing there as divine Judge. He speaks with authority, saying, "Do not make My Father's house a house of buying and selling." He overturns the tables of the money changers. Then the people turn to Christ and ask Him to bless them. He hears every cry, and with the pity of a loving mother bent over her little ones, He looks at each one and heals all those around Him.

Questions: Are you willing to share your food with other people? How much of it?

July 16

We know that whoever is born of God does not sin.—1 John 5:18, NKJV

Nicodemus. *Jesus accepted an invitation from Nicodemus, a Pharisee, to have a private meeting with him at night.* Jesus spoke to him with dignity and respect, and in look and tone He expressed deep, earnest love for him. Repentance comes through Christ as truly as pardon does. By faith we receive the grace of God, but faith is not our Savior. It earns nothing. It is the hand by which we lay hold on Christ and His merits. Then the Holy Spirit produces a new life in the soul, and the thoughts and desires are brought into obedience to the will of Christ. In none of His other talks and conversations did Jesus explain so fully, step by step, the change necessary in the heart to inherit the kingdom of heaven. Nicodemus emerged from this night meeting a changed man and came boldly to the forefront, helping the disciples and the infant church.

Questions: Are you willing to talk privately to an important person and tell them they must be born again? How would you go about it?

JULY 17

*I will praise You, O Lord my God, with all my heart,
and I will glorify Your name.*—Psalm 86:12, NKJV

"He Must Increase." *Jesus' purpose in His life was the same as John
the Baptist's, who called for people to repent and give their hearts to God.* The
people's attention was fixed on John's preaching, but he directed it to
Jesus. It was his joy to witness the success of the Savior's ministry. "I
rejoice," he said, "to see Him increase and myself decrease." Willingly
he accepted silence and obscurity, for he knew that love of self must be
swallowed up in love for Christ. This was the same spirit that Christ had
when He was human and said, "I seek not Mine own will, but the will
of the Father who sent Me." Jesus knew that some would spare no effort
to create a division between Him and John, so He quietly withdrew
and went to Galilee.

Questions: Are you willing to leave where you are and move to help
others? How far—to the mission field?

JULY 18

Give thanks to the LORD, for He is good! . . . Let the redeemed of the LORD say so.—Psalm 107:1, 2, NKJV

At Jacob's Well. *On the way to Galilee, Jesus passed through the province of Samaria and was very tired and thirsty.* When He got to the beautiful valley of Shechem, He sat on the little wall around the city well to rest, while the disciples went to buy food. A woman came to draw water from the well. She filled her pitcher and turned to leave. Jesus, with great tact and love, asked her for a drink of water. The woman stopped, turned, and asked Jesus, being a Jew, talking to a Samaritan. Patiently Jesus allowed her to lead the conversation while watching for a chance to speak to her heart. The woman was so impressed with what He said and the tone of His voice that she felt He was her friend. He told her of God's love and grace.

The spiritual response of the woman was refreshing to Him, and her gratefulness brought joy to His heart. As a mother watches for that special smile from her little child which shows the dawning of intelligence, so Christ watches for expressions of grateful love, which shows that spiritual life is begun in the soul. Then the woman went and told the townspeople about Jesus, and they came out and invited Him to stay with them. Though He was a Jew, He mingled freely with them, accepted their hospitality, slept under their roofs, ate with them at their tables, taught in their streets, and treated them with the utmost kindness and courtesy.

Questions: Are you willing to help others even if you're misunderstood? Have you thought about this?

July 19

So then faith comes by hearing, and hearing by the word of God.
—Romans 10:17, NKJV

"Except You See Signs and Wonders." *Jesus did not refuse the request for help by an army officer in the service of King Herod.* This officer had heard about Jesus' miracles, so he decided to go to Him and ask Him to heal his young son, who was suffering from an incurable disease. The physicians had given him up to die. The father was determined to get help. When he saw that Jesus was just a common man, he was disappointed, yet he talked to Jesus, told Him the problem, and asked Him to come to his house to heal his son. Before the father had left the house, Jesus knew that he was coming to ask Him to heal his son. Jesus not only longed to heal the boy but to bring salvation to the whole family.

The officer had a degree of faith, so Jesus looked at him and said, "Except you see a miracle, you don't really believe who I am." Like a flash of light, those words penetrated the heart of the officer. Suddenly he realized that his thoughts and motives were not totally right and that they might cost the life of his son. So with his whole heart and by faith, he reached out to Jesus and would not give up. Jesus looked at him and said, "Be on your way—your son is healed." With strong confidence the officer took hold of what Christ said and accepted Christ as his own Redeemer. At home, the family members, who were by the side of the young man, suddenly saw a change in his face. His fever was gone, and his eyes opened. With intelligence he looked at the family and then fell into a deep, restful sleep.

At first the officer wanted to see the fulfillment of his prayer before he would believe, but he had to accept what Jesus said. When we come to Jesus asking for help, every request reaches the heart of God. We need to believe this and then go about our duties, assured that the blessing will come when we need it the most.

Questions: Are you willing to help an army officer occupying your country? Would you do this kindly or because you had to?

JULY 20

If my father and mother desert me, Yahweh will care for me still.—Psalm 27:10, JB

"Is Not This the Carpenter's Son?" *During His childhood and youth, Jesus worshiped with His family at the synagogue in Nazareth.* After He began His ministry, He came back home for a visit and to worship with them again. The people who had known Him from childhood were all there, eager to see Him as He came in and took His place among the worshipers.

During the service, the rabbi who was present gave the sermon, and any Israelite might be asked to give the Scripture reading. On this particular Sabbath, Jesus was asked to come up front and give the reading from the prophets. As Jesus stood before the people, He explained the meaning of what He read. His words thrilled the hearers with a power that they had not felt before. Their hearts were moved by the Holy Spirit, and they responded with a loud "Amen."

When they were told that they needed salvation and a Savior, their pride was offended. They said to themselves, "Who does this Jesus think He is? He's just the son of a carpenter. His father is Joseph. We've seen Him working by the carpenter's bench and in the fields. We've seen Him grow up." And when Jesus mentioned blessings going to the Gentiles, a fierce national pride was aroused, and the worship service broke up. The people grabbed Him and hurriedly pushed Him to the edge of a precipice, ready to push Him over. Some were ready to stone Him. Suddenly He disappeared. Heavenly messengers surrounded Him and conducted Him to a place of safety.

Questions: How would you feel if, after having done good, you came back to your home church where you grew up and they didn't want you? Can you imagine something like this happening?

JULY 21

He said to them, "Come aside . . . and rest a while."—Mark 6:31, NKJV

The Call by the Sea. *Jesus hoped to get a little rest from the multitude that followed Him day after day.* He stepped into Peter's boat to get away from the crowd so He could talk to them away from the shoving and pushing and be better seen and heard. Aged men leaning on their canes, hardy peasants, fishermen, merchants, priests and rabbis, the rich and learned, old and young were all there. Many had brought their sick and suffering ones to be healed.

In addition to the crowds Jesus saw on the beach, prophetically He looked down the ages and saw some of His followers being tempted, afflicted, suffering, and put in prison. Also He saw that there would be believers who would come to help His followers and bring them messages of comfort and hope. And through the Holy Spirit, Jesus Himself would be with them to the close of time and enable them to bear much fruit to the glory of God.

Questions: Are you willing to go to the afflicted to give them comfort and hope? What would you do to help them?

July 22

I will praise You, O Lord, with my whole heart;
I will tell of all Your marvelous works.—Psalm 9:1, NKJV

At Capernaum. *Jesus never flattered anyone for their wisdom or cleverness, which He knew would only increase their pride.* But those who were ready to listen marveled at the spiritual truth expressed in His simple language. The most highly educated were charmed by His words, and the uneducated and illiterate profited by what they heard. Jesus' tender compassion fell with a touch of healing on troubled hearts. The purity of His character and the love expressed in look and tone is what drew people to Him. Had it not been for the sweet, sympathetic spirit that shone out in every look and word, He would not have attracted so large a crowd. Those afflicted saw in Him a faithful and tender friend.

While the congregation sat there spellbound, Jesus came down from the rostrum and quietly left the synagogue and went to the home of Peter for a little rest. The news of where Jesus was staying quickly spread throughout the city. The sick were carried there, some came leaning on staffs, and others supported by friends tottered feebly into His presence. Hour after hour they came, and the air was filled with the voices of triumph and deliverance. Jesus rejoiced to restore them to health. When the long day was over, Jesus needed some rest. He quietly made His way into the hills to spend the night in prayer, talking with His heavenly Father and preparing Himself for the next day's work.

Jesus was not satisfied just to attract attention to Himself as a healer, but to draw people to Himself as their Savior. In His life there was no self-assertion. Position and talent and wealth had no attraction for Him. To have the Father revealed in the character of His Son was the great desire of Jesus.

Questions: Are you willing to work long hours helping people? Would you do this day after day?

JULY 23

If we confess our sins, he who is faithful and just will forgive us our sins and cleanse us from all unrighteousness.—1 John 1:9, NRSV

"You Can Make Me Clean." Jesus did not shy away from lepers and healing them, even though He was accused of being unclean by touching them. Nor did He stop forgiving sins and being accused of playing God. A severe case of leprosy was considered incurable and very contagious. One such leper heard about Jesus' power to heal and was determined to go to the Savior—this was his only hope. Being guided there, he sees Jesus healing the sick, the lame, the blind, and the paralyzed. Faith strengthens in his heart. He's a terrible spectacle—his decaying body is horrible to look at. People back away, and some even try to prevent him from coming close to Jesus. When he gets closer, he throws himself at Jesus' feet and cries out, "Lord, if You will, I know You can make me clean!" Jesus places His hand on him and says, "I will—be clean." Immediately a change took place. His nerves became sensitive and his muscles firm. The rough, scaly surface disappeared, and his skin became as smooth as that of a child.

Also there was a paralytic who was entirely helpless and had lost all hope. He was brought to Jesus, and the Savior healed him as He had the man with leprosy. But the paralytic wanted the forgiveness of his sins and the peace of heaven more than physical healing. While he was still at home, he repented of his sins and believed in the power of Jesus to make him whole. His friends agreed to take him to the house where Jesus was. They got on the flat roof, opened a place, and lowered him down on a stretcher in front of Jesus. When the Savior saw the pleading look in the man's eyes, He said to him, "Son, be of good cheer—your sins are forgiven." Jesus' words fell like music on the man's ears. Then Jesus said, "Get up, pick up your stretcher, and go home." Strength came into the man's body. He stood up, picked up his stretcher, and walked home. The people glorified God, and the Pharisees stood there amazed.

Questions: As a physician, what would you do if you had such miracle-working power? Would you use it rightly or recklessly?

July 24

Let us love one another, for love is of God.—1 John 4:7, NKJV

Levi-Matthew. *The Savior did not hesitate to reach out to tax collectors who collected taxes for the hated Romans.* The only people who were more despised than the Romans were their tax collectors. These taxes were a constant irritation to the people. One such Jewish tax collector was Matthew. He was hated, but Jesus saw in him a man whose heart was open to truth. Walking by his tax booth, Jesus looked at him and said, "Come, follow Me." Without a question, Matthew turned the job over to his helpers and left to follow Jesus, exchanging his lucrative business for poverty. He did so with his whole heart and longed to bring his fellow tax collectors to Jesus also.

So he held a feast at his house for his relatives and friends in honor of Jesus, who accepted the invitation with courtesy, even though this would offend the Pharisees and the people. No question of policy could influence Jesus. With Him, external distinctions meant nothing. By accepting the place of an honored guest, Jesus gave recognition to the dignity of humans, and men longed to become worthy of His confidence.

Questions: How would you relate to dishonest tax collectors? Would your friendship be able to win them to Christ and honesty?

July 25

*"Anyone who does not welcome the kingdom of God like
a little child will never enter it."*—Luke 18:17, JB

He Ordained Twelve. As Jesus was preparing His disciples for their ministry, Judas pushed his way into their circle to be one of them, and though Jesus knew Judas would betray Him, He did not turn away from him. Jesus withdrew from the confusion of the city to talk to His disciples among the quietness of the trees and hills. The Savior knew the character of these men. Each one was different from the others. They sat together in groups of three or four, and Jesus talked to them about getting them ready for ordination. Judas was there professing to be a follower of Christ. With earnestness he said, "Master, I will follow You." Jesus did not repulse him. Judas believed that Jesus was the Messiah and by joining the disciples, he hoped to receive a high position in the new kingdom, and Jesus knew this.

But the disciples wanted Judas to become one of them because he had great executive ability. How tenderly the Savior dealt with the man who would betray Him. Jesus presented to Judas the principle of benevolence that would root out covetousness, but Judas would not change his ambition, which he didn't see as being wrong. Christ's life was a living example of what He taught, but lesson after lesson fell on the deaf ears of Judas. The Savior read Judas's heart like an open book. When Jesus ended His instruction to the disciples, He gathered them close to Him. Then He knelt among them, and, laying His hands on their heads, He offered a prayer of dedication and ordained them.

Questions: How would you relate to someone you knew would accuse you falsely? What if they had you arrested?

JULY 26

Let this mind be in you which was also in Christ Jesus.—Philippians 2:5, NKJV

Sermon on the Mount. The measure of attention that Jesus gave to His disciples and to the people who followed Him was in proportion to their great value in His eyes and in the eyes of the universe. The Sermon on the Mount was given primarily to the disciples but in the hearing of the multitude. They always sat close beside Him. There was pride and hope in the air as the disciples and the people anticipated that the kingdom would come, Israel would be honored above all nations, and Jerusalem would be the capital of God's universal kingdom. But Jesus disappointed their hopes and undid the work of false education. He did not make a direct attack on this misunderstanding, but He told them the conditions of entrance into this new kingdom, leaving them to draw their own conclusions.

He said, "Blessed are those who recognize their spiritual poverty, sorrow for their sins, submit to God, and are humble, meek, self-controlled, and calm in the face of rebuff and cruelty." This is the highest evidence of nobility. After explaining what constitutes true blessedness and happiness, Jesus made it clearer to His disciples that they were chosen to lead others in the path of righteousness, even though they would often suffer from disappointment and discouragement as they were insulted and their testimony rejected. Jesus knew what this was like, and in addition, He was hungry, thirsty, tired, and needed food and sleep just as they did.

Questions: How would you feel if you were insulted and rejected as you spread the gospel? Would you give up?

JULY 27

You, O Lord, are a God full of compassion, and . . . abundant in mercy.
—Psalm 86:15, NKJV

The Centurion. *Jesus responded to the faith of strangers and reached out to widows who had lost family members.* A centurion is a commander of one hundred troops in the Roman army. He was stationed in Capernaum with his men and had a servant who was stricken with palsy and was at the point of death. Among the Romans their servants were slaves bought and sold in the marketplace, and they often were treated abusively and with cruelty. But this officer love his servant, was tenderly attached to him, and wanted him healed. He believed that Jesus could heal him. He showed kindness to the Jews and felt unworthy to come into the presence of Jesus. He simply said to Jesus, "Just give the word and my servant will be healed. I am a man of authority, and my soldiers obey me. I just have to speak, and they do what they're told." When Jesus heard this, He marveled at the centurion's great faith, a faith that He had not found in Israel. Then Jesus said to him, "As you have believed, so be it." At that same hour the centurion's servant was healed.

Twenty miles from Capernaum was the village of Nain, and Jesus made His way there. As He and His disciples got close to town, a funeral procession was coming out, making its way slowly to the place of burial, accompanied by mourners filling the air with their groans. They were carrying the body of a young man, the only son of a widowed mother and her only support. When Jesus saw this, His heart of compassion reached out to her. He stopped the funeral procession, came close to her, and gently said, "Don't cry. Your son is not dead but only sleeping." He touched the bier carrying the body and said with an authoritative voice, "Young man, I'm telling you to get up!" The young man opened his eyes; Jesus took him by the hand and helped him up. Then He watched as the mother and her son were united in a long, clinging, and joyous embrace.

Questions: What would you do if you had the power to raise the dead? How would you know which ones to raise and which ones not to raise?

JULY 28

I bow my knees to the Father of our Lord Jesus Christ, from whom the whole family in heaven and earth is named.—Ephesians 3:14, 15, NKJV

"Who Are My Brothers?" *Jesus loved His family, even when He was misunderstood and treated unfairly.* Joseph had sons from a previous marriage who were older than Jesus (Joseph's first wife had died). They heard about Jesus' labors, His entire nights in prayer, and His constantly being crowded with people demanding His attention. They were worried about Him wearing Himself out. In fact, His brothers thought that Jesus' mind was becoming unbalanced, as shown by His claiming divine authority and by His attitude toward the Pharisees, who were accusing Him of casting out demons by using the power of Satan. This reproach of Jesus fell on His brothers and the entire family. The brothers thought that Jesus needed their counsel and that He should listen to their ideas. This pressure by them was most painful to Jesus. He found relief only through communion with His heavenly Father, yet His heart was full of love and kindness toward His brothers.

The brothers decided that Jesus would have to be stopped from what He was doing, and they talked Mary into helping them. They went to where Jesus was teaching, and His disciples gave Him the message that His mother and brothers wanted to see Him. Jesus knew what was in His brothers' hearts and said to His disciples, "Who is a mother to Me, and who are My brothers? It is those who do the will of My Father; they are closer to Me than an earthly family." The responsibility of redemption had been given to Him when He became part of the human family. We should recognize and appreciate His relationship to us, for we are His brothers and sisters!

Questions: What would you do if you had brothers who were against you because you were good? Would you stay away from them or try to get close to them?

JULY 29

"Peace I leave with you, My peace I give to you."—John 14:27, NKJV

"Peace, Be Still!" *Jesus trusted His Father and rested in His love and care in the midst of storms at sea and while facing evil spirits.* All day long Jesus had been teaching and healing, with scarcely a moment to eat or rest, and the Pharisees were constantly criticizing Him. When evening came, He was tired and utterly worn out. So He decided to get some rest across the lake in a solitary place. Overcome with weariness and hunger, he got into the boat, lay down, and fell asleep.

Soon the sun set and the night settled on the rough sea. The waves lashed against the disciples' boat as the winds picked up, and soon they were helpless in the middle of a terrific storm. Absorbed in saving themselves and the boat, they forgot that Jesus was on board. Finally, they realized that Jesus was at one end of the boat sleeping, and they called out, "Master, don't you care?" Their cries woke Him up, and as the lightning flashed again, they saw the peace of heaven on His face. Jesus, trusting in His Father's care, stood up, lifted His hand, and said to the angry sea, "Peace, be still!" Immediately the storm stopped, the waves quieted down. Awe filled their hearts, and the storm was forgotten.

In the morning the boats landed on the other shore. What greeted them was terrifying. Two devil-possessed men came charging down the hill, their eyes glaring. They looked like wild beasts. The disciples ran, and when they turned to look back, Jesus was still standing there. He raised His hand, and the men could not come closer. Then Jesus commanded the demons to come out, and the men fell at the Savior's feet. When Jesus turned to go to the boat, they begged Him not to leave or to let them come with Him. But Jesus asked them to go home and tell the people what great things the Lord had done for them. They did and were the first missionaries to their people.

Questions: What would you do if devil-possessed men were coming at you? How would you respond?

JULY 30

Be an example . . . in word, in conduct, in love, in spirit, in faith, in purity.
—1 Timothy 4:12, NKJV

The First Evangelists. Jesus never compromised the truth but always spoke with love and tact. When challenged by the priests, there were tears in His voice as He responded. Now the apostles were like members of Jesus' own family. They went with Him as He traveled on foot throughout Galilee and shared toils and hardships with Him. They listened to His teachings and learned from Him how to work in helping people. But they also needed to learn how to work alone. In the training of the disciples, the example of Jesus' life was far more effective than any instruction.

As the Savior's eye penetrates the future, He sees the experience of His followers through the ages until His second coming. He sees the conflicts they must meet and how they will have to contend with spiritual forces and will need supernatural help. Angels will be in their ranks to help them, and the Holy Spirit will direct the battle. Jesus said to His disciples, "I send you out as sheep among wolves, so be wise and harmless in what you do." The Savior Himself did not suppress one word of truth, but He always spoke it in love, exercising the greatest tact and thoughtful and kind attention. He was never rude, never needlessly spoke a severe word, and never gave needless pain to a sensitive soul. He never censured human weakness, yet He did denounce hypocrisy and sin, and there were tears in His voice when He had to do so. He never compromised truth to secure peace, but His heart overflowed with love for the whole human family.

Jesus said to His disciples, "If you acknowledge Me to others, I will acknowledge you before the Father and the angels. You are My witnesses and channels through which My grace can flow out to others for spiritual healing. I will be your representative in heaven, and the Father does not see your faulty character, but He sees you clothed in My perfection."

Questions: Are you willing to never compromise truth? Are you sure? Where do you get such commitment?

July 31

Though I bestow all my goods to feed the poor . . . but have not love, it profits me nothing.—1 Corinthians 13:3, NKJV

"Give Them to Eat." *While Jesus could work miracles to feed many hungry people, He was never motivated to draw attention to Himself.* Christ had gone with His disciples to a secluded place to get some rest and quietude, but soon the peaceful atmosphere was changed. People noticed the direction they were going and followed them. Soon there were five thousand men grouped together, not counting women and children. From the hillside Jesus looked at this large multitude of people, and, interrupted as His rest was, He was not upset or impatient with them. He went and began teaching them, and as the people listened, Jesus' words of love and mercy flowed out so simply and plainly that they brought gladness to their hearts.

Jesus had worked all day without rest or food, and He was pale from weariness and hunger. The disciples tried to persuade Him to stop, leave the people, and go to a secluded place to get some rest. Jesus said, "Let's feed the people." The disciples responded, "Where are we going to get food to feed such a huge crowd? Besides, it would cost a lot of money, and we have so little. The only food available is what a little boy has—five small loaves of bread and two small fish." Jesus asked to see the little boy, who willingly gave Jesus his lunch. Jesus thanked him and said to His disciples, "Tell the people to group themselves together by fifties or hundreds." Then the Savior blessed the little lunch. It multiplied, and the disciples passed the food out to the people, who ate until they were full.

All day the conviction among the people got stronger that Jesus is the long-looked-for Deliverer. In their enthusiasm they were ready to crown Him king, and the disciples united with the people to do so. Jesus called His disciples together and told them to get into the boat and cross the lake to Capernaum. Then Jesus commanded the multitude to disperse. His manner was so decisive that they dared not to disobey. Then Jesus went up into the hills to pray.

Questions: Are you willing to get involved in feeding the hungry? Have you ever been hungry, really hungry? Would you be grateful for someone helping you?

AUGUST 1

He is despised and rejected by men, a Man of sorrows and acquainted with grief.
—Isaiah 53:3, NKJV

The Crisis in Galilee. Because of the spiritual application that Jesus made to the miracle of feeding the people, many turned against Him, which brought great pain to His heart. The news of the miracle of feeding thousands of people with five little loaves and two small fish spread everywhere. People came from near and far, by land and sea, to Bethsaida and to Capernaum, looking for Him. Meanwhile, He had gone to Gennesaret. There the people found Him in the synagogue and learned from the disciples how He had walked on water to the disciples' boat and gotten in. The people wanted to know more, but He did not satisfy their curiosity. The fact that He claimed to be sent by God and yet refused to be crowned king was a mystery the people could not understand. Jesus tried to explain that He is their Savior and that they must feed on Him and receive Him into their hearts. His life must become theirs, and His love and grace must be assimilated. He was so surrendered to the will of God that the Father alone appeared in His life, and they must do the same.

When the people heard this, many of them turned away from Jesus, and a different spirit took control. They now saw nothing attractive about Jesus that they had once seen, and they were now in harmony with His enemies. The news spread that Jesus was not the Messiah, and popular feeling turned against Him. His compassion and love were not appreciated, and His mercy and salvation were rejected. This filled Jesus with a sorrow inexpressible, and He wept.

Questions: Are you so surrendered to the Father that people see Him reflected in what you do? How do you do that?

AUGUST 2

"You have made the commandment of God of no effect by your tradition."
—Matthew 15:6, NKJV

Tradition. Jesus did not hesitate to gently but firmly point out the self-interest by which the scribes and Pharisees interpreted the law. They expected Him to come to the Passover at Jerusalem, and they laid a plot for Him. Jesus knew this, so He stayed away, but they came looking for Him. Many people kept looking for Jesus to carry out their expectations of the Messiah to restore Israel to greatness, which, together with the disciples' commitment to Him, excited the jealousy of the Jewish leaders. So they sent spies to watch His every move. They did not challenge Jesus directly but criticized His disciples, accusing them of not following the tradition of the elders. Jesus made no attempt to defend Himself or His disciples but pointed to the spirit and attitude that motivated these Jewish leaders.

The people had been told by their leaders that they could decide to dedicate all their property to the support of the temple by calling for it to be "Corban" [a gift] and use it all for themselves, while neglecting the needs of their parents. Jesus pointed out that tithes and offerings were important but the priests and rabbis, in their false zeal for God, supported the temple selfishly. It was the purpose of Jesus to free the people from this bondage of tradition and false teaching.

Questions: Are you willing to give up traditional beliefs and go by the Bible alone? Are you sure?

AUGUST 3

"God made no distinction between them and us,
since he purified their hearts by faith."—Acts 15:9, JB

Barriers Broken Down. *Jesus never discriminated against races or cultures but loved all people and treated them as being of equal value.* After the encounter with the Pharisees, Jesus left Galilee and went to the hill country of Phoenicia to find some rest and to prepare His disciples for their mission. In the Phoenician area, there was a woman of Canaanite descent who had heard about Jesus. Hope sprang up in her heart that she could present her sick and demon-harassed daughter's case to Him. Jesus knew this mother's situation and purposely placed Himself in her path. Jesus did not immediately respond to her request. He related to her as the Jews would, to illustrate to His disciples how not to despise people of another race. When Jesus did not at first respond to her plea, the disciples asked Jesus to send her away. But she did not lose faith, for she saw compassion in Jesus' face and bowed at His feet, urging her case with increased earnestness.

Testing her faith, Jesus said, "It's not right to take food from the children of the family to feed the dogs." The woman responded, "But the dogs are fed with the family's crumbs." Then Jesus had tested her faith in Him and said, "Woman, great is your faith; your daughter is free and is healed." At that moment it happened. The woman had trusted in the Savior's love, and to this love and faith He responded, showing that all people, no matter of what race, are created equal.

Questions: Do you accept and treat all people equally? Do you do this no matter what background or race they may be?

August 4

I have said before that you are in our hearts.—2 Corinthians 7:3, NKJV

The Foreshadowing of the Cross. *Jesus did not hide anything from His disciples that they needed to know, not even His coming crucifixion.* The work of Christ on earth was hastening to a close. Everything was before Him in clear outline. Even before He became a man, He saw the whole length of what He must do to save us. His life of toil, the insults, the heartbreak, and every privation from the manger to Calvary was open before Him prior to stepping down from the throne. But He also saw the results of His self-sacrifice and was cheered by the prospect and the joy of bringing redemption to the lost race.

Jesus desired to prepare His disciples for what lay ahead. They left Galilee to escape the influence of Judaism and went north to Caesarea Philippi. Christ wanted to more fully tell His disciples about the sufferings that awaited Him. But first He went to be alone to pray for them. When He came back, He asked them, "Who do people say that I am, and who do you believe that I am?" Peter answered, "You are the promised Christ, the Son of the living God." Jesus said, "Let Me tell you that the keys to the kingdom of heaven are My words and the words of Holy Scripture."

Then Jesus told His disciples not to tell anyone what they had talked about, because the people had the idea that the Messiah would come in power to set up His kingdom. He first had to go to Jerusalem, suffer many false accusations from the scribes and Pharisees, and then be killed. When Peter heard this, he was willing to use his sword to defend Jesus, but Christ rebuked him for thinking this way. Then Jesus explained to His disciples that He would accept all this for them. He did not count heaven a place to be desired if they were not there. This same spirit of love for people must also motivate His disciples.

Questions: How much do you love people? What motivates you?

AUGUST 5

Render therefore to all their due: taxes to whom taxes are due.
—Romans 13:7, NKJV

"Who Is the Greatest?" Jesus avoided confrontations with the Pharisees about their continual emphasis on the importance of paying the temple tax, but Jesus ignored their accusations and continued teaching His disciples what they needed to know. Then, returning to Capernaum, Jesus temporarily settled in a house with His disciples. But even though they were very sorrowful about the sufferings of their Master that would soon come, there was still a spirit of rivalry among them that they tried to conceal from Jesus. He knew He had to talk to them, so He waited for a quiet time when their hearts would be open to listen to Him.

Soon after they reached town, the collector of the temple tax came and asked Peter, "Does your Master pay temple tax?" This was not a tax but a contribution that every Jew was expected to give annually to show their loyalty by supporting the temple. Jesus did not let Himself get into an argument with the Jews over this. He asked Peter to go to the lake, catch a fish, and open its mouth, where he would find two coins, enough to pay temple tax for both of them, which Peter did.

When this was done, Jesus again tried to prepare His disciples for His soon coming death and how it would test their faith. The disciples still did not understand the nature of Christ's kingdom, and they differed about its interpretation. But this was not the real cause of their contention. The real problem was self-exaltation. With that spirit the disciples could never enter heaven. What they needed was a change of heart and a spirit of self-forgetfulness. Their hearts must change, and gratitude must spring up for what He had done and would do for them.

Questions: Are you financially honest with the church? How about with the government?

AUGUST 6

You are my hope, O Lord God.—Psalm 71:5, NKJV

At the Feast of Tabernacles. Jesus did not respond to the demands of His brothers to go to this Feast, but waited for directions from His Father and then went. Three times a year the Jews assembled at Jerusalem for a special occasion. God wanted them to remember His goodness and mercy. This was a time to remember God's protection over them in the wilderness after leaving slavery in Egypt, as well as thanking Him for the various harvests during the year. People came with rejoicing from far and near and brought some form of thanksgiving. They celebrated the Feast with songs of praise: "O give thanks to the Lord; for He is good; for His mercy endures forever" (Psalm 106:21).

As the sons of Joseph prepared to go to the Feast, they saw that Christ made no preparations to go. They watched Him with concern. They were gratified with the work that Jesus had done in Galilee and were proud of it. That's why they wanted Jesus to go to the Feast and, with tones of authority, urged Him to go. Jesus responded, "You go ahead. My time has not yet come." He did not want to be presumptuous, rush into danger, and hasten the crisis. He must patiently wait; to prematurely expose Himself to danger would not be the will of His Father.

Finally, directed by the Father, Jesus quietly made His way to Jerusalem. In the middle of the week, He came into the temple, surprising everyone. Every voice was hushed, and the people marveled at His dignity and courage in the presence of His enemies. Every day Jesus taught the people, and on the last day of the Feast He lifted up His voice, which rang through the temple: "Come to Me and drink of the water of life!" The people had enjoyed the festivities of the Feast, but there had been nothing to satisfy the thirst of the soul. When Jesus invited them to drink from what He said, they listened, and through the Holy Spirit their minds were kindled with new hope.

Questions: Are you presumptuous? Do you at times rush into danger without thinking beforehand?

AUGUST 7

*"Come now, and let us reason together
[about your sins]," says the LORD.*—Isaiah 1:18, NKJV

Among Snares. Jesus did not expose the plots of the Pharisees against Him but tried to reach their hearts with the truth, and He continued healing people and forgiving their sins. All the time Jesus was in Jerusalem during the Feast, He was shadowed by spies. Day after day, new schemes were tried to silence Him, as the priests and rulers were watching to entrap Him or even to stop Him by violence. They brought up the question of His right to teach. Jesus said, "My teaching is not Mine, but His who sent Me." Then He told them that the appreciation of the truth depends not so much on the mind but the heart. If truth depended on reason alone, pride would be no hindrance to its reception. But truth is to be received through the work of God's grace in a heart that's open.

Finally, they decided to send officers to arrest Him, but they came back without Him and said, "No man ever spoke like this." The rulers were upset and responded angrily, "Are you also deceived?" In the meantime, Jesus left the temple to find a quiet place to be alone and pray. In the morning He returned to the temple. When the Pharisees saw Him, they came dragging a terror-stricken woman with them, whom they had trapped into prostitution to challenge Jesus with the question of whether she should be forgiven or put to death. Jesus did not respond to their question but stooped down and began writing something in the dust of the pavement. The Pharisees went over and looked at what He was writing. Each one read his own sins, and one by one they left. Then Jesus looked at the frightened woman and said, "Where are your accusers? No one is here to condemn you. Neither do I. Go and sin no more." The woman fell at His feet, sobbing out her grateful love. This was the beginning of a new life for her, a life of purity deeply devoted to God.

Questions: Do you know how to avoid enemy traps and yet help others? What precautions would you take? Would you limit the help you would give?

AUGUST 8

The LORD is my shepherd; . . . and I will dwell in
the house of the LORD forever.—Psalm 23:1, 6, NKJV

The Divine Shepherd. *Jesus was the example of a good shepherd, knowing each sheep personally, identifying with it, and calling it by name.* He said of Himself, "I am the Good Shepherd, and I know My sheep, and they know Me. A good shepherd gives his life for the sheep." Never could the disciples see a shepherd with his flock without thinking of Jesus. David wrote, "The Lord is my shepherd" (Psalm 23:1). Then Jesus set before the people the contrast between the Pharisees and the Good Shepherd, pointing to Himself, the real keeper of the Lord's flock. He said, "He who does not go through the gate into the sheepfold, but climbs over the fence or gets in some other way, is a thief and a robber." Christ is the gate into the fold of God.

A good shepherd knows his sheep by name. Each one responds to its name when called, and the shepherd leads them to grassy areas and the riverside, and tenderly cares for the sick and feeble; his life is one with theirs. Jesus knows and identifies with each of us like that. He knows us individually and by name, the very house we live in and the name of each occupant, and His heart is touched by the feelings and hurts of each one. Every soul is as fully known to Jesus as if we were the only one for whom the Savior died. The one who has given himself to Christ is more precious to Him than the whole world. The Savior would have gone through the agony of Calvary for one to be saved in His kingdom. He will never abandon one of His followers and will hold them tightly, unless they choose to leave Him.

Though we can't see Him, by faith we hear Him say, "Fear not, I am with you." We are the gift of His Father, the reward of His work, and Jesus loves us. So we can trust Him. Jesus said, "My Father loves Me even more for laying down My life for you, because He loves you so much."

Questions: How close are you to your heavenly Father? Do you have a deep relationship with Him?

AUGUST 9

"You have sent Me, and have loved them as You have loved Me."
—John 17:23, NKJV

The Last Journey From Galilee. *Jesus was committed to carrying out the Father's will, regardless of the agony and pain of Calvary.* As the ministry of Jesus was drawing to a close, there was a change in His work. Until now He had shunned excitement and publicity, even when He went to Jerusalem. He simply went from place to place, carrying out His ministry. But now He made His way to Jerusalem in a most public manner. It was painful for Him to do this against the fears and anguish of His disciples of what might happen in Jerusalem. Why should He die now and leave the work of the gospel when it was just beginning? Had Jesus yielded for a moment and changed His course in the least particular to save Himself, Satan would have triumphed and the world would have been lost. Jesus set His face steadfastly to go to Jerusalem, for the one law of His life was to do His Father's will.

It was not a part of Christ's mission to make people accept Him. When Jesus sent out His disciples with the gospel, they were not to urge their presence on any place where they were not welcome. Christ only desired voluntary and willing service with a heart motivated by love and gratitude for Him. So as He looked beyond Calvary with its agony and shame, He saw Satan conquered and knew that one day evil would be gone. With Jesus there can be no such thing as failure, loss, or defeat.

Questions: Is your life motivated by gratitude to God? If not, why not?

AUGUST 10

The law of his God is in his heart; none of his steps shall slide.
—Psalm 37:31, NKJV

Not With Outward Show. Christ did not come to reform the government but to reform and change men's hearts, to make them good men through which to have a good government. Some of the Pharisees came to Jesus and asked Him when the kingdom of God would come. Jesus responded, "The kingdom of God does not come with outward show, but begins in the heart and is within you." The gospel of God, with its self-surrender to Him, can never be in harmony with the spirit of the world.

The government under which Jesus lived was corrupt and oppressive; everywhere there was abuse, extortion, intolerance, and cruelty. Yet the Savior attempted no civil reforms. He attacked no national abuses nor condemned the nation's enemies. He did not interfere with the authority of those in power, not because He was indifferent to the hurts of people but because the ultimate remedy was not in human actions. For the remedy must first begin in men individually and regenerate the heart. Not by decisions of courts or councils or legislative assemblies, not by patronage of the great men of the world is the kingdom of Christ established, but by the work of the Holy Spirit implanting Christ's nature in the heart. Here is the only power that can uplift mankind and bring about peace and harmony.

Questions: Are you a truly peaceful and harmonious person? Could you make improvements? How?

AUGUST 11

Behold, children are a heritage from the L<small>ORD</small>.—Psalm 127:3, NKJV

Blessing the Children. Jesus loved the little children, took them in His arms, blessed them, and understood the hard work and concern of every mother. He accepted the sympathy and love of the children, and their grateful praise was music to His ears and refreshed His spirit. The love for them seen in His face and His kind and gentle spirit won their love and confidence. He took the children in His arms, laid His hands on them, and blessed them. The mothers who brought their children were comforted and returned home strengthened and blessed, taking up their work with new cheerfulness.

The Savior knows the burden of every mother, for He had a mother who struggled with poverty, and He sympathizes with every mother in her work. In His agony on the cross, He remembered His mother, was touched by her sorrow, and committed her to the care of John.

As a mother prays for her children and teaches them to obey because they love her, she is teaching the little ones the first lesson of the Christian life, to trust and obey their Savior. Jesus was the pattern for children, mothers, and fathers. He was never rude and did not use an unkind or discourteous word or expression. His grace will impart heaven-born dignity and soften whatever is harsh, coarse, and unkind. He will lead fathers and mothers to treat their children as intelligent beings, as they themselves would like to be treated. Christ's heart is drawn out not only to the best-behaved children but to those who by inheritance have objectionable traits of character. Nothing gives Him greater joy than for children to give themselves to Him in the bloom and freshness of their years.

Questions: Do you love all children, even the misbehaving ones? How do you do that and show it?

AUGUST 12

There is no work, . . . nor knowledge, nor wisdom, in the grave, whither thou goest.
—Ecclesiastes 9:10, KJV

"Lazarus, Come Forth." *The Savior felt the pain of losing a friend like Lazarus at death, and He comforted the family.* At the home of Lazarus, Jesus was always welcomed and found deep and pure friendship. But sorrow entered that peaceful household. Lazarus got sick, and it looked as though he might die. So his sisters sent a message to Jesus, asking Him to come quickly to heal their brother. Jesus sent a message back, "This sickness is not unto death." Tenderly, the sisters tried to speak hope and encouragement to their brother, but before Jesus came, Lazarus died. When Christ got the message, He said to His disciples, "Lazarus is sleeping, so let's go, and I'll wake him up."

When Jesus got to Bethany, the messenger whispered the news to Martha. She slipped out of the house, and when she saw Jesus, she noticed the tender expression on His face and burst out, "Lord, if You had only been here, this wouldn't have happened!" Jesus looked into her care-worn face and said, "Your brother will live again." Martha responded, "I know he will at the resurrection." Jesus said, "I am the resurrection." Martha quickly went to get Mary, who was followed by weeping family and friends.

Jesus said, "Show Me where he's buried." They all went to the grave, weeping, and Jesus wept with them. When they got to the tomb, He said, "Someone roll away the stone from the opening." The sisters said, "Lord, he's been dead for four days, and the smell will be awful." With gentleness Jesus said, "Do you believe what I've told you?" Then He prayed, "Father, I thank You for hearing Me." When the stone was rolled away, Jesus called out, "Lazarus, come out!" And he who was dead came out, not the same sickly man but full of vigor. They took off his grave wrappings, and in adoration he threw himself at Jesus' feet.

Questions: How do you feel when a loved one or a good friend dies? How do you comfort the family?

AUGUST 13

On whatever grounds you judge another, you condemn yourself.
—Romans 2:1, NET

Priestly Plottings. *Jesus knew that the Jewish judicial council was plotting against Him, but He did nothing to hinder or hasten the process.* Bethany was not far from Jerusalem, so the news of the raising of Lazarus spread quickly. Immediately a meeting of the Sanhedrin, the Jewish high judicial body, was called to decide what should be done, now that Christ had showed the people that He had control over death. Though the Sadducees were not favorable to Christ, they were not so full of hatred as the Pharisees. Now they were totally alarmed because they did not believe in the resurrection, that a dead body could be made alive. So now they agreed with the Pharisees that Jesus had to be put to death, and the two groups became friends opposing Christ.

While the discussion was at its height, Caiaphas, the high priest, spoke up with authority and said, "You haven't considered the future of our country. Isn't it better for one man to die than the whole nation to perish?" Then Caiaphas pointed out that even if Jesus were innocent, He had to be put out of the way or there would be no more Jewish nation. Satan was there, urging the council to put Jesus to death. Although one or two spoke against it, the decision was made, and under the leadership of Caiaphas, the council decided that Christ had to be put to death. The members considered themselves to be patriots who were seeking the good of the nation.

Jesus knew what was going on. He had given three years of public labor. His example of self-denial and benevolence, His life of purity, of suffering and devotion, was evident to all. Yet this short period of three years was all that the world could endure of its Redeemer. Jesus knew that what the council had decided would be carried out. But it was not His place to hasten the crisis, so He withdrew from the area of Bethany, taking His disciples with Him so as not to imperil their lives.

Questions: Are you willing to protect the life of your friends? How far would you go with this?

AUGUST 14

Let the peace of God rule in your hearts, . . . and be thankful.
—Colossians 3:15, NKJV

The Feast at Simon's House. *Christ was ever polite and considerate of others, no matter who they were or what position they held.* Simon of Bethany was one of the few Pharisees who had openly become a follower of Christ. He had been healed of leprosy and wanted to show his gratitude to Jesus. So he planned a feast and invited Jesus and His disciples, as well as Lazarus and his sisters. Only six days remained before the Passover, and people were expecting to see Jesus and Lazarus during the Passover in Jerusalem and to hear from Lazarus the story of his sickness, death, and resurrection. When Jesus and Lazarus went, the people were surprised when Lazarus said nothing about it.

The priests and Pharisees realized it would be dangerous to arrest Jesus openly, so they decided to somehow do it secretly and to have a trial as quietly as possible. While this was going on, Jesus and His disciples came to Simon's house. The Savior sat on one side of Simon, and Lazarus sat on the other side. Martha served, while Mary sat at Jesus' feet, she wanted to do something to honor Him one last time. So she took a very small bottle of expensive ointment and poured it on the Savior's head and feet. Then as she knelt, her tears fell on His feet, and she wiped them with her long hair.

Judas, who was there, was upset over this waste—the perfume could have been sold and the money put into the treasury for the poor. Mary heard his words of criticism and got scared, but Jesus knew her heart and that what she did was an expression of her gratitude. So He said, "Leave her alone—she has done this for My burial." Christ valued every act of heartfelt courtesy shown to Him, and with heavenly politeness He blessed the one who did it. The Savior's heart is grieved when His followers neglect to show their gratitude to Him.

Questions: How far would you go to forgive and protect a prostitute? What if she continues her prostitution?

AUGUST 15

I will praise thee, O LORD, with my whole heart; . . .
I will sing praise to thy name.—Psalm 9:1, 2, KJV

"The King Cometh." *The Savior knew the time had come to publicly let the people know who He was before He was crucified.* During the Passover, Jesus decided to ride into Jerusalem riding on a borrowed colt. Throughout Jewish history, this is what a new king did before taking the throne. The hope of Jesus' declaring Himself king filled their hearts and minds. In their imagination they saw the Roman armies driven out and once again Israel's being a free and independent nation. They hailed Him as the Messiah, the Liberator of Israel, and Jesus accepted their homage. He knew this entrance into Jerusalem would take Him to the cross, but it was needful to proclaim Himself as the Redeemer.

Never did the world see such a triumphal procession of a king! There were no enemy captives, but a procession of the blind who had been healed were leading the way; those who could not speak and were healed were shouting His praises; healed cripples were jumping for joy; widows and orphans were exalting His name; the healed lepers were spreading their garments on the road ahead of Him; and Lazarus was leading the colt that Jesus was sitting on.

Many of the Pharisees witnessed the scene and were burning with envy and hatred. They tried to silence the people, but their appeals and threats only increased the people's enthusiasm. As the sun was setting and shining on the gates of Jerusalem, Israel's King was in tears and groaned in agony. The people were struck with a sudden gloom, the shouts of praise ceased, and they wept in sympathy with a grief they could not understand. Jesus did not weep over His soon-coming agony and death. This was not some selfish sorrow, but it was over Jerusalem, His own city, which had rejected Him; and this pain pierced His heart.

Questions: How much emotional pain and hurt would you be willing to take from those who hate you? How deep is your love for people? Is it deep enough to love even those who hate you?

AUGUST 16

All nations shall call Him blessed.—Psalm 72:17, NKJV

In the Outer Court. Jesus gladly went to the Gentiles' outer court of the temple when He was told that Greeks had come to Jerusalem to worship and that they wanted to see Him and talk to Him. There were certain Greeks who came to worship in the outer court of the temple during the Passover at Jerusalem, where the Gentiles worshiped. When Philip greeted them, they said to him, "We would like to meet Jesus." Philip went and told Andrew, and together they told Jesus, who eagerly went to the outer court to meet the Greeks. These men from the West came to find the Savior at the close of His life, as the wise men from the East had come to the baby Jesus at the beginning of His life.

The Greeks had heard about Christ's triumphal entry into Jerusalem, that He had driven out the priests and that He was ready to take David's throne. The Greeks wanted to know the truth about all this. So Jesus went out to see these men to personally explain things to them. On His way there, He looked for a moment into the future, and in His mind He heard people from all parts of the earth say, "Behold the Lamb of God, who takes away sin from the earth." And in these men Jesus saw a representation of a great harvest from all nations, tongues, and peoples who will hear and accept the message of salvation.

In His teaching among the people, Christ had illustrated His own future by the things of nature. He said that when a kernel of wheat falls into the ground and dies, it brings forth a harvest. If it doesn't die, it produces nothing. As the seed of grain has to be buried and die to bring forth a harvest, so the death and burial of Christ will produce fruit unto eternal life. The meeting of the Greeks was a foreshadowing of the gathering in of a harvest of Jews and Gentiles, which was the purpose of the mission of Jesus. This will be His reward and His joy throughout eternity.

Questions: How do you relate to visitors from other countries?

August 17

*"Whoever wants to be first among you
must be the slave of all."*—Mark 10:44, NET

Servant of Servants. *The Savior did not hesitate to do anything that
needed to be done, even washing people's feet when no one else was available.* It
was Thursday evening during the Passover week, and Jesus wanted to
be alone with His disciples. He would die the next day on Friday, when
the Passover lamb was to be killed, representing Him. Special meetings
with His disciples were usually times of quiet joy, highly treasured. On
this occasion Jesus was troubled, His heart burdened. It could be seen
on His face, and His disciples were concerned, sympathizing with the
grief He showed. Christ was now in the shadow of the cross and knew
that the time had come for Him to die and return to the Father. Leaving
His disciples and other believers broke His heart. He knew He would
be betrayed and be subjected to a most humiliating process to which
criminals were subjected.

As the disciples were preparing the upper room for the Passover
supper, they still had resentful feelings toward each other, Judas being
the most vocal of all—he was determined to have the highest place
in the kingdom to be set up. Another cause of division among the
disciples was who would wash the dirt off their feet; there was no
household servant there to do it. They all sat there in silence, not one
of them offering to do it. Jesus' heart was breaking. He did not get into
a discussion and argument over it but gave them an example that they
would never forget. He took off His outer garment, wrapped a towel
around His waist, and began washing their feet, including the feet of
Judas. Peter did not like Jesus lowering Himself like this and refused
to have Him wash his feet. Jesus looked at him and said, "If you don't
surrender and let Me do this for you, you can't have a true relationship
with Me." Peter said, "If that's the case, Lord, wash me all over." Christ,
in His life and ministry, gave a perfect example of unselfish ministry,
representing the Father, and He wants us to live that way too.

Questions: What kind of servant or worker are you? Do you have the
attitude of a willing servant?

August 18

Do not take your Holy Spirit away from me!—Psalm 51:11, NET

"Let Not Your Heart Be Troubled." Jesus had committed Himself to modeling the Father's love and promised He would continue to be with His people through the Holy Spirit. After Jesus had used the bread and wine as a symbol of His body and blood and instituted the communion service, He looked at His disciples with divine love and tender sympathy and said, "I'll only be with you a little while longer. Then I'll go away, and where I go, you can't come." Their Master and Lord, their beloved Teacher and Friend, was to leave them! So Jesus turned their thoughts to their heavenly home and said, "For your sake I came into the world, and for your sake I am going to the Father to build beautiful houses for you to live in."

Then Philip spoke up: "Lord, please show us the Father before You leave." Jesus responded, "Don't you men believe what I've just said? You've seen Me, haven't you? So you've seen the Father." Christ did not cease to be the Son of God when He became a man. He was still a part of the Godhead. As the disciples were being drawn to Him in deeper love, they were drawn to one another, and they felt that heaven was very near.

Before leaving His disciples, Jesus wanted to give them a gift. He said, "I won't leave you alone. I will be with you through the ministry of the Holy Spirit, who is the third Person of the Godhead. He will be with you and comfort you. He will come and glorify Me and point you to what I have done for you." The Savior came to glorify the Father, and the Spirit will glorify Christ, reproducing through a new spiritual birth a reflection of God in humanity. The Lord is disappointed when His people place a low estimate on themselves and each other. He wants them to value themselves according to the price that Jesus paid for them.

Questions: Do you know how to value yourself without becoming proud? How do you do that?

AUGUST 19

"I am not alone, because the Father is with Me."—John 16:32, NKJV

Gethsemane. Jesus was so weak that He couldn't get to the Garden of Gethsemane by Himself. He had to be supported by two of His disciples, and when He got there, the battle with Satan began. He had often visited this place for meditation and prayer, but as He neared the garden this time, He became strangely silent. The guilt of fallen humanity would soon be placed on Him, and He began to fear that it would forever shut Him out of His Father's love. Never before had His disciples seen Him so sad and silent. This strange sadness deepened, and His body began to sway as if He were about to fall. He groaned aloud, and twice He would have fallen if His disciples had not supported Him.

At the entrance of the garden, Jesus asked His disciples to stay there and pray for Him. He took Peter, James, and John with Him into the garden and also asked them to pray for Him. Then He went a little distance and fell prostrate on the ground. He feared that He would not be able to endure the coming conflict. If He could only know that His disciples were praying for Him. But as He went back, He found them sleeping. He shook them awake and asked them why they couldn't stay awake and pray for Him. This happened three times. Jesus' final prayer was one of submission to His Father, and His decision was made—He would save humanity at any cost to Himself.

When Jesus came back to His disciples, He said, "You need to get up, because my betrayer is coming, leading a mob to arrest Me." Jesus' face showed no sign of His recent struggle, and He went forward to meet the mob and asked, "Who are you looking for?" They said, "Jesus of Nazareth." He said, "I'm the one." Then Judas stepped forward, greeted Him, and kissed Him on His cheeks. Jesus said, "Are you betraying Me with a kiss?" Then under the direction of the priests, the temple police stepped forward and arrested Jesus. When the disciples saw that Jesus allowed Himself to be arrested, they all ran.

Questions: Are you willing to stay committed to Jesus no matter what? How can you make sure?

AUGUST 20

Before Annas and the Court of Caiphas. *During the trial, Jesus was physically and mentally abused.* It was just past midnight when the soldiers hurried Jesus into the city with the shouting mob following Him. The Savior was tied up, and it was painful for Him to be forced to walk so fast. He was first taken to Annas, the retired high priest, for a preliminary hearing. There were two charges against Jesus that the priests wanted to prove: one, that Jesus was a blasphemer because of His claim to be sent by God, which was an issue with the Jews; and two, that Jesus was establishing a secret society to set up a new kingdom, which would be a threat to the Romans. Annas asked Jesus what He was teaching. Jesus said, "If you don't believe Me, you can ask My disciples." One of the temple officers slapped Jesus across the mouth and said, "Is that the way you talk to a high priest?" The priests and rulers were determined that Jesus should be given into the hands of the Romans. So Annas ordered Jesus to be taken to Caiphas, the ruling high priest, for a legal trial.

By this time it was early morning but still dark, so Jesus was taken by the light of torches to the courtroom of Caiphas. As the members of the Jewish high court were coming together, Caiphas took his seat as judge, and Roman soldiers were stationed near the front. False witnesses who had been bribed were called on to accuse Jesus of starting a rebellion and trying to set up a new government, but their testimonies contradicted each other. Then another witness who had been bribed was called on, and he accused Jesus of planning to destroy the temple and rebuild it. On this charge the Romans and Jews agreed, for they all respected the temple.

Questions: What would you do if you were threatened with arrest because of your faith in Christ? Would you give up your faith in Him?

AUGUST 21

If we confess our sins, He is faithful and just to forgive us.—1 John 1:9, NKJV

The Trial Continued. Jesus had patiently listened to the conflicting statements of the witnesses but did not say one word in self-defense. At last Caiaphas raised his right hand toward heaven and asked Jesus to take an oath that He was the Son of God. On this Jesus could not keep silent, because His relationship to the Father was being called into question. He knew His answer would mean His death, but He said to Caiaphas, "What you said is correct—I am the Son of God." When the high court members who were present heard this, they pronounced the death sentence on Jesus. But this was contrary to Jewish law—to convict a prisoner during the night.

But a deeper pain tore at Jesus' heart. One of His own disciples denied being His follower. Peter was in the courtyard, standing by the fire with others to keep warm. When he was recognized and ridiculed, that's when he denied being a disciple of Christ. Peter would have fought to defend Jesus, but ridicule he could not handle. When Jesus was being transferred from the one courtroom to the other, He looked at Peter with love and pity. At that moment, what Peter had just done hit home. He quickly left the courtyard, made his way to Gethsemane, wept bitterly, confessed his sin, and wished he would die.

As soon as it was day, the high court assembled again with all members present. They needed to hear for themselves Christ's claim to be the Son of God. Jesus gave the same answer He had given before and added, "Soon the Son of God will be seated on the right hand of God." This confirmed His condemnation. Then there followed more abuse and mockery, even worse than before, and the mob rushed forward, ready to kill Jesus. The Roman officers stopped it and said that it was illegal for the Jews to pronounce a death sentence on anyone. Then Jesus' persecutors spit in His face, placed an old garment over His head so He couldn't see, and mockingly asked Him to prophesy who had done it. The angels witnessed all this and recorded it, which will be brought up at the final judgment.

Questions: How much ridicule about your faith in Christ are you willing to take? Would you be willing to die for Christ?

August 22

The Lord is King forever and ever.—Psalm 10:16, NKJV

In Pilate's Judgment Hall. Though Jesus was human, He was still divine and could have protected Himself, but He was willing to suffer because He loved us. The Jewish leaders took Jesus as a prisoner to Pilate, the Roman governor of Judea, to confirm their sentence and have Him executed. Pilate was not happy, because he had been called out of bed early in the morning, and he was determined to get this trial over with in a hurry. He saw on Jesus' face no sign of guilt or defiance as he expected a criminal would have. This made a favorable impression on Pilate, who had heard about Jesus and His ministry. So he asked the Jews what their accusations were. They didn't answer his question but said, "We wouldn't have brought Him here if we didn't need to." In Pilate's estimation, a prisoner's life was worth nothing. But there was something about this Man that kept Pilate from acting quickly.

The Jews accused Jesus of forbidding the people to pay taxes to Caesar, and proclaiming Himself to be their King. Pilate did not believe that Jesus had plotted against the government like that. So he asked Jesus, "Are You claiming to be the King of the Jews?" Jesus said, "What you said is correct." When the Jews heard His answer, they shouted abusively and demanded His execution. Standing behind Pilate, Jesus heard all this and said nothing. So Pilate took Him inside and privately asked Him if He claimed to be the King of the Jews. Jesus answered, "Do you personally want to know, or are you asking because of what they said about Me?" Pilate said, "Am I a Jew? Why should I care?"

Jesus spoke up and said, "My kingdom is much greater than this world, and this is the truth." Pilate responded, "Truth? What is truth these days?" He did not wait for an answer because of the shouting outside. So he went out and emphatically said, "I don't find Him guilty of anything worthy of death." When the priests and rulers heard this, they went into a rage. They denounced Pilate, and Pilate dreaded what could happen to him if he didn't carry out their wishes.

Questions: How do you relate to unreliable leaders in little things and big things? Is there a limit to your forgiveness and acceptance?

AUGUST 23

"The Holy Spirit will teach you in that very hour what you ought to say."
—Luke 12:12, NKJV

Pilate's Wife. When Pilate was told that Herod, the ruler of Galilee, was in town, Pilate sent Jesus to him, for He was from Galilee. Herod had put John the Baptist to death, so this seemed like a good solution. Herod was glad to see Jesus and ordered Him to be freed from His bonds. He charged Jesus' enemies with cruelty for the way they were handling Him. Herod asked Jesus a lot of questions, but the Savior said nothing. Then Herod ordered Jesus to perform a miracle to prove who He claimed to be, but Jesus would not work a miracle to save Himself. This irritated Herod, and he took Jesus' silence as a sign of indifference to his authority. So he and his soldiers made fun of Jesus, and some from the mob joined in, bowing in mockery to Jesus. Then Herod sent Him back to Pilate, who decided to have Jesus scourged, which means being beaten with a whip that had sharp metal points at the end of leather strips, to pacify His accusers, and then release Him. When the Jews saw Jesus' upper body dripping with blood, it only increased their demand for His execution.

Now Pilate's wife had been visited by an angel during the night and was given a dream in which she saw Jesus' trial, how He was being treated, His scourging, His crucifixion, and His second coming. She let out a scream and woke up. Then she sent an urgent message to her husband, saying, "Have nothing to do with this just Man—I have suffered a lot this night because of a dream about Him." When Pilate got this message, he got scared and his face grew pale.

Questions: How do you relate to messages from the Holy Spirit? How do you test the reliability of messages brought to you? If proven true, are you willing to obey them?

AUGUST 24

Consider Him who endured such hostility from sinners against Himself.
—Hebrews 12:3, NKJV

The Trial Continued. It was customary at the Passover to release a prisoner. So Pilate decided to give the Jews a choice and asked, "Do you want me to release to you Jesus or Barabbas?" Barabbas was a hardened criminal and murderer who claimed to be the Messiah, and he was determined to help the nation by setting things right. The people shouted, "Give us Barabbas!" Pilate asked, "What, then, should I do with Jesus?" They shouted, "Crucify Him!"

Pilate responded, "Why? What has He done? I'll scourge Him again and let Him go." Jesus, still covered with wounds from the first scourging in the sight of the people, was led inside the hall by the soldiers for mockery and a second scourging. Once inside, they saluted Him, called Him "King," spit in His face, covered Him in a purple robe, and put a crown of thorns on His head, forcing it into His skull as the blood trickled down His face. Satan thought that Jesus would retaliate and save Himself, thus ending the plan of salvation, but Christ calmly submitted to the coarsest insult and outrage. When Jesus was brought out, He was stripped to the waist, showing the people the long, deep scars from the scourging, the blood still flowing freely.

Pilate again asked the people what he should do with Jesus. They shouted, "Crucify Him! Crucify Him!" Losing his patience, he firmly said, "I find no fault in Him," and again proposed to release Jesus. But the priest and people shouted, "If you let Him go, you're not Caesar's friend." Pilate knew that if he was reported to Caesar, he would be removed as governor. Finally, he said, "Look, here is your king!" The people shouted back, "We have no king but Caesar." Then Pilate turned to Jesus and said, "Forgive me for not saving You," and ordered Him to be crucified. Not long after the crucifixion, Pilate killed himself.

Questions: What would you do if you were beaten because of your faith in Christ? Would you be willing to die a horrible death because of your faith?

AUGUST 25

"If anyone desires to come after Me, let him . . . take up his cross, and follow Me."
—Matthew 16:24, NKJV

Calvary. Jesus could also have reduced His pain and agony on Calvary and could have decided not to die, but He chose to complete His agreement with the Father to save us. The news of Jesus' conviction had spread throughout Jerusalem, and a large multitude of all kinds of people followed the soldiers and Jesus from Pilate's judgment hall to Calvary. The cross that had been prepared for Barabbas was placed on the bleeding shoulders of Jesus. Two companions of Barabbas were to be crucified also. But since Jesus was thought to be the worst criminal, His cross was to be placed in the middle. Since the Savior had been scourged twice and had the heavy cross placed on His shoulder, human nature gave way, and He collapsed. He was laughed at, and no one tried to help Him.

At this time a Jew from Cyrene named Simon had come to Jerusalem for a visit. When he heard the crowd calling out, "Make way for the king of the Jews," he stopped, saw Jesus on the ground, and felt compassion for Him. Then the people grabbed Simon and placed the cross on him. Carrying the cross for Jesus proved to be a blessing for him, and he gave his heart to Christ, and was grateful for this providence ever after. There were women in the crowd who were weeping and expressing their sympathy. Jesus was not indifferent to their grief but looked at them with compassion and kindly said, "Don't weep for Me but for Jerusalem."

When Jesus and the two companions of Barabbas got to Calvary, all three were stripped naked. The Roman soldiers had to force two of them down on the crosses, but Jesus gave no resistance. Jesus' mother was there watching all this and, seeing His shame, the hammer and the nails being driven through the tender flesh, she couldn't take it anymore, and the disciples had to carry the fainting mother away. Then the Savior prayed for the soldiers who were nailing Him to the cross. He pitied their ignorance and asked the Father to forgive them, for they didn't realize Jesus was the Son of God. Pilate had ordered a sign to be nailed over Jesus' head which read, "Jesus of Nazareth, the King of the Jews."

Questions: Would you resist being arrested and publicly stripped naked because of your faith? Or would you resist and fight as much as you could?

AUGUST 26

"Nor is there salvation in any other . . . by which we must be saved."
—Acts 4:12, NKJV

The Other Criminals. The government allowed those who were crucified to be given a pain-killing drink, but when it was offered to Jesus and He tasted it, He refused to swallow it and spit it out. The priests who were there were making fun of Jesus, saying, "He saved others, but He can't save Himself. Let Him come down from the cross, and we'll believe Him. He trusted in God—let God deliver Him." Through all this agony there was one ray of comfort for Jesus. One of the crucified thieves repented. When during the trial he heard Pilate say, "I find no fault in Him," and later heard Jesus pray for and forgive His tormentors, the Holy Spirit touched his heart. He looked at Jesus and said, "Lord, remember me when You come into Your kingdom." In a soft voice full of love, Jesus answered, "One day you will be with Me in paradise."

As the weight of the guilt of the world was placed on Jesus, the Father hid His face and looked away from His Son. Jesus feared that this might separate Him from His Father forever, and the resulting emotional pain was so severe that His physical pain was hardly felt. Suddenly the midday sun seemed to be blotted out, and a deep darkness covered the land for the next three hours. But the Father was still with His Son. God was using the darkness to cover the last hours of agony of His Son, and silence fell on Calvary and a sense of terror came upon the people. At three o'clock the darkness lifted, yet occasionally lightning would flash, seemingly aimed at the cross. Jesus cried out, "My God, My God, why have You forsaken Me?" Then in a clear trumpet-like voice, the Savior called out, "It is finished!"

Questions: How much physical pain are you willing to take for Jesus? How about emotional pain?

AUGUST 27

"Remember the Sabbath day, to keep it holy."—Exodus 20:8, NKJV

In Joseph's Tomb. *The long day of shame and torture was over, and at last Jesus was at rest.* As the sun was setting, Jesus lay quietly in the tomb, His work completed, His hands folded in peace. He rested during the hours of the Sabbath from the work of redemption as He and the Father had rested on Sabbath at the time of creation. All through eternity, heaven and earth will unite in praise from one Sabbath to another.

The priests and rulers were amazed to find that Christ was already dead. It was unheard-of for a person to die after six hours. The priests wanted to make sure Christ was dead, so they suggested that a soldier thrust his spear into Jesus' side, which he did. When blood and water flowed out, the priests knew that Christ was dead. The disciples were heartbroken as they looked at Jesus with His eyes closed, His head drooping, His hair matted with blood, and nails in His hands and feet. The future looked dark.

Jesus had been convicted and condemned to death for treason against Rome, and those who were executed for this were to be buried in a criminal's cemetery. This is when Joseph of Arimathaea and Nicodemus came to help. Joseph went to Pilate and begged for the body of Jesus. When Pilate was assured by the commander that Jesus was really dead, he let Joseph have the body. So Joseph went back and, together with Nicodemus and the apostle John, gently and reverently took Jesus' body down from the cross, straightened the limbs, folded the bruised hands on His breast, and placed the body in Joseph's personal tomb. A great stone was rolled in front of the opening, and the soldiers sealed it with the Roman seal. A guard was then stationed there to make sure that no one tampered with it.

Questions: Are you willing to keep the seventh-day Sabbath? Would you keep it no matter what people say or do to you?

AUGUST 28

If Christ has not been raised, then our preaching is futile and your faith is empty.
—1 Corinthians 15:14, NET

The Lord Is Risen. *Jesus could have resurrected Himself but was obedient to the Father and stayed in the tomb until His Father called Him.* The night slowly wore away. The Roman guards were still there, and hosts of evil angels were surrounding the place, which, if they could, would have kept the tomb sealed. Suddenly, just before daybreak, there was a great earthquake as Gabriel, who had taken the position previously held by Satan until he was thrown out of heaven, descended, with the glory of God illuminating his way. His face was like lightning, and the soldiers shook, fell down as dead men, and saw him remove the stone as though it were a pebble. Then they heard him cry out, "Son of God, Your Father calls You!" and Jesus came out of the tomb in majesty and glory, saying, "I am the resurrection and the life." Then the soldiers got up, staggered like drunken men, and hurried into the city to tell the people and Pilate what had happened. When Pilate had confirmed the report, in terror he locked himself in his house, determined to see no one, and not long afterward killed himself.

At Christ's resurrection there was a large earthquake, and the graves of many who had labored for God and testified for Him at the cost of their lives were resurrected and taken to heaven with Him as trophies of His victory over death. Before Christ ascended, these witnesses went into Jerusalem and appeared to many people, testifying of His resurrection. Their resurrection was an illustration of the final resurrection of the righteous at the end of time. To the believer, death is but a small matter. Christ speaks of it as if it were of no consequence, for it is but a quick sleep, just a moment of silence. The believer's life is hidden in Christ with God.

Questions: Do you believe in the resurrection of Jesus as a tradition of the Christian faith? Or do you believe it as described in Scripture?

AUGUST 29

We are God's children . . . [so] then heirs of God and also fellow heirs with Christ.
—Romans 8:16, 17, NET

"Why Weepest Thou?" *The Savior's love for others was seen after His resurrection, when He stayed near the tomb to comfort Mary before ascending to the Father, whom He had not seen for thirty-three years.* The women who had been at the cross and who had watched Jesus being laid in the tomb went home late Friday afternoon to pray and keep the Sabbath. On the first day of the week, early in the morning, they made their way back to the tomb. They had forgotten His words, "I'll see you again." As they neared the tomb, they realized they couldn't remove the large stone covering the entrance, but they at least wanted to honor Jesus' burial site. As they neared the tomb, suddenly the heavens lit up, the earth trembled, and they saw that the stone had been rolled away. They looked inside and saw that the tomb was empty. The women had come from different directions. Mary, the sister of Martha, got there first, and when she saw that the tomb had been opened, she turned and ran to tell the disciples. Meanwhile, the other women got there, saw the open tomb, and saw someone else there; it was an angel disguised as a man. The women got scared, but the angel said, "Don't be afraid. Jesus was crucified and buried, but He is not here—He has risen! Go tell His disciples that He'll meet them in Galilee."

Questions: Do you believe in the power of angels? Do you believe what they can do as described in Scripture?

AUGUST 30

Let the nations be glad and sing for joy!—Psalm 67:4, NKJV

The Race to the Tomb. In the meantime, Mary got back to the disciples and quietly told Peter and John about the empty tomb. The two of them raced there, looked inside, and saw that it was empty. The Lord's body was gone, but as they looked more carefully, they noticed that the grave clothes had been neatly folded and laid to one side. They knew that this was not the work of thieves. Of the two angels who had come, one had rolled away the stone, and the other had taken the grave clothes off Jesus' body. But Jesus Himself had folded them up and laid them in place.

Mary (the sister of Martha) slowly followed Peter and John, and she arrived at the tomb after they had already raced back to tell the other disciples about the empty tomb. When Mary got there, with a heavy heart she looked inside and saw two angels disguised as men sitting there. They asked her why she was crying, and she said, "Because someone stole the body of my Lord, and I don't know where it is." Then she turned around and saw a Man standing there. She thought it was the caretaker. She didn't even look up and with a tear-filled voice said, "Sir, tell me where you've taken the body, and if it's in your way, I'll see to it that it's taken." That's when she heard a familiar voice as Jesus lovingly said, "Mary." She looked up, and in her joy she forgot that He had been crucified. She got on her knees and was ready to hug His feet. Jesus said, "Don't touch Me—I have not yet gone up to see My Father and your Father." Then Mary got up and joyfully ran back to tell His disciples what happened.

Jesus ascended and entered the heavenly courts. But He refused to receive any homage from the angels until He had heard from the Father that His sacrifice had been accepted, the covenant officially ratified, and that the Father loved the redeemed as He loved His own Son.

Questions: Do you believe that God loves you as much as He loves His Son? Are you sure?

AUGUST 31

We through the . . . comfort of the Scriptures . . . have hope.—Romans 4:3, NKJV

The Walk to Emmaus. Jesus returned from heaven and took a personal interest in those who were troubled about what had taken place over the weekend. Late in the afternoon after Christ's resurrection, and after He had been to the Father, two of His followers were on their way home from the Passover in Jerusalem. They felt they needed to have time alone to pray after they had heard that the body of Jesus was stolen. As they talked about the trial of Jesus, His crucifixion and burial, the future looked hopeless, and they often stopped and wept together. They had not noticed a stranger walking a short distance behind them. Jesus heard what they were saying and longed to comfort them and fill them with joy. So He moved closer, greeted them, and asked what they were talking about. They said, "Are you a stranger here and haven't heard what happened in Jerusalem this past weekend?" Then they told him everything that had happened to their Master—the trial, the crucifixion, the burial, and now the stolen body.

Jesus said to them, "You need to believe what the prophets have said." Then beginning at Moses, Christ explained from the Scriptures the things that were said about Him. The two men wondered who this stranger was who knew the Scriptures so well and spoke to them with such sympathy and hopefulness. Jesus did not reveal Himself. His first work was to explain the Scriptures to back up their faith. The two men urged Him to stay overnight with them. He agreed, so they went in, sat down, and waited for supper. Soon the evening meal was ready. Jesus sat at the head of the table, and folded His hands to say the blessing. When He did that, the men saw the wounds in His hands, and they sat back, speechless. They looked at each other and said, "This is Jesus, our Lord! He has risen from the dead!" They stood up, ready to throw themselves at His feet and worship Him, but instantly He disappeared. The two men couldn't believe it. They had to go back to Jerusalem and tell the disciples. When they got to Jerusalem, they found the upper room where the disciples were staying and told them how Jesus had appeared to them. Suddenly Jesus appeared and showed them His hands and feet.

Questions: How familiar are you with Scripture? Do you believe what it says?

SEPTEMBER 1

Love . . . is kind; love does not envy; love does not parade itself, is not puffed up.
—1 Corinthians 13:4, NKJV

By the Sea Once More. After Christ's resurrection and return from the Father, He first restored the faith of the disciples in Peter and then made it clear that each follower is given his own work. Immediately after His resurrection, before ascending to the Father, Jesus had told Mary to go and tell the disciples that He would meet them in Galilee. So as soon as the Passover ended, they went to where they had met many times before. While they were waiting, Peter suggested that they go fishing. They fished most of the night and caught nothing. As the morning dawned, the disciples were discouraged and decided to go back to shore. Jesus was there and called out, "Have you caught anything?" They said, "No!" He said, "Throw your nets out again but on the right side of the boat." They did, and they caught so many fish and their nets were so full that they could hardly pull them in.

John realized that the stranger on the shore was Jesus, and he said to Peter, "It's the Lord!" Peter got so excited that he jumped into the water and was soon standing by the side of his Master. The other disciples came in their boat, dragging their nets. When they came ashore, they noticed coals of fire with fish, and bread on the side. Jesus said, "Come and eat." While they were eating, Jesus looked at Peter and said, "Peter, do you love Me?" Peter answered, "Lord, you know that I love You." Then Jesus asked him again, and Peter gave the same answer. For a third time Jesus asked him, "Are you sure you love Me?" Peter knew that Jesus had a reason for asking three times. So this time he said, "Lord, You know my heart better than I do. You know that I love You." During Jesus' trial, Peter had denied knowing Him three times, so three times Christ drew from him the assurance of his love and loyalty. Peter loved his Master and was even willing to die for Him.

Questions: How much do you love Jesus? What do you think of Peter's response?

September 2

"Our Father in heaven, may your name be honored."—Matthew 6:9, NET

"To My Father, and Your Father." *The Savior's thoughts were not on the joys of finally being home in heaven but with His disciples and His people on earth.* The Savior had finished the work the Father had given Him to do, so it was time for Him to ascend. The place He chose was the Mount of Olives, where at its base He had often gone to meditate and pray. He would ascend near Bethany, on its eastern slope, and when He comes back, His feet will touch the summit of the mountain. As He was about to ascend, He reviewed in His mind the ingratitude of the people He came to save, but He will not withdraw His sympathy and love from them and only set His affections on the place where He is appreciated and where angels wait to do His bidding. He promised His people, "I will be with you always, even to the end of the world."

With His hands outstretched in blessing, He slowly ascended, accompanied by a group of angels. The awestruck disciples looked with straining eyes for a last glimpse of their Lord. Two angels from the group stayed behind. These were the same two angels who had come to the tomb at Christ's resurrection. They longed to be with the other angels to welcome the Son of God into the holy city, but in sympathy and love for the disciples, they stayed behind to comfort them. They talked with the disciples and said, "Why are you gazing up into heaven? The same way Jesus went up into heaven, He will come again."

Questions: Do you believe that Jesus will come again? How will He come?

SEPTEMBER 3

Blessed be His glorious name forever!—Psalm 72:19, NKJV

Back in Jerusalem. The disciples went back to Jerusalem, and the people expected to see them sorrowful and depressed, but instead they looked happy and triumphant. They did not mourn over disappointed hopes but were full of praise and thanksgiving, no longer distrusting the future.

When the Son of God with the angels approached the city of God, the challenge was given by the accompanying angels, "Lift up, you gates and you everlasting doors—the King is coming in!" Then the gates opened, and the group was welcomed by the most rapturous music. There was the throne and the rainbow of promise, and the commanders of the angelic host and the representatives of unfallen worlds were assembled to welcome the Son of God. But not yet. Christ waves them back and first goes to the Father, lifts up His hands as evidence of His triumph, and says, "Father, it is finished." The Father's arms encircle His Son, and the word is given, "Let all the angels worship Him!"

Questions: Do you believe that the Father's arms will encircle you and welcome you home? Will He do it as He welcomed His Son, Jesus?

How to Live Like Christ

Insights From Ellen White's Book *Christ's Object Lessons*

September 4

These things . . . the Holy Spirit teaches, comparing spiritual things with spiritual.
—1 Corinthians 2:13, NKJV

Teaching in Parables. Christ taught in parables to make His teachings easier to understand. In these parables we see His mission to the world and know more about His divine character and life. The best way people learn about the unknown is through what they see and know. Jesus used parables from the natural world to teach spiritual things. These parables and the teachings from Scripture were given to help us understand God, but they had been so twisted that God could not be truly understood. Christ's words opened the teachings of nature and Scripture to help us understand God better.

One day Jesus took some beautiful lilies and placed them in the hands of children, and as the children looked into His smiling face, radiant with the light of His Father's love, He said, "Look at these lilies, how beautiful they are. God made them grow that way. If God can do that for little plants, how much more can He do for you and give you beautiful little hearts." These words were spoken not only to children— they were spoken to the multitudes. Our heavenly Father knows our needs, so the first thing we need to do is to open our minds and hearts to the Holy Spirit.

Through His parables Jesus said things He could not say directly, as people would not understand and would just walk away. But by using parables, He could condemn sin, hypocrisy, and false teachings. As the works of God are studied in Scripture, the Holy Spirit brings conviction to us. But this is not conviction that comes only from logical reasoning. It is much deeper than that—it touches the heart and the soul, and in the process our minds are strengthened and character is developed. It is so easy to forget God, but Jesus, through His parable teaching, would have the thought of God run like threads of gold through all our home cares and daily occupations.

Questions: When you speak to people or share your faith with someone, do you use illustrations or explanations that they can understand and relate to? How do you make sure?

September 5

Whoever has been born of God . . . His seed remains in him.—1 John 3:9, NKJV

The Sower and the Seed

By using this parable, Christ illustrated the work of the heavenly Sower. It has never been appreciated as it should be. Jesus wants us to think of the gospel seed and the sowing as bringing people back to their loyalty to God. The same law that governs earthly seed-sowing governs the sowing of heavenly truth. The crowd that came to hear Jesus continued to increase, and the people pressed so close to Him that He was almost forced off the beach into the lake. So He got into a boat, pushed away from the shore, and taught the people from there. As He looked up to the hillside, He saw sowers throwing out their seed and others harvesting an early crop. That's when He gave the parable of the sower and the reapers.

Christ came to sow the seeds of truth, but the Pharisees focused on traditions and theories that they put in place of the Word of God. Today many professed ministers of the gospel do not accept the whole Bible as God's Word. The portions of Scripture that they do teach rests on their own authority, and the Bible is robbed of its power to create spiritual life. Jesus taught that the whole of Scripture is of unquestionable authority. Instead of discussing false theories or trying to correct the opponents of the gospel, follow the example of Christ. His favorite theme was the abundant love and grace of our heavenly Father and the holiness of His character and law. When faith is lost in God's Word, there is no heavenly guidance, no safeguard. Teachers of truth must make the Word of God their own by daily personal experience and know that Christ is their wisdom, righteousness, and redemption.

Questions: Do you have a daily experience with Christ? Is it deep and personal or just casual? How can you know?

September 6

Your word I have hidden in my heart, that I might not sin against You.
—Psalm 119:11, NKJV

Part 1: The Soil by the Wayside. The seed that falls on the edge of the road next to the field represents the hearts of inattentive hearers. Their selfish aims and ambitions have made their hearts like a hard-beaten path. Their spiritual faculties have become paralyzed, so they hear but don't understand. As the birds quickly come to eat the seed on the road, so Satan and his angels quickly come into the assembly where the gospel is being preached to take away any positive impression that is made. They lead the people to criticize the speaker by pointing out his defects and to sit in judgment on the sermon. The respect for God's messenger and reverence for the message is destroyed, and as a result they lightly regard the Word of God.

Questions: Do you have a problem along this line of evaluating the speaker? What can you do to solve this problem?

September 7

Today, if you will hear His voice: "Do not harden your hearts."
—Psalm 95:7, 8, NKJV

Part 2: The Stony Places. The stony places in the field represent those who hear the Word and receive it with joy. This lasts for a while, but when troubles come because of their faith, they give up. The Word of God doesn't go very deep into their hearts. Like the rock underneath the shallow soil on top, natural selfishness is underneath the top layer of good intentions and desires. These people appear to be bright converts to the gospel but only have a superficial religion. They do not face all the habits of their life and yield themselves fully to the control of the gospel. They trust to their good works and impulses and feel they are strong without having the deep power of Christ. They accept the gospel as a way to escape from difficulty and trial, instead of as a deliverance from sin. They rejoice for a little while in their newly found faith, but when troubles come, or when the Word of God points out some cherished sin, they are offended and give up.

They do not believe that Christ can give them power to overcome such sins.

It is one thing to accept the Holy Spirit in a general way, but it's another thing to accept Him as a Corrector of selfishness and sin. There must be unreserved consecration and undivided service. Love must be the foundation of the believer's character and the principle of action. Christ gave His all for us, and we must be willing to give our all for Him. If we love Jesus, we will love to live for Him, and His glory and honor will come before anything else. We cannot serve self and Christ—that is what would make us a stony-ground hearer.

Questions: How do you respond when a sin is mentioned by a speaker that is personal to you but that only you know? How do you emotionally deal with it?

September 8

Here we have no continuing city, but we seek the one to come.
—Hebrews 13:14, NKJV

Part 3: Among Thorns. Some seed fell among thorns and weeds. It sprang up and grew, but its full growth was prevented by the thorns and weeds, which can grow almost anywhere. So it is with us—the pressures, cares, and perplexities of life keep us from fully growing in Christ. God's grace must be cultivated, and the Holy Spirit must be allowed to refine and ennoble us. But the cares of this life that should drive the thorny-ground hearers to the Savior actually separate them from Him, and they neglect to put the spiritual things of life first. They must go to work and carry on their business, and they may do that without committing sin, but they become so absorbed that they have no time for prayer, the study of the Bible, or seeking and serving God. Devotional time is crowded out, and what should be made first is made last.

The culture of today is fast becoming like Sodom and Gomorrah. The many holidays with an emphasis on pleasure, exciting sports, media productions, horse racing, gambling, drinking, and partying, sweep people away, especially the youth. They may repent and change, and God may pardon them, but they have hurt their ability to recognize the guiding voice of the Holy Spirit. If any love the world and the things of this world, the love of Jesus and their heavenly Father is not in them.

Questions: How do you evaluate whether you love the world more than you love Jesus? And if you find out that you do, what will you do to correct it?

September 9

Part 4. Preparation of the Soil. In this parable Jesus speaks of the different results of sowing seed, depending on where the soil is. But in every case the Sower and the seed are the same. Jesus is saying that the problem of the Word of God's failing to accomplish its work in our hearts and lives is found in ourselves and the choices we make. The garden of the heart must be cultivated by cooperating with the Holy Spirit. Even in the ministry of the Word, there is too much sermonizing and too little personal, heart-to-heart work for the people and those who are lost. Logic and arguments may be powerless to convince, but the love of Christ communicated through us to others will soften the stony heart so that the seed of truth can take root. The sowers have something to do so that the seed is not choked with the thorns or doesn't dry up because of the shallowness of the soil. The new believer is not only to be taught that he will be saved by Christ's sacrifice but that he is to make the life of Christ his life and the character of Christ his character.

Questions: Does your heart have to be soft to soften the heart of others? If so, how do you know that your heart is soft enough to do so?

September 10

Wait on the L‌ord; . . . He shall strengthen your heart;
wait, I say, on the L‌ord!—Psalm 27:14, NKJV

Part 5: In Good Ground. The Savior said that the seed which fell into good ground will bring forth fruit, whether a hundredfold, sixty, or thirty. The "honest and good in heart" are those who are honest with themselves and yield to the convictions given by the Holy Spirit. They feel the need of the mercy and love of God and want to know the truth in order to obey it. A good heart is a believing heart. The good-ground hearer receives the Scriptures as the voice of God speaking to him. A knowledge of the truth does not depend so much on the power of intellect as on purity of purpose, a simple faith, humility of heart, and a longing for divine guidance. Just to hear and read the Word of God is not enough. We must meditate on what we read, learn its personal meaning with prayer, and drink in its spirit. Those who do this will be transformed. The good-ground hearers accept all the requirements in God's Word and gladly submit to their heavenly Father.

This does not mean that good-ground hearers are exempt from difficulties and trials, but when afflictions come, they do not cast away their confidence in God, and their spiritual life is strengthened. Faith, meekness, and love mature best in the storm clouds of life. So God's people are to wait on the Lord with patience, for He often answers our prayers by allowing circumstances that develop good fruit, the fruit of the Holy Spirit: love, peace, long-suffering, kindness, goodness, faithfulness, gentleness, meekness, and self-control.

Questions: Do you read the Bible just for information, to know what it says, or to find a closer relationship with Jesus? Do you pray about this before you read the Bible?

September 11

Grow up in all things into Him who is the head—Christ.
—Ephesians 4:15, NKJV

First the Blade, Then the Ear. The parable of the sower raised a lot of questions, because the people expected Jesus to set up an earthly kingdom, and from what He said, it didn't sound as though He was going to do that. Then Jesus used other illustrations to turn their minds from an earthly kingdom to the work of God's grace on the heart. It's like the seed that is sown which sprouts, grows, and produces first the blade, then the ear, and finally the full corn in the ear. It is then that the harvest is reaped. The sowers are those who take the place of Christ in sowing, but it is Christ who will do the reaping. It is the power of God that is at work in nature—the seed has no power in itself. But men and women have a part to act to cultivate the ground, plant the seed, and fertilize it. However, there is a point beyond which they can't do more than that.

As it is in the natural world, so it is in the spiritual world. The germination of the seed represents the beginning of spiritual life, and its growth is a figure of the growth of a Christian. In nature, if the seed doesn't grow, it dies; and so it is with God's grace in the heart. Every stage of our Christian development that we reach may be perfect, but God's purpose for us is not yet complete. His purpose for us is continual advancement. Feeling our helplessness, we are to daily open our heart to the Holy Spirit and take advantage of all opportunities to gain a fuller spiritual experience. With longing desire, Christ is seeking to reproduce Himself in us and claim us as His own.

Questions: What part do you think you have in making the spiritual seed grow in your heart? What point is it beyond which you can't do more? Then what?

SEPTEMBER 12

"Judge not, . . . condemn not. . . . Forgive, and you will be forgiven."
—Luke 6:37, NKJV

Weeds. Jesus used another parable. He pointed out that the kingdom of heaven is like a man who sowed good seed in his field, but during the night, his enemy came and sowed weeds in the field. When the good seeds came up, so did the weeds. The good seed represents those who have been born again. The weeds are the errors in the hearts of people, sown there by Satan. Just as weeds injure the crop, so the errors from the Evil One injure the church. Christ has not given us the work of judging other people's characters and motives. However, if there are those in the church who are living in open and known sin, their church membership needs to be discontinued, but they are not hopeless and lost. Then there are some who have joined the church but have not joined Christ. They may be living good lives and appear to be true disciples but are not so in heart. On the other hand, those who were living in sin may repent, and if they do, they will be saved.

Satan is the great deceiver. When he sinned in heaven, even the loyal angels did not fully detect his real character. This is why God did not at once destroy him. Had God done so, the angels would have misunderstood His justice and love. They would have doubted His goodness and been like an evil seed among them. Through long ages God carried in His heart the pain of watching the development of evil, and He gave His Son to die on Calvary to save humanity and to reveal Satan's wickedness and his hatred of Christ. At the time of the end, the Son of Man shall send forth His angels to take out of His kingdom all that do iniquity, and, together with Satan, they will suffer the second the second and final death.

Questions: At the end of time, when the weeds in God's garden will be pulled up, how will the angels know which are weeds and which are not? Would you be able to tell? How?

We are receiving a kingdom which cannot be shaken.—Hebrews 12:28, NKJV

Like a Grain of Mustard Seed. Among the people who listened to Christ's teaching that day were Pharisees, who pointed out how comparatively few accepted Him as the Messiah. They questioned how this unpretending Teacher could exalt Israel to universal power, which they believed the Messiah was supposed to do. Earthly governments established themselves by physical force and war. The Jews looked for the kingdom of God to be established the same way. But Jesus compared the beginning of His kingdom to a mustard seed, which is one of the smallest seeds, and when it grows, it becomes a giant plant. So the kingdom of Christ, in its beginning, seemed insignificant. Yet the seed of the gospel had divine life and power, and as it grew, it would spread its branches all across the world.

In every generation God has a special emphasis on truth, and His church has a special work to do. John the Baptist had his work to do, Paul had his work, Martin Luther had his, John Wesley had his, and we who are living at the end time have ours. The special emphasis on truth in our day will build on the truth that has come before, built on the Word of God and not on church authorities. In this last generation before Jesus comes, the mustard seed of truth will reach its full growth and will become a giant tree covering the world. This means that the gospel will go to every nation, kindred, and language to bring people to Christ, and the earth will be lightened with His glory.

Questions: How is the gospel being spread across the world today? Media? Does this mean you don't have to do anything to help spread it? What can you do?

SEPTEMBER 14

Train up a child in the way he should go.—Proverbs 22:6, NKJV

Other Lessons From Seed-Sowing. From the parable of seed-sowing, precious lessons are taught for the family and the school. The material world is under the control of the Creator. All nature obeys His will. There is an invisible power at work to feed and clothe people. God employs many avenues to do this, including people helping people. We have a part to act, but we need power from above to help us with our efforts. Jesus gave us the parable of seed-sowing to illustrate by the natural order the spiritual order of things. He was born as a babe, grew as a helpless infant, and became an obedient child as He spoke with the wisdom of a child. He honored His parents, carrying out their wishes, but at each stage, His development was perfect, as He lived a simple and sinless life. He grew, became strong in spirit and full of wisdom, and the grace of God was with Him.

The work of parents and teachers is here suggested. They should aim to cultivate the natural beauty and grace appropriate for each stage of development, as children unfold like the plants in the garden. Children are most attractive who are natural and not influenced by wrong principles. Also, it is not wise to give them special notice and repeat their clever sayings, and pride should not be encouraged by unduly praising their looks, words, and actions, nor should they be dressed in an expensive, showoff manner, as this also encourages pride. Children need to be educated and given every opportunity to form characters after the example of Christ. They should be taught liberality, helping the cause of God and relieving the needs of others. Like the natural soil worked by the farmer, the soil of the heart must be worked by the Holy Spirit to bring forth fruit to the glory of God.

Questions: Do you have children? What schools are you sending them to? Are you personally teaching them at all? If so, what are you teaching them, and how are you doing it?

September 15

The righteous shall flourish like a palm tree,
[and] grow like a cedar.—Psalm 92:12, NKJV

Like Unto Leaven. Many educated and influential men came to hear Jesus, the Prophet of Galilee. There were also the poor, the illiterate, the beggar, the thief, and the robber among the listening multitude. Jesus compared His kingdom to yeast that women put in dough to make it rise for baking bread. The Jews saw yeast as a symbol of sin, and during the Passover, people were to remove all yeast from their houses. Jesus compared yeast to the hypocrisy of the Pharisees, which can grow in the heart so silently. But yeast also represents the work of the Holy Spirit, which silently grows in the heart, and to all who submit to the Holy Spirit, a new principle of life is implanted. Man cannot transform himself by the power of his will. The yeast of heaven must be implanted; the renewing power of spiritual energy must come from God.

A profession of faith and the possession of truth are two different things. Just to know the truth is not enough. The man who attempts to keep the commandments from a sense of obligation because he is required to do so will never enter heaven. He does not obey with a willing heart out of love for His Savior and loyalty to Him. The yeast of truth works silently and secretly and transforms the whole man—his thoughts, feelings, and motives—and sweetens the disposition. He is kind and thoughtful of others and humble in the opinion of himself. Self is not looking for recognition. He does not love others because they love and appreciate him, but is kind, polite, and thoughtful of others, yet always full of hope, trusting in the mercy and love of God. When angels see these changes, they break forth in song, and the Father and Son rejoice as man is remade after the divine likeness.

Questions: Are you humble in the opinion of yourself when you think of how the Lord has blessed you and what you have done, even done for Him? What's the difference between being joyous in what you have done or are doing for the Lord and having a high opinion of yourself? How can you tell the difference?

SEPTEMBER 16

Salvation [and] the fear of the LORD is His treasure.—Isaiah 33:6, NKJV

Hidden Treasure

The kingdom of heaven is also compared to a treasure that is buried in a field. When a man discovers it, he quickly buries it again and then sells all he has to buy that field. In ancient times it was customary to hide treasure in an unknown place in the field, because thefts and robberies were frequent. Also, the country was in constant danger of foreign armies. Sometimes death would claim the owner of the field, and it was not uncommon in Christ's day that treasures of coins or gold and silver was found as the new owner plowed the field. The parable of Jesus illustrated the value of heavenly treasure, and the field represents the Holy Scriptures where the gospel treasure is found.

Questions: Do you consider the salvation you found in Christ a treasure? How about the Bible you have? Do you consider it a treasure? How do you treat it? How much do you value it?

SEPTEMBER 17

"If the blind lead the blind, both fall into a ditch."—Matthew 15:14, NKJV

Part 1: How Hidden. The treasures of the gospel are hidden by those who are wise in their own estimation, puffed up by teaching philosophy, and they are not able to perceive the value of Scriptures and the gospel. They sit down and rest under a tree, so to speak, and don't realize that these riches are under the roots. When they do read the Scriptures, they read them from a human perspective but do not see the spiritual meaning of the sacred writings. God does not conceal His truth, but they themselves make it obscure. They do not want to give up their own opinions. The natural man can't receive the things of the Spirit of God, because those things need to be spiritually understood.

Questions: Do you read the Bible from a human perspective, or from the perspective of God speaking to you? Are you listening or just reading? Do you pray before you read the Bible, asking the Holy Spirit to help you apply what you read to yourself?

SEPTEMBER 18

Thy word . . . is light; it gives understanding.—Psalm 119:130, NEB

Part 2: Value of the Treasure. The value of this treasure from God is of more value than silver or gold. Its value cannot be estimated. It is found in the Scriptures, the Bible, God's great educator and lesson book. True higher education is gained by studying and obeying the Word of God. But when it is laid aside for other books that do not lead to God, the education gained is a perversion of the word education. God's lessons are also seen in nature, but these lessons do not impress the mind of those who do not accept the Word of God and who see it as old-fashioned, stale, and uninteresting. But those who have been made alive by the Holy Spirit see the Word of God as a priceless treasure, given to us by the greatest Author and Teacher the world has ever known, who gave His life for us.

Questions: What do you think is a well-rounded education? Is it based on the degree or various degrees you got? Do they make you feel important? Did this rounded education include an exposure to and knowledge of the Scriptures? If so, was it just biblical knowledge or a personal knowledge and relationship with Jesus Christ?

SEPTEMBER 19

We must pay closer attention to what we have heard.—Hebrews 2:1, NET

Part 3: Results of Neglecting the Treasure. Satan works on human minds, leading men to think that there is wonderful knowledge to be gained apart from God. By deceptive reasoning and a false theory about God, Satan led Adam and Eve into disobedience and sin. A student may go through all the grades in school and college and acquire much knowledge, but unless he gains a knowledge of God and is willing to obey, he will lose his God-given sense of self-appreciation and self-respect. He will lose full control of himself, will not reason or think correctly, and will acquire habits that will injure him for this life and for the life to come. By making the Bible secondary in his life, he is sacrificing a treasure worth more than anything that can be imagined.

Questions: Have you ever thought about losing your self-value and respect? What does self-respect include? Is it just thinking highly of yourself? How do you measure self-respect? What's the standard you measure it against? Is it society, your friends, or what God expects?

SEPTEMBER 20

I commune with mine own heart, and my spirit makes diligent search.
—Psalm 77:6, KJ21

Part 4: Search for the Treasure. The Word of God is to be our treasure and study. Our affections and capabilities must be focused on the search for spiritual treasure hidden in the Word. The Scriptures can be understood only by those who humbly search for knowledge of the truth to know it and obey it. Do you want to know what to do to be saved? Put aside your preconceived ideas and opinions, and don't search the Scriptures to vindicate what you think. If conviction comes to you as you read and study, don't misinterpret the Scripture to suit yourself. Faith in Christ is inseparable from a needed change and transformation of character. Except a man be spiritually born again, he cannot see the kingdom of God. We need the enlightenment of the Holy Spirit in order to discover and appreciate the truths hidden in God's Word. The Holy Spirit will reveal them to us, impress them on our minds, and make them so plain to us that no one who believes in Christ needs to be lost.

Questions: Have you been spiritually born again? How do you know? How can you tell? What's the evidence for it?

SEPTEMBER 21

Leap for joy: for, behold, your reward is great in heaven.
—Luke 6:23, KJV

Part 5: Reward of Searching. When once we know the truth in God's Word, let us not think there is no more to learn. There is endless knowledge still to be gained. We are only working the surface of the mine of knowledge and wisdom. There are still more riches further down to reward those who will dig deeper. No one will go unrewarded who searches the Scriptures in the spirit of Christ and is willing to be taught as a little child, submitting wholly to God. If men would be obedient, heaven would open its chambers of grace and glory for them, and they would be totally different from what they are now. In His prayer to the Father, Christ said, "That they might know Thee, the only true God." This is true education. It imparts power and transforms man into the image of God. It gives him mastery over himself and makes him a son of God and an heir of heaven. This is the treasure that may be found by those who will give all to obtain it.

Questions: Do you have control of yourself? All the time? If not, what's the problem? Do you get angry? Is there a difference between being angry and being upset or frustrated? Can you explain the difference?

SEPTEMBER 22

I have rejoiced in . . . thy testimonies, as much as in all riches.
—Psalm 119:14, KJV

The Pearl. Jesus compared the blessings of redeeming love to a precious pearl. He illustrated this by the parable of a merchant looking for genuine pearls, and when he found one, he sold all that he could and bought it. Christ is the pearl of great price, and His righteousness is like a pure, white pearl, more precious than anything else. In the parable the pearl is not spoken of as a gift, but Christ is a gift to us from the Father. However, it is only a gift to those who give themselves to Him. When we give ourselves totally to Him, Christ gives Himself totally to us, and we have the Pearl of Great Price in our hearts. Giving ourselves to Him, we become His purchased possessions. We cannot earn salvation, but we can seek for it as if we're looking for a precious pearl. We should not think that our spiritual advantages constitute the pearl; God calls for total surrender and a willingness to obey. To just have a feeling of being saved means still being lost.

Christ saw in lost humans a pearl of goodly price. Hearts that have been the battleground of Satan and that have been rescued by the power of His love are more precious to Him than those in the universe who have never fallen. God did not see humans as worthless, but He willingly gave all the riches of heaven embodied in Christ to buy the pearl. The Holy Spirit gives us insight into the value of this precious heavenly gift. Christ is our Friend and Redeemer. Every Christian should see in his brother the value of a precious pearl. This is what makes up the church. And the outpouring of the Holy Spirit as it was on the day of Pentecost will in the last days be even more abundant, and men will see the extreme value of the precious pearl, which is Christ.

Questions: What is the precious pearl? What does the Holy Spirit say it is? Do you know? Read this last paragraph again. What a gift! What are you doing to make sure you don't lose this pearl or forget where you placed it?

SEPTEMBER 23

But they have not all obeyed the gospel.—Romans 10:16, NKJV

The Net. The kingdom of heaven is also compared to a fishing net. When it's thrown into the lake or sea, it pulls in all kinds of fish. Then it's pulled to shore and the fish are sorted. The good fish are kept, and the bad ones are thrown away. Jesus said that is how it will be at the end of the world. He compared the casting out of the net to the preaching of the gospel, which brings all kinds of people into the church. The angels will separate the bad from the good, and the final judgment will do the final work. There will be no probation after the separation. When the work of the gospel is finished, immediately the separation takes place. It is only those who reject His pleading and cling to sin that will be separated out. God has no pleasure in the death of the wicked; He wants them to turn to Him and be saved, just as He wants you to be saved.

Questions: Are you trying to tell the difference between the good fish and the bad fish caught in the gospel net and pulled into the church? Are you that wise? And who gave you the ability and the authority to do that? If you have fallen into the habit of evaluating others, how do you stop it?

SEPTEMBER 24

I have rejoiced in the way of Your testimonies, as much as in all riches.
—Psalm 119:14, NKJV

Things New and Old. While Christ was teaching the people, He was also educating His disciples about their future work. He taught them that the truth committed to them is to be communicated to the world. He asked them if they understood what He was saying, and they said, "Yes, Lord." All who receive the gospel message into their hearts will be eager to share it and relate their experience, tracing step by step the leading of the Holy Spirit in their life so that others can receive the same blessing. The truth as it is in Jesus can be experienced but never fully explained, for it is a love that is higher than the heavens. It is possible for us to understand God's divine compassion as we search the Word of God in humility of heart.

If we keep the Lord always before us and let our hearts go out to Him in thanksgiving and praise, we will have a continual freshness in our religious life. Our prayers will be a conversation with God as we talk to Him as we would to a friend. When this is our experience, there will be humility, meekness, and lowliness of heart in our lives. People will be able to see that we have been with the Father and with Jesus. There will be no dull teaching or sermonizing. Old truths will be seen in a new light, which the Holy Spirit will use to work on the minds of others, especially the youth, whom He loves so much. As we near the close of this world's history, the prophecies of Scripture especially need our study, not excluding the love of God in redemption, which will continue throughout eternity as new insights into God's love unfold to our minds.

Questions: How can people tell whether or not you've been with the Father? If it's not evident that you have been with the Father, what do you think is missing in your life? How do you make it evident?

SEPTEMBER 25

In the morning my prayer comes before You.—Psalm 88:13, NKJV

Asking to Give. Christ was continually receiving new insights from the Father to share with us. He always lived, thought, and prayed for others. In the early hours of a new day, the Father would awaken Him, and after spending hours with the Father, Christ would receive a fresh baptism of the Holy Spirit and come forth in the morning to bring new light to the people. The disciples were impressed by Christ's habit of communion with God. One time He was so absorbed in talking to His Father that He wasn't aware of the presence of the disciples. They waited till He finished praying and then said, "Lord, teach us to pray like that." Christ repeated to them the Lord's Prayer, which He had given in the Sermon on the Mount. He wanted the disciples to ask for bread so they could give it to their friends who come to them in need. This is also true for spiritual bread. God loves us to address Him as Father, asking for a blessing to bless others; it's music to His ears.

God does not say, "Ask once, and you'll receive." He wants us to persist in prayer and press our petitions with determination and with a more earnest attitude, realizing our own needs. The Father longs to have us reach out to Him in faith and expect great things from Him. We should talk and act as if our faith and trust in Him is invincible. In a Spirit-filled prayer, there is a pledge from God that He is ready to answer our prayers, especially the prayer that is offered in the name and spirit of Jesus.

Questions: How persistent should we be with God in prayer or become a pest with our petitions? How do we tell the difference? Can we ever tire Him? No. But could our prayers simply become meaningless repetitions? How can you tell the difference?

SEPTEMBER 26

Not to think of himself more highly than he ought to think.
—Romans 12:3, KJV

Two Worshipers. Christ gave this parable to point out the difference between the one who prays and has a high opinion of his commitment and the one who feels his spiritual need. Whoever thinks that he is good and righteous by comparing himself to others is judging them. On the other hand, those who come and worship the Lord feeling unworthy and in need of help are the true worshipers. There is nothing so offensive to God and dangerous to the soul as pride and self-sufficiency. Of all sins, it is the most hopeless and incurable. Peter's fall was gradual; self-confidence led him to believe that he was saved and secure against temptation. Those who accept Jesus as their Savior and are converted should never say that they are saved and beyond the reach of temptation, for they are the ones who are in the greatest danger of losing sight of their own weakness and their constant need of divine strength. While praying to God, our hearts may be proud of our humility. True faith renounces all self-trust.

Questions: What kind of worshiper are you? Do you know for sure? Not just being in church and kneeling to pray, but what is on your mind during the worship prayer? Is it on someone you know who is kneeling next to you, or on the person up front doing the worship prayer? Are you comparing yourself to him or her? If so, how do you change that?

SEPTEMBER 27

What is man that You are mindful of him?—Psalm 8:4, NKJV

Human Limitations. No man can empty himself of self—he can only consent for Christ to do the work for him. The language of the soul will be, "Lord, save me in spite of myself. Take my heart; I can't really give it, because it is Your property. Keep it pure—I can't do it. Mold me, fashion me, raise me up to where the rich current of Your love can flow through my soul." This reaching out to a power outside of ourselves is not only to be seen at the beginning of the Christian life but at every step along the way.

There are seven spiritual dangers that we need to be concerned about: (1) that your will is not in subjection to Christ's will; (2) that self will come between you and your Master; (3) that self will hinder the high purpose that God wants to accomplish through you; (4) that you will trust in your own strength; (5) that you will withdraw your hand from the hand of Christ and walk alone; (6) that you will receive flattery and praise and won't direct such praise to God; (7) that you will feel no need of a living, personal union with Christ. We must humble ourselves in order to be exalted. We need Christ in our heart, for He is the true source of power and joy.

Questions: Are you concerned about any of these seven spiritual dangers in your life, or all of them? How can you—how can we—overcome them? Any suggestions?

September 28

He is my defense; I shall not be moved.—Psalm 62:6, NKJV

Shall Not God Defend His Own? Christ spoke to His disciples and the people about the time just before His second coming and the need to pray. He told the story of a judge who didn't care about God. A widow was brought before him who asked for protection from her enemies. The judge wanted to show his power, so he made her come again and again, pleading for his help. Finally, he got tired of listening to her and decided to help her because of her persistence. Christ then draws a sharp contrast between the unjust judge and God. If this unjust judge finally took action, how much more will God, who is a loving Father and has His people close to His heart, take action on our behalf.

Satan is like a prosecuting attorney. He loves to accuse us before God as being sinful, unworthy, and full of ingratitude. The Lord's people cannot answer the charges of Satan. They appeal to Jesus, their Defense Attorney, and with confidence they cry out to Him for help. He responds and says, "The Lord rebuke you, Satan! These are the ones I have pulled out of the fire." Then He says, "Take away their unclean clothes, and I will cover them with clean clothes and put a crown on their heads." In spite of the defects of His people, Christ does not turn away from them but writes "Pardon" beside their names.

Questions: Can you imagine standing before a judge for whatever reason, with only a prosecuting attorney present, accusing you of what you did, knowing he's right, and with no defense attorney present? That would be hopeless and terrifying. How thankful for the defense attorney who also is there speaking on your behalf. How grateful you would be to such a defense attorney when he won your case. How often do you thank Jesus for having won your case?

"My people have been lost sheep."—Jeremiah 50:6, NKJV

The Lost Sheep. "The people whom you despise," said Jesus to the Pharisees, "are the property of God by creation, as you are." By redemption they are His and are of value in His sight. They may wander away from God, but He longs to bring them back. It's like a shepherd who goes after a lost sheep who has wandered away from the fold. The shepherd goes looking for it because it can't find its way back on its own. When it gets dark and stormy, the shepherd is all the more concerned and anxious to find that sheep. When he finds it, he does not scold it because it has caused him so much trouble or drive it home with a whip. He is so happy that he found it that he takes it in his arms and holds it close to his chest. He returns to the fold with gratitude that his search was not in vain. Christ will rescue from the pit and thorns of sin everyone who submits to be saved.

The Pharisees taught that before God's love could be extended to a sinner, he must repent—that's how he could earn the favor of heaven, and come close to God. Jesus taught that salvation does not come to us because we seek God, but because God is seeking us. We do not repent so God can love us, but He shows His love for us so we will repent. When the shepherd comes back with the lost sheep, gratitude fills his heart, and he breaks out in songs of rejoicing. He calls his friends together and says, "Rejoice with me, for I have found the sheep that was lost!" This world is the one lost sheep in God's great universe. If the religious leaders had been true shepherds, they would have done the work of a shepherd and would have shown the mercy and love of God in what they did.

Questions: Do we have to earn the favor of heaven, or has God loved us from the beginning? Did you go searching for God, or did He go searching for you? What did He do to find you, or what does He have to do to find you?

September 30

"For the Son of Man has come to seek and to save that which was lost."
—Luke 19:10, NKJV

The Lost Piece of Silver. After giving the parable of the lost sheep, Christ gave His listeners the parable of the lost coin: There was a woman who had ten pieces of silver, and when she lost one of them, she lit a candle and swept the house until she found it. In a one-room house with no windows that is hardly ever swept, a coin falling on the floor would quickly be covered up by dust and trash. Like the lost sheep and the lost coin, people cannot recover themselves. The lost piece of silver is still precious and has not lost its value. In a family, a son or daughter may be lost and not even be aware of their need. They are the heritage of the Lord; they belong to Him. The education and training of their children to be Christians is the highest service that parents can give to God. They must not give up on their children.

Christ risked all for our redemption. Christ would have laid down His life for one soul, so by this we can estimate the value of one person. If we have a relationship with Christ, we will place the same value on every human being that He does, and feel the same love for them that He has. We are to reach out to others in sympathy, and our courage and steadfastness will help them to stand firm. The angels are ready to help us in this work of helping others.

Questions: What are you doing to educate your children? Are they receiving the right education? How do you know? Have you asked them? If the education they're receiving is not the right kind, what will you do and how will you go about changing it?

OCTOBER 1

"The Father Himself loves you."—John 16:27, NKJV

The Lost Son. The parable of the lost sheep and the lost coin ends with the parable of the lost son.

The younger of the two sons in the family had become tired of restraints, thought his freedom was restricted, and decided to follow his own feelings and inclinations. He didn't feel any obligation to his father. The inheritance that would be his at his father's death, he wanted now. The father gave him what he wanted, and with plenty of money in his pocket and the freedom to do what he liked, the son flattered himself and left home. Soon he made friends who led him down the wrong path, and he spent his money on drinking, partying, and having a good time. His money was soon all gone, and he had to get a job to survive. The only job he could get was feeding pigs.

This is a classic picture of a sinner, who claims that the good things of God are his right but goes and does his own thing. Whatever the situation, every life centered in self is squandered. The heart and mind that God created for companionship with Him and the angels becomes degraded and unfit for heaven. This is what happens to the self-serving person. But God sets in operation things that draw the sinner back home, just as the love of his father that the son remembered was drawing him home. So the son decided to go back and be a servant in the house of his loving father. The father sees him coming and runs to meet him with a hug and kiss, and he holds a welcome party. What a wonderful picture of our loving heavenly Father!

Questions: How do you see yourself fitting into this picture? Are you the older or the younger brother? If you don't fit into this picture at all, where would you place yourself in relationship to your heavenly Father? Can you give the reasons for where you would place yourself and why you would do so?

OCTOBER 2

All have sinned [are sinful] and fall short of the glory of God.
—Romans 3:23, NKJV

The Older Brother. The older son was working on the family farm, when he came home from the field and heard this celebration. It made him angry, for he had been obedient and faithful, and he would not go in to welcome his younger brother back. The father went out to meet his older son and expressed his love for him, telling him the reason for his joy in having his younger son back home.

The older son represented the Jews in Christ's day and those in every age who look down on sinners, feeling they are so much better than they are. Such people serve Christ not out of love but out of obligation and the hope of reward. They may claim to be children of God, but the spirit they have toward others shows they are influenced by the evil one. When we see ourselves as sinners saved by the love of God and His grace, we will have love for others who are living in sin and will not censure them for what they have done. We should greet the lost with joy that they have come home to the Father's house.

Questions: If you've been a faithful church member for a long time and no one has expressed appreciation for what you have done, how do you feel? Is it wrong to expect a thank-you? Will you continue to be a faithful, supportive church member whether someone says "thank you" to you or not?

OCTOBER 3

You also be patient. Establish your hearts, for the coming of the Lord is at hand.
—James 5:8, NKJV

Spare It This Year Also. In His teaching Christ linked the warning of judgment with God's mercy. Jesus illustrated this mission of mercy in relation to God's justice by the parable of the barren fig tree. Christ was drawing the people's attention to the coming kingdom of God. The people were quick to notice the signs in the sky to tell them the approaching weather, but they could not understand the signs that pointed so clearly to Christ's mission. People were as ready then as men are now to think of themselves as the favorites of heaven, and that any reproof was meant for someone else, especially pilgrims and strangers.

Jesus said that a certain man had a fig tree, which he had planted among the other trees in his vineyard. After three years, he expected fruit, and he went to look for it but didn't see any. So he decided to cut the fig tree down. God is also looking for the fruit of obedience from His people but doesn't see any. He wants His people to be trees of righteousness. The people had a show of piety, but they were destitute of the graces of the Spirit of God. They were misrepresenting God to others. As the worker in the vineyard pleaded to give the tree another chance and the owner agreed, so Christ pleaded for His people, and still does. The Father and the Son were one in their love for their people. So it is today. How long does God have to wait for a return of His love and the fruit of the sweet graces of the Spirit?

Questions: Have you ever thought of thanking God for His patience, particularly with you? How long does God have to wait to see the fruit of grace in your life? How long do you expect Him to wait?

OCTOBER 4

"Go therefore and make disciples of all nations, baptizing them . . . ; and lo, I am with you always, even to the end of the age."—Matthew 28:19, 20, NKJV

Go Into The Highways and Byways. One day the Savior was invited to be a guest at a Pharisee's house during a feast of Israel's national rejoicing. In choosing his guests, the Pharisee was thinking about his own selfish interests. Jesus told him that he should not always invite just his friends and rich neighbors, but he should also include the needy. The point that Jesus was making is that the spiritual blessings given to Israel were not for them alone. They needed to share those blessings with other people.

Jesus illustrated this with the story of a man who prepared a feast and sent his servants out to tell the expected guests that it was time for them to come. But they all had excuses: one had to go and close the deal on buying a farm, one had to test new oxen, one had to prepare for an upcoming wedding, and so on. None of them could come. Similar reasons are given today, whether business or family hindrances, not to give ourselves fully to Christ, and the very blessings God gives us become excuses.

The message of Christ's soon coming is an invitation to the whole human family, with whom pastors and church members are to share God's word of grace. Those who stand high in society are seldom approached directly, but they should be. If a man is drowning, we must save him, no matter who he is. The success of the gospel does not depend on learned speeches and eloquent, deep arguments but on the simplicity of the message and its adaptability to its hearers. In the needy and those living in sin, we are to see those whom Jesus came to save and, by kindness and compassion, draw them to Christ. When He returns, they will stand next to Him in His kingdom.

Questions: What excuses do you have for not responding to God? Are you too busy? What is most important in your life? Do you just give God a passing nod, or are you willing to come to Him with your whole heart and soul? What's holding you back?

OCTOBER 5

For You, Lord, are good, and ready to forgive.—Psalm 86:5, NKJV

The Measure of Forgiveness. Peter came to Jesus with a *question:* "How many times should I forgive my brother, seven times?" The priests allowed three times, and Peter, extending it to seven times, thought that he was being generous. But Christ responded, "Not only seven times, but seventy times seven!" Then Jesus told the parable of a king who was informed that a servant had embezzled a great sum of money. When the servant was found out, the king ordered him to be sold as a slave. The servant came, fell at the king's feet, and begged for forgiveness. The king was moved with compassion and forgave him and told him not to do it again. Later, the servant who had been forgiven went to one of his fellow servants who owed him a small sum, took him by the throat, and demanded to be paid. The other man begged for forgiveness and promised to pay, but the servant had him thrown into prison.

When the king heard about it, he called the servant in and said, "You are a wicked man. I had compassion and forgave you a large sum. Couldn't you have done the same with a fellow servant who owed you a small sum?" The king represents Christ and God's compassion and forgiveness. "If God so loved us, we should also love one another." How many today show the same spirit as the servant in the parable? We have sinned—what a great debt we owe to God! The Lord's Prayer says, "Forgive us as we forgive," not *because* we forgive, but *as* we forgive. So let this mind be in us, as it was in Christ.

Questions: How far are you willing to go to forgive others, especially if they have repeatedly lied to you? Do you keep forgiving them? Would there be a limit? If so, when and where would you draw the line? How patient and forgiving are you? Do you really know? If you forgive a person once, is it easier or harder to forgive him or her again?

OCTOBER 6

"What good is it for someone to gain the whole world, yet forfeit their soul?"
—Mark 8:36, NIV

Gain That Is Loss. As Christ was teaching His disciples, others came to hear Him. He told the disciples that they should share the truths He had given them. They might be taken to court, but He promised that the Holy Spirit would give them the wisdom of what to say. Also, they would find that many would desire the grace of heaven for selfish purposes. As Jesus was speaking, one man in the crowd came up to Him and said, "Master, tell my brother to divide the inheritance with me." Jesus knew that the brothers were arguing over the inheritance because they were covetous. But Christ was not to be distracted from His work to settle temporal affairs—neither were His disciples. Only the gospel can.

Jesus gave another parable about a rich man whose farm brought in plenty of money. The man said to himself, "I know what I'll do. I'll pull down my barns and build bigger ones." But God spoke and said, "How foolish can you be! Tonight you will die—then whom will your riches go to?" The man didn't realize that God had made him a steward of His goods in order to help the needy. To live for self is to perish, because it cuts off the soul from God and life. It is the spirit of Christ to give, to sacrifice for the good of others.

Questions: Are you saving up for the future? Are you being reasonable about it or thinking only of yourself? What would be an acceptable balance? How would you use the funds you can spare? Whom would you give them to and why, or why not?

OCTOBER 7

"Freely you have received, freely give."—Matthew 10:8, NKJV

A Great Gulf. Another parable that Jesus told was the parable of a rich man and Lazarus, the sick beggar full of sores who was sitting at the rich man's gate. The parable draws a contrast between the rich who have not depended on God and the poor who have done so. There were no hospitals in those days where the sick could be cared for. Lazarus suffered day after day, while the rich man went through life thinking only about himself. So it is today. There are many homeless, hungry, and sick near us who need help. To neglect to give of our means to help them is covetous and offensive to God. We are God's stewards of the means we have, and it is our obligation to use what we have to uplift humanity.

In figurative language, when the rich man died, he pleaded with God for a second chance, but no second chance was given to him, while Lazarus, the beggar, was safe in the arms of Abraham. There was a great gulf between the two which could not be crossed over. It is not a sin to be rich, but it is sinful if we are selfish with what we have. Money cannot be taken into the next life; even if it could, it would not be needed there. The closing scenes of this earth's history are seen in the closing of the rich man's history. There are many today who are like the rich man, living for themselves. There are church members who come to church and sing hymns to God but who are unconverted. God is not uppermost in their thoughts. If they do not serve God here, they would not serve Him there. To receive God's grace in order to be saved, we need it here.

Questions: Are you in a saving relationship with God? How do you know? Will there be a time when it's too late to begin having such a relationship? Are you waiting for a better time? What's the reason for waiting? Is that a safe thing to do?

OCTOBER 8

Faith without works is dead.—James 2:20, NKJV

Saying and Doing. Jesus told the experience of a man with two sons. He said to the first son, "Please go and work in my vineyard today." But the son said, "No!" Then the man said to the second son, "Please go and work in my vineyard today." And the second son said, "Sure." But he didn't go. Then the first son had second thoughts and decided to go and work in the vineyard. So Jesus asked, "Which son did the will of his father?" The people answered, "The first son." The test of sincerity is not in words but in deeds. Words are of no value unless they are followed by appropriate deeds.

In the parable, the father represents God and the vineyard represents the church. The two sons represent two kinds of church members. God is calling the church members to be coworkers with Him. In joining the church, they have pledged themselves to obey the Word of God and to keep His commandments, but some have not surrendered their will to God. Let's not think that because we are not against Christ that we are for Him. There is no such thing as a truly converted person living a useless life. Those who do not work together with Christ on earth would not work together with Him in heaven. Good works won't purchase the love of God, but they show that we love Him. God's love to us is a free gift, and out of our gratefulness for that gift, we are happy to obey Him and keep His commandments.

Questions: Are you someone who quickly responds to God and then doesn't follow through, or turns from God and later changes his mind? Have you at times had second thoughts about what God wants you to do and then changed your mind and obeyed Him? Do you remember such times? What did you learn from them?

OCTOBER 9

*I will praise You, O L*ORD*, with my whole heart.*—Psalm 9:1, NKJV

The Lord's Vineyard. The parable of the two sons is followed by the parable of the vineyard, which represents Israel. God expected Israel to honor Him by representing His character in the midst of a wicked world. It was His purpose to bless all nations through His people and for His people to be the means to restore the moral image of God in men and women. This parable also applies to the church today. God has blessed this church and has given us great spiritual privileges, and He expects corresponding returns. The church is very precious to God. He values it, not because of the advantages He has given it, but because of the spiritual progress the people are making. The congregation may be the poorest in the land, but if the members have the spirit of Christ, angels will join them in worship, and praise will ascend to God from grateful hearts as sweet incense. Praising God is our duty as much as is praying. We need to speak of the precious experiences in our life and recount His goodness.

God is looking for gratitude of the heart, as well as the tithe and offerings to help send the gospel to the world. Through the grace of Christ we may accomplish everything that our heavenly Father is asking us to do and His name be glorified. The sin of today is the sin of ingratitude to God for what He has done for us. This was the sin that brought destruction on Israel. Time is nearly over, and the day of mercy is almost ended. There are members whose names are on the church books but who are not under the rule of Christ. Let us be grafted on to Christ, the divine olive tree.

Questions: How do you show your gratitude to God for what He has done to redeem you, to give you hope and a future? Would words be adequate if there are other ways to express it? What are the ways for you to express your gratitude to God?

OCTOBER 10

*"Blessed are those who are called to the
marriage supper of the Lamb!"*—Revelation 19:9, NKJV

Without a Wedding Garment. The parable of the wedding garment has a lesson of the highest value. It was the highest honor to have received an invitation to the wedding of the king's son. Yet it was not appreciated by some, and the king's invitation was despised. Then the king told his servants to go out and invite as many as they could to come to the wedding, and everyone was given a wedding garment at great cost to the king. The king was glad to see those who did come, and he greeted them warmly. But there was one person there who was not wearing the wedding garment that the king had given the guests to wear. So the king asked the man, "How did you get in without being properly dressed?" The man had no answer, and the servants came and took him away.

Christ's marriage takes place at the second coming of Christ when He comes to take His bride, the church, home with Him. But not all who claim to be Christians are true followers of Christ—they are only human moralists, and the Lord can't trust them. So there has to be an inspection of the guests and their real motives ahead of time, which takes place in heaven before the Lord comes. Only the robe that Christ provides will allow us into God's presence. It is Christ's perfect obedience that has made it possible for every human being to be so united with Him that our will and mind are linked with His. This is what it means to be clothed with the wedding garment of His righteousness. The end is near, and the day of our probation is fast closing. Soon Jesus will come.

Questions: Can you imagine that Christ thinks of the church as His bride? How do you relate to a bride getting ready for her wedding? You know. She does everything that needs to be done with the help of her attendants, and you're there to help as well. What can we do, what can you do, to help the church be ready for the Bridegroom to come and pick up His bride and take her to the wedding? Will people be there who had no interest, or just a casual interest, in the wedding? Will you be there? How are you involved in getting the bride ready?

October 11

Do you not know that your body is . . . from God, and you are not your own? . . .
Therefore glorify God in your body.—1 Corinthians 6:19, 20, NKJV

Talents. On the Mount of Olives, Christ had talked to His disciples about His second coming and the different talents that God gives to people. This He illustrated by a man who gave talents to his servants. To one person he gave five, to another he gave two, and to another he gave one. Then he left for a far country, and when he came back, he called his servants together to see what they had done with their talents. God gives to every person his/her work. Just as surely as there is a place prepared for each of us in heaven, there is work for us to do on earth.

In the parable, each one is honored for the improvement made with what he or she had been given. Our physical, mental, and moral powers all belong to Him. Let us not disappoint Him who loved us so much that He gave His life for us. This is especially important for ministers and teachers. Our words, our actions, our dress, and even the expressions on our face all have an influence. Our time, health, strength, and money all belong to God, but of no other talent will He require a stricter accounting than that of our time. Concerning health, we must keep ourselves in the best physical condition that we can. By neglecting physical exercise or by overworking, we unbalance the nervous system and are guilty of robbery toward God.

In the parable, the man with the one talent buried it, showing he did not appreciate the gift of heaven that was given to him, because it was so small. But God is honored by faithfulness, even in little things. To neglect doing what we can for God is a sign of disloyalty to Christ. Faithfulness and loyalty go together. Our heavenly Father requires no more or less than He has given us the ability to do, and He is pleased when we take up our duties with gratitude.

Questions: How many talents do you think you have? Five? Two? One? What are you doing with what you have? Is what you're doing making your talent multiply for the kingdom? Have you been able to influence others who are advancing the kingdom? If so, that's multiplying your talent(s). Are you afraid to try something new for the Lord with the ability that you do have? What is it? Why?

OCTOBER 12

Provide things honest in the sight of all men.
—Romans 12:17, KJV

Dishonest Living. Christ came to change the order of things, directing men's thoughts from the present to the future. In the parable, Jesus told of a rich man who had a steward who defrauded his master. When it was discovered what he had done, the steward was called to account and then fired. So the steward said to himself, "What am I going to do? How am I going to make a living? I know what I'll do. I know who owes my master money—I'll reduce their bill and obligate them to me." When his master heard about it, he commended the steward on his shrewdness and forethought. In listening to this parable, the tax collectors recognized some of their own dishonest practices. The Savior was speaking to the Pharisees about their spiritual self-interest. However, of the people who heard what Jesus said, many took it to heart, and under the influence of the Holy Spirit, they became followers of Christ.

After giving the parable, Jesus said, "The worldly-wise men show more wisdom in serving themselves than the people of God do in their service to Him." So it is now. Look at the life of many who claim to be Christians. The Lord has given them many gifts to be used to bless others that they have used for themselves. They are supposed to make a heavenly investment and enter into partnership with the Lord, helping those in need. Riches wisely used will accomplish a great amount of good. The ransomed will be grateful as they meet those who have been instrumental in their salvation, and together they will praise the Lord.

Questions: How honest are you—in little ways as well as in big ways? Do you have to tell all the truth about everything you know? Do you have to answer every question you're asked? If you think it's not right or that it would be hurtful to someone, what do you say? Are there times when you should say all you know? When?

OCTOBER 13

Do not withhold good . . . when it is in the power of your hand to do so.
—Proverbs 3:27, NKJV

Who Is My Neighbor? Among the Jews there was always the question, "Whom should I consider to be my real neighbor?" So Christ applied the news of the Good Samaritan, which was fresh in the minds of the people, to show that our neighbor does not mean only a person in the same church or of the same faith to which we belong. A man was going from Jerusalem to Jericho when robbers attacked him, beat him, stripped him naked, and took all he had, leaving him half dead. Later a priest came by and kept going, and so did a Levite. They were interested in getting to the temple in Jerusalem to worship. But then a Samaritan came by, saw the man, took pity on him, washed his wounds, bandaged them up, helped him onto his own donkey, and took him to the first rest stop he came to. He asked the one in charge to take care of the wounded man, left some money to pay for it, and promised that he would pay for the rest on his way back. Then Jesus asked, "Who was being a neighbor to the man who was attacked?" The Jewish lawyer said, "The one who was kind and had mercy on him." Jesus responded, "Go and do the same."

Many today are making the same mistake as the priest and the Levite did. They are focusing on going to church to worship and forgetting the commandment to "love your neighbor as yourself." They do not notice the poor, the needy, and the distressed. They think they are advancing the cause of God by choosing what is more comfortable to do. Or they will bend energy to have a part in some great work of the church and turn from the needy that are nearby. With this attitude we can never come into the spirit of the love of Christ. Christlike character shows in the impulse to help and bless others, no matter the race or nationality, that springs from within and the sunshine of heaven fills the heart, as seen in actions.

Questions: Do you get excited only about some great work that you might do for the church? How about helping your neighbor and those in need, either through direct or indirect involvement? Isn't that great in God's sight also? Do you have plans for helping? What are they?

OCTOBER 14

"Behold, I am coming quickly, and My reward is with Me."
—Revelation 22:12, NKJV

The Reward of Grace. The truth of God's free grace had almost been lost among the Jews. The priests and rabbis taught that God's favor must be earned. Even the disciples were not totally free from this misunderstanding. One day, as Jesus was walking along with His disciples, a young rich man came running up to Him and, kneeling down, asked, "Good Master, what good thing should I do to have eternal life?" Jesus responded, "Why do you call Me good? No one is good but God. If you want to have eternal life, keep the commandments." The young man said that he had done so all his life. Then Jesus told him to use his money to help the poor. But the young man turned and walked away. All our money is to be held in trust to be used as God directs. When Peter saw this, he spoke up and said, "Lord, we have forsaken all to follow You. Will we be rewarded for what we have done?" Jesus looked at him and said, "A rich man cannot enter heaven just because he's rich, but through the grace of God, all things are possible."

It is not the amount of labor performed with its visible results that's most important, but the spirit in which it is done with hearts full of gratitude. This is what makes the labor of value to God. When Christ abides in the heart, the thought of reward is not uppermost in the mind. Love to God and for our fellow men should be the most important motive. In the parable of men looking for work, the last ones who were hired received the same reward as the first ones who were hired. At the end of the day, the first ones complained, but the Lord is the one who pays the laborers and who has the right to decide. It is the spirit in which they work that's important to Him, not the length of time. For the Lord it is our willingness and faithfulness that makes our work acceptable. The smallest duty done in sincerity and self-forgetfulness is more pleasing to Him than the greatest work done with self-seeking.

Questions: Is your heart full of gratitude for any opportunity to do something for the Lord, whether great or small? With what spirit do you do it? If it's small, do you do it grudgingly? If so, how do you plan to change that?

OCTOBER 15

Building yourselves up on your most holy faith, praying in the Holy Spirit.
—Jude 20, NKJV

To Meet the Bridegroom. One evening when Jesus and His disciples were seated on the Mount of Olives, they saw a house down below with lights streaming from doors and windows for a wedding. It was the custom for the bridegroom to leave his father's house and go to meet the bride, to bring her home to his father's house. In the scene below, Jesus points out the ten young women dressed in white, each with a lamp, eagerly waiting for the bridegroom and his party to come. But there was a delay, and all the young women fell asleep. Suddenly they hear: "The bridegroom is coming!" They get up and light their lamps. Soon the lamps of five of the young virgins start going out—they're out of oil. So they ask the other five if they could borrow some, but they have none to spare. They told them to hurry and go to buy some, and then went with the wedding party into the bridegroom's house. When they got there, they were welcomed in and the door was locked. A little later, the other five young women came and knocked on the door. The master of the festivities came to the door and said, "Sorry, it's too late—I can't let you in."

This represents God's people just before Christ's second coming. There will be some who prepared for the delay and some who will be foolish and won't. All members have a knowledge of the Scriptures and know about Christ's soon coming. But a time of waiting tests their faith. Some have the Holy Spirit and stay ready, and some do not and are not ready. Knowing the truth alone cannot change the heart. To love the truth and not yield to the Holy Spirit is to be unprepared for Christ's coming. The church does not know the exact time when probation closes, which occurs before Christ comes. There is nothing that Christ desires so much as having a people who are prepared for His coming, because they have heaven in their hearts.

Questions: Do you have a yielding spirit, a yielding to the Holy Spirit? Or do you feel as though you have to yield to Him in order to make it to heaven? How do you evaluate the spirit you have? Would relating to people, whether superiors or equals, be an indication? If you need to change, how do you do it?

Faith and Works

Insights on How to Live a Balanced Life From the Ellen White Book
Faith and Works

OCTOBER 16

Here is the patience of the saints; here are those who keep the commandments of God and the faith of Jesus.—Revelation 14:12, NKJV

Clarifying Issues. The love of God needs to be constantly cultivated. One group overemphasizes free justification by faith and neglects the conditions laid down, such as, "If you love Me, keep My commandments." Another group claims to obey the commandments but neglects the love of God reflected from the cross of Calvary. If we accept Christ as a Redeemer, we must also accept Him as Ruler, acknowledging Him as our King and obeying His commandments. Speak it from your heart: "Lord, I believe You have died to redeem me. If You have placed such value on me so as to give Your life for me, I will respond and give my life, with all its weaknesses, to You."

We hear many things from the pulpit in regard to conversion that are not true. People are led to think that by having faith and by repenting they can buy their way into heaven. There is danger in placing merit on faith. Is faith our savior? What is faith? Faith is giving our heart and mind to God, accepting Christ as the only door to heaven, and then doing our part. Man must yoke up with Christ and learn His meekness and lowliness. There must be a Power that comes from outside of us. And while God through Christ must be the One to build the church, there must be a co-partnership with Him.

Questions: Have you been converted? How do you know? Can others tell? What do they see? Have you been tempted to emphasize one aspect of theology at the risk of minimizing or neglecting the others, as it says in the first paragraph? How do you stay balanced?

OCTOBER 17

Search me, O God, and know my heart.—Psalm 139:23, NKJV

True Sanctification. Sanctification is obtained only in obedience to the will of God. Many claim holiness of heart and do not have a saving and experiential knowledge of God or His law. For them sanctification is nothing more than self-righteousness. Jesus said, "I have kept My Father's commandments." God has not given His Son to a life of suffering and a shameful death to release man from obedience. Through His sacrifice Christ gave man another opportunity to obey Him. God's government and His grace are inseparable. They go hand in hand. Man looks at the outward appearance, but God looks at the heart.

In every congregation there are souls who are listening to popular discourses but not what satisfies the heart. They are taught to make feeling their criterion, without an intelligent faith. The minister may profess to be very sincere, but he is giving them a false hope. Spiritual poison can be sugarcoated with a false doctrine of sanctification, and thousands swallow it, but their sincerity will not save them. Men may make whatever excuses they please for not accepting and living by God's law, but no excuse will be accepted in the Day of Judgment, which is not far hence.

Questions: Do you just look at your outward actions and appearance and feel good about yourself? How about your heart? How carefully do you look at the inside of yourself? How are things there? Are there any changes that need to be made? What are they? What are your plans to make those changes?

OCTOBER 18

Looking unto Jesus, the author and finisher of our faith.—Hebrews 12:2, NKJV

Christ Our Righteousness. God requires that we confess our sins and humble our hearts, but at the same time we should have confidence in Him as a tender Father who will not forsake those who put their trust in Him. We cannot dishonor God more than by not trusting Him and what He says. God does not give us up because of our sins and mistakes. When we come to Him, He will not turn us away.

But we must not accept feeling for faith. In Christ is our hope. We dishonor Him by not believing His promises. It is astonishing how little confidence we place in what He says. Is this the way to treat our very best Friend? When we realize our condition, we must not become discouraged. That's how Satan would have it. Confront him and say, "I have a risen Savior—in Him I do put my trust."

We need to remember that repentance, as well as forgiveness, is a gift from God through Christ. He will help us when we come to Him. But there are those who are conscientious and trust partly to God and partly to themselves. God accepts everyone who comes to Him totally trusting in the merits of a crucified Savior. There may be no ecstasy of feeling, but there is an abiding peaceful trust.

Questions: How do you feel about your relationship with Jesus? How about your relationship with God? Do you feel good about it? How far should you go in measuring your relationship with Christ by how you feel?

OCTOBER 19

"I am the Lord, I do not change."—Malachi 3:6, NKJV

Clear Lines Drawn. Are the professed followers of Christ complying with the conditions upon which His blessings rest? Satan is ever ready to present reasons why it would not be best to totally trust what God says or to go to the other extreme and claim promised sanctification while disobeying God's commandments.

We can always come up with excuses for not obeying God. The conditions of eternal life are so plain that no one needs to be deceived. Will we be doers and not just hearers of God's Word? God's law is as unchangeable as His character. He will have a people on earth who will vindicate His name by respecting and obeying all His commandments.

There is no change when Christ returns. Character building is to go on now—it is now that we must copy the pattern given us by Jesus. Those who are watching, praying, and searching the Scriptures with an earnest desire to do the will of God will not be led astray by any deceptions of Satan. When Christ returns, it will be said of them, "Blessed are those who keep His commandments; they have a right to the tree of life and may enter through the gates into the city."

Questions: Have you ever been tempted by excuses not to obey God? If so, what were they? What did you do with those excuses, use them as legitimate reasons to disobey, or tell yourself that there are no excuses to disobey God and follow through on obedience and loyalty to Christ?

OCTOBER 20

Jesus answered them, My Father worketh . . . , and I work.
—John 5:17, KJV

Faith and Works. There are many who claim that all that is necessary for salvation is to have faith and that works have nothing to do with it. But God in His word tells us that faith without works is dead—it means nothing. Faith must have a foundation on which to build, and that foundation is the promises given to us by God based on conditions. In order to have the benefits of God's grace, we must do our part and bring forth fruits to the honor of God. He will help us. We grow in grace by improving upon the grace and blessings we already have. While works will never save us, Christ will make our efforts acceptable to God.

There is no excuse for indolence and laziness. But we need not be discouraged, for Jesus led the way, and it is by His grace that we are being transformed. When it is in the heart to obey God, when efforts are put forth to this end, no matter how feeble, Jesus accepts this disposition and effort as man's best service and makes up the deficiency with His own divine merits.

Questions: What have been your best efforts to obey God? Are you sure they have been your best efforts? Could you have done better? What lessons have you learned from those experiences?

OCTOBER 21

What does the Lord require of you but to do justly, to love mercy, and to walk humbly with your God.—Micah 6:8, NKJV

A Warning. Counterfeit sanctification has its origin in selfishness and not in submission to the will of God. This is one of the deceptions in the last days, and those who are deceived by it seldom find their way back to a true relationship with Christ. True faith wholly in Christ, and not partly in self, will lead us to conform to and obey the law of God. It is unsafe to trust to feeling or impressions. Some say, "Only believe that Jesus saves you—that's all that's necessary." But true sanctification will be seen by a conscious regard for all His commandments and will reveal the meekness of Christ in every act.

The true follower of Christ will make no boastful claims to holiness and sanctification. We become reconciled to God through the blood of Jesus Christ, and as we walk with Him, we gain a clearer sense of God's character and the nature of His requirements. Those who walk with Christ and have a sense of His presence will not indulge in self-confidence. The nearer we come to the character of Christ, the less worthy we view ourselves. It's all about Him and not about us.

Questions: How do you make sure that what you do is all about God and not about yourself and your commitment to Him? What motivates your loyalty to God? Is it to present yourself as a good Christian and Bible student, or are you trying to be a good Christian and Bible student to glorify Him? How do you make sure that you're doing it the right way?

OCTOBER 22

Resist the devil [by Scripture] and he will flee from you.
—James 4:7, KJV

How to Tell if God Is Leading. God is speaking to us through His word when He tells us that at the end time, we will hear many voices telling us that we can find Christ here or that we can find Him there. The only way we can know the truth of such claims is by knowing the Scriptures for ourselves.

The time is coming when Satan will work miracles right in our sight, claiming to be Christ. He will even look like Christ and talk like Him. Unless our feet are firmly standing on the truth in Scripture, we will be deceived and led away from the foundation on which we stand. It is important that you study the Word of God for yourself and store the truth in your heart and mind, because you may be separated and placed where you will not have the privilege of meeting with your brothers and sisters in Christ.

Questions: Can you imagine what it will be like to see what appears to be Christ speaking in love and working miracles? Should miracles convince you of the genuineness of what you see? Didn't miracles convince the people in Christ's day that He was the Messiah? So what's wrong with that today? What else should you look for besides miracles?

OCTOBER 23

For [in] the LORD will be your confidence.—Proverbs 3:26, NKJV

God's Commandment–Keeping People. All heaven is looking with intense interest to those who claim to be God's people. We have received the rich blessing of God about Jesus and the time of the end. There has never been a time when we can have more courage and confidence in God's work than at the present time. Why should not those who are keeping God's commandments hold on to His promises that have been given to them?

Truth and righteousness must be presented with the love of God as manifested in Jesus. Why have our hearts been so insensitive to the love of God? Satan has misrepresented Him in every possible way. We cannot afford to listen to him putting our heavenly Father in a false light. What kind of recommendation do we give to the world if we go around complaining with sorrowful thoughts? We are representatives of Christ and a living testimony of God's love, mercy, and graciousness in forgiving our sins. So let us go forth to show and proclaim the goodness of God and reflect His character and glory.

Questions: Would you be willing to stand for Christ and keep His commandments if you were the only one in the world? Are you sure? Have you made such a decision? If not, why not?

OCTOBER 24

Submit yourselves . . . to God.—James 4:7, KJV

The Quality of Our Faith. There is nothing more definite in Scripture than in John 3:1–16 to point out to us the way to heaven, what conversion is, and what we must do to be saved. It strikes directly at the surface work done in the churches that we can become a child of God without making a change. There has to be a change of life to show that we have been born again and have given ourselves to Christ.

Being saved is as simple as "ABC," but we don't understand it as we should. How can the natural heart stir itself up to repentance? It can't. What is it that brings man to repentance? It is Jesus Christ who gives us repentance. So the Spirit of God is working on human minds all the time to draw them to Christ. Some say, "I want to think this through and reason it out." We can't explain all the moving of God's Spirit on the human heart. We can't rationally explain faith to some who question us as we reach out and lay hold on the merits of the blood of a crucified and risen Savior.

We need the faith of the paralytic who asked his friends to carry him to Jesus, or the faith of the man unable to move his limbs to respond to Christ's command to stand up and walk. This is the kind of faith we need, but to try to stop and explain everything and reason out every point to your satisfaction will never happen. We need the faith of submission in regard to our salvation through Christ, for He is our Savior. If we try to work out our own righteousness, we will surely fail.

Questions: Is your faith a reasonable faith? Is it logical? If not, why not? Shouldn't it be? Is the logic of the mind an adequate measure of faith? Should we have a thoughtless faith? How do you answer this?

OCTOBER 25

Without faith it is impossible to please Him, for he . . . must believe that He . . . is a rewarder of those who diligently seek Him.—Hebrews 11:6, NKJV

Exercising Faith. However, we are not saved by indolence without some response on our part. Didn't our Savior have Satan's temptations to overcome? Will we be like Jacob who wrestled with Christ, who appeared to him in the form of an angel, held on to Him, and said, "I will not let You go until You bless me"? Christ did bless him. Let's not keep talking about the power of Satan, but talk about Jesus and His power to save and about our heavenly Father who loves us. Our hope is not in ourselves and in what we can do, but our hope is in Christ and what He has done and can do for us, so let's hold on to Him.

We need to talk faith, live faith, and act out faith. God wants us to be filled with joy and His blessings. Let us not go on our way to heaven moaning, groaning, and complaining. We need to learn to sing to God here if we are going to sing to Him there. When Christ comes, we will sing the song of triumph, joined by heavenly angels. Let our churches ring with songs of praise and glory now, for soon we will be singing with the angels in the city of our God!

Questions: Are you filled with joy in your relationship with Jesus Christ? Is it a legitimate joy? How do you show this joy in Him during times of difficulty? Is that even possible? What is the root of such joy? Can you explain this to others who would think that there is something wrong in such quiet joy?

OCTOBER 26

Enter into His gates with thanksgiving [gratitude],
and into His courts with praise.—Psalm 100:4, NKJV

Response to a Sermon. As a minister preached, light flashed from the Scriptures about the righteousness of Christ available to the people that seemed almost too precious to believe. Soon there was a surrendering of the heart and mind to God. Afterward, the young minister said that he had enjoyed more of the blessing and love of God during the meeting than in all his life before.

There is another message that we need to take into consideration. It is the Spirit's message to church members living in the last days. Here are people who pride themselves in their possession of spiritual knowledge and advantages. But they have not responded to God with gratitude as they should have, and in spite of their ungratefulness, our loving Father has spoken to them as His sons and daughters.

Christ sees that which man does not see. He sees the sins that, if not repented of, will eventually end the patience of a waiting God. Our Savior says, "Behold I stand at the door and knock; if you open the door, I'll come in." In every meeting held by our church, people have accepted the precious message of the righteousness of Christ freely offered to them. We thank God that there were those who realized that they did not possess the precious gifts of the gold of faith and love, the white robe of Christ's righteousness, nor the eye salve of spiritual insight, and gave their hearts to Christ. When they did, they freely received these precious gifts as their own.

Questions: What is God's message to the world in the last days? Can you share it with others in such a way that they can understand it? The basic question is: Do you believe it deep down in your heart?

OCTOBER 27

"Oh, that they had such a heart in them that they would respect Me and always keep all My commandments."—Deuteronomy 5:29, NKJV

Obedience and Sanctification. Christ gave Himself for us as a full and free Sacrifice, and each one should accept Him and love Him as if the price had been paid only for him or her. Respect and grateful obedience is true sanctification. It is not instantaneous but progressive and continuous, with a relationship growing deeper and deeper.

Yes, there is always the danger of falling into sin—that's why Christ has told us to watch and pray. We must not allow ourselves to become self-confident and forget our human weakness, but daily apply the merits of the death of Christ to our lives. There are two lessons to be learned: self-control and self-sacrifice. Through these two lessons the Savior gives us gentleness and love. Some will require the slow discipline of suffering that cleanses the heart of pride and self-reliance. Sanctification is nothing more or less than to love God with all the heart and live according to His commandments.

There is always danger of putting our trust in men, even if they have been used as instruments by God to do a great and good work. Christ must be our strength and refuge. From some pulpits in our land we hear: "Only believe, only believe." But we must have a faith that works and is motivated by love. Obedience was expected by God from Adam and Eve. They failed to obey, and we have been given a second chance to obey in the strength of our Redeemer.

Questions: Do you have self-control all the time, even under pressure? If you do, how do you do it? What's the secret? If not, how can you get it and keep it under all circumstances? Explain.

OCTOBER 28

"For the Father Himself loves you."—John 16: 27, NKJV

Appropriating the Righteous of Christ. Those who trust wholly to the righteousness of Christ, looking to Him in faith, will know that they are known by Christ. We are saved by faith in the grace that was given to us as the gift from God. There are many who find satisfaction in false doctrines where there is no disturbance between themselves and the world. But Christ calls our attention to the world to come.

The Christian must contend with supernatural forces, but he is not left to do so alone. The power of God is at the service of those who put their trust in Him. The voice of the Captain of our salvation is saying, "Be of good cheer—I have overcome the world. I am your defense, so move on to victory."

Through Christ, restoration as well as reconciliation is provided for us. Through the merits of Christ's sacrifice by which our complete ransom was paid, we are pardoned and accepted by the Father as if we had never sinned. Individually, I can claim Him and rejoice in Him as my loving heavenly Father.

Questions: What are you doing to get ready to live in the world to come? Are you aiming for that? If so, can you explain how you do it and what's involved?

OCTOBER 29

Blessed is the man . . . [whose] delight is in the law
of the LORD.—Psalm 1:1, 2, NKJV

Faith and Works Join Hands. We should study the Word of God carefully that we may come to right decisions, for then we obey the Lord in harmony with His holy law. But we cannot possibly keep God's commandments without the regenerating grace of Christ. He does not save us by the law, and neither will He save us in disobedience of the law. The gospel of Christ does not give us permission to disobey God, for that's how evil began in heaven and then in the world.

Self-righteousness separates us from Christ. Those who trust their own right-doing don't understand how salvation works. That's why there are so many conversions that are not genuine. The teaching of sanctification based on belief alone is deceptive and can lead to self-satisfaction and pride.

In the Word of God the honest seeker for truth will find the guidelines for genuine sanctification. As the apostle says, "There is no condemnation of those who walk not according to themselves, but according to the Spirit." God sent His Son into the world not only to save us but also that the law might be fulfilled in us.

Questions: If you're doing everything in your power that you know is right, shouldn't that be good enough to go to heaven? What else is needed, if anything? What happens if you fail once in a while? Then what? How do you solve the problem for yourself?

October 30

Having made peace through the blood of His cross.—Colossians 1:20, NKJV

The Experience of Righteous by Faith. There is no salvation without repentance, which is godly sorrow for sin committed. It has no merit in it but prepares the heart for the acceptance of Christ as the only Savior from sin. The law makes the sinner's guilt plain to him, and the only comfort and hope is found in looking to the cross of Calvary.

God requires the entire surrender of the heart before justification can take place; and in order for us to retain God's justification, there must be continued obedience through an active, living faith that's motivated by love. Without the grace of Christ, man is in a hopeless situation. It is through grace that we are brought into fellowship with Christ, and faith presents Christ's perfect obedience in our place. We need to remember that God loves us as much as He loves His own Son.

Many think that they must climb to heaven by themselves. If by our own effort we could take one step on heaven's ladder, then the words of Christ would not be true. We need Him—He is our Savior. And when we accept Him as such, good works will appear as the fruitful evidence that Christ's example is our way of life.

Questions: Have you surrendered yourself totally to Christ? If not, why not? How do you tell the difference? And if not, what is keeping you from a total surrender? What are the results of your total surrender? Can you explain it?

OCTOBER 31

Being justified freely by His grace through the redemption that is in Christ Jesus.
—Romans 3:24, NKJV

This Is Justification by Faith. Pardon and justification are one and the same. Through faith we are changed from a child of the world to the position of a loyal follower of Jesus Christ. Our heavenly Father says, "This is My child—I saved him from the condemnation of death and have given him My life insurance policy, which gives the assurance of eternal life. It is the Father's prerogative to forgive us our sins, because Christ has taken them upon Himself. It is through Jesus that we are brought into harmony with God and into the strong hope of eternal life.

God so loved us that He gave His Son to die for us. Christ is our Sacrifice, our Substitute, our Surety, and our Intercessor. He is presenting His merits on our behalf to the Father. As the apostle John said, "Herein is love, not that we loved God, but that He loved us and sent His Son to die for us." We should not torture our soul with the fear that God will not accept us because of our sins and sinful nature. Yes, we need to admit that we have a sinful nature, but that's the reason we need a Savior. Jesus gives us access to the Father, whose ears and heart are open to our quietest pleading.

It is the righteousness of Christ that makes us acceptable to God, and we can stand spotless before Him, because through Christ we are clothed in His righteousness. We have a living Savior, and His death on the cross is a pledge to us of our acceptance with the Father. We are incomplete in and of ourselves, and our repentance and faith by themselves will not save us. We come in humility to the foot of the cross, and a voice speaks to us from the Word of God, saying: "You are complete in Him."

Questions: Do you believe that God hears you all the time, even whispered prayers, and prayers in your mind? Are you daily in an atmosphere of prayer? What are you most concerned about in your life today? When is it hardest to maintain an atmosphere of prayer, in times of difficulties or in times of prosperity? Should there be a difference? If not, why not? Isn't it logical that there would be and should be a difference?

NOVEMBER 1

What good is it, my brothers and sisters, if someone claims to have faith but does not have works? Can this kind of faith save him?—James 2:14, NET

A Leading Minister. A minister was presenting the subject of righteousness by faith. He repeated several times that works amount to nothing. When a woman heard him say that, she knew that the people would be confused. He presented the subject too strongly, as if there are not conditions to receiving justification and sanctification. If this minister would understand the subject as he should, he would not present the matter so radically against works as he does. He needed to know the conditions for salvation laid down in Scripture, for there was no consistency in what he was saying.

Never should we place one pebble of stumbling in the pathway of those who are weak in the faith. Do not go to extremes in anything, but keep your own feet on solid rock. Jesus said, "He who keeps My commandments is loved by My Father, and I love him and will reveal more of Myself to him." Oh, my brothers and sisters, walk with God, and remember that people are watching you, so in humility and dependence keep close to Jesus. There is no place in the school of Christ for graduation. Through His grace, we need to work for Him on the plan of addition, and He will work for you on the plan of multiplication.

Questions: Will there ever be a time when we graduate from the school of Christ? If yes, when? If not, why not? How about when Jesus comes and takes us home—isn't that like a graduation? Isn't that recognizing what we have achieved? If not, why not? What about the learning that continues throughout eternity? In that sense, will we ever graduate, or will we be ever learning new things?

NOVEMBER 2

If we hope for what we do not see, we eagerly wait for it.—Romans 8:25, NKJV

We May Be Pure in Our Sphere. John said, "Beloved, now are we the sons of God; it does not always outwardly appear as such, but we know that when He shall return, we shall be like Him, for we will see Him as He truly is." Through faith we cherish the hope of Christ's appearing when the sleeping saints will be called from their graves, and we who are alive will be caught up with them and together see and admire the Lord. Everyone who has this hope will purify his life. They will realize that it is not enough to hold on to the doctrines of truth, but they must apply them to the heart and practice them in life. We should not be just hearers of the truth but doers of the truth.

The sons and daughters of God will not be like the people of the world. If Christ is in the heart, He will appear in the home, in the workshop, in the marketplace, in the business, and in the church. The power of the truth will be felt and seen in all we do. It will elevate the mind and soften and subdue the heart.

Whoever sins breaks the law, and God could not and will not change the law one bit to help man in his fallen condition. But He loved us so much that He gave His Son to come and save men and women and make them prisoners of hope. The death of Christ has forever settled the question of the validity of the law of God. Calvary vindicated God's law, to show that it is holy, just, and good, not only for us but for the entire universe, and has given us grace to keep it.

Questions: What will it be like to meet loved ones again, seeing them young, healthy, and strong? What evidence can you give from Scripture that this will happen? If so, what a wonderful hope we have. As the song says, "It's burning in our hearts." Is it burning in yours? If so, what started it? What are you doing to keep it burning?

NOVEMBER 3

Being then made free from sin, ye became
servants of righteousness.—Romans 6:18, KJV

Opinions and Practices. The expression "I am saved, I am saved" does not prove that the person is saved. People flatter themselves that they are saved because they feel happy, but they stop their ears from hearing the whole truth as found in the Word of God. Excitement is not sanctification. Total commitment to doing the will of our Father is sanctification, and the will of God is expressed in His law. Being obedient children seen by keeping His commandments is sanctification.

To be a Christian means living by the words of the Bible. We are to believe in Christ and live by Him and for Him, because He is the way, the truth, and the life. We say that we love and trust God, but this will be seen when we obey Him by keeping His commandments. We are judged according to the light of truth that has come to us, and if we follow the light, we will be free men and women through Jesus Christ our Lord.

Questions: How does keeping God's commandments set us free? Can restrictions of a law be called freedom? Free from what, and protection from what? How do you explain this?

Keeping the Sabbath

Insights About the Sabbath From Ellen White's Writings

November 4

All things were made through Him [the Son of God], and without Him nothing was made that was made.—John 1:3, NKJV

Lucifer Wanted to Be Consulted About Creation. Before the fall of Satan, the Father consulted with His Son concerning the creation of the earth and man. When Satan heard about it, he envied Christ, because the Father had consulted His Son but had not consulted him. Lucifer did not like Christ to be preferred before him. He would not submit to the Son of God. Unless the Father granted his wish, Lucifer said, he would rebel and defend his position in heaven by force, which he did. So there was war in heaven. The Son of God and His angels fought against Satan and his supporters, and the latter were defeated and forced to leave heaven. Then the Father immediately consulted His Son to proceed with the planned creation.

When the earth was created, the angels looked with admiration at what God through Christ had done, and they shouted for joy. At the end of the six-day creation, God blessed the seventh day and sanctified it, setting it apart as holy. The fourth commandment says, "In six days the Lord made the sky, the earth, the sea, and then rested on the seventh day and blessed the Sabbath day." The Sabbath was instituted in Eden before the fall, and Adam and Eve, together with the heavenly host, kept the day in honor of Christ the Creator. The Sabbath will never be done away with, but the redeemed and the angels will keep it throughout eternity. There are three dimensions of deeper meaning about the Sabbath: (1) the conflict in heaven with Lucifer wanting to have a part in creation; (2) the visible demonstration of the divine power of Christ creating the earth; and (3) the angelic host's observing the Sabbath to honor Christ. This includes much more than simply worshiping on the seventh day to remember Creation.

Questions: What impact has the Sabbath made in your life besides just having a day of rest? What spiritual significance does it make in your life? Does it give you a deeper connection with Christ? If so, how? If not, why not?

NOVEMBER 5

And no wonder! For Satan himself transforms himself into an angel of light.
—2 Corinthians 11:14, NKJV

Lucifer's Deceptive Strategy. For Lucifer to exalt himself above the Son of God to diminish His authority would take some bold and strategic moves. From Scripture we know that Lucifer has the ability to transform himself into an angel of light from heaven, which he did when he came to tempt Christ in the wilderness. Lucifer pretended that he had a commission from God to tell Jesus to end His fasting and praying. During these temptations, he misquotes Scripture, and even asks Jesus to worship him. Then he tells Him that one of the most powerful angels has been banished from heaven and suggests that it looks as though He might be the one. He asks Jesus to prove this to be untrue by using His divine power to work a miracle. Jesus refuses.

Not only does Satan have the power to appear as an angel of light but also to appear as someone who is dead. Such was the case when Saul visited the witch of Endor and asked to see Samuel, the prophet who had died years before. A man appeared who looked like Samuel and talked like him, but it was not really Samuel. This appearance of Samuel was produced by the power of Satan. Jesus said that the time will come when many would claim that they are Christ and deceive many (see Matthew 24:3–5). This is what Satan will do—actually appear as Christ. He will personify Jesus and will present the same wonderful truths in beautiful language, work miracles, and make it look as though he is the divine medical missionary sent by God. Men will fall down and worship him, and those who do not will be commanded to worship him. As the impersonated Christ, Satan will then declare that he personally changed the Sabbath to Sunday and that keeping it is a test of loyalty to him.

Questions: What will you do when you are commanded to worship on Sunday as a sign of loyalty to Christ? Will you do so to save your life? If absolutely not, how can you make sure about this? When you do stand firm, how will you explain this to neighbors, friends, and family members who worship on Sunday? What if they see you as being stubborn and unreasonable? What answer will you give them?

November 6

That the name of our Lord Jesus Christ may be glorified in you.
—2 Thessalonians 1:12, NKJV

We Make Three Important Statements by Keeping the Sabbath

1. We uphold Christ's divinity and equality with the Father, which Satan denies.

2. We uphold Christ as Savior, who paid for our sins on Calvary, which some people do not believe.

3. We uphold Christ's promise to come again, destroy this world, and make a new heaven and earth.

Think carefully about these statements, and pray for strength to keep the Sabbath for the right reason and not just for fellowship with brothers and sisters, as important as that is.

Questions: Do you agree? Have you thought about what statement you are making about Jesus when you keep the Sabbath? Are those your reasons for keeping the Sabbath now? If not, are you willing to deepen and expand your reasons for keeping the Sabbath?

NOVEMBER 7

Watch, stand fast in the faith, be brave, be strong.—1 Corinthians 16:13, NKJV

The Sabbath Is Our Banner. Considering the great controversy between Christ and Satan, we are to raise the banner on which is inscribed, "The commandments of God and the faith of Jesus." The Sabbath is a sign of loyalty to Jesus Christ and His kingdom and may be compared to a loyal army. A sleeping army would be unthinkable, and so is a lukewarm church! When we think of veterans, what comes to mind? First, we expect a veteran to be loyal to his country, to obey his commander, and to put his heart and spirit into all that he is asked to do. So it is with us: we are loyal to God's kingdom; we obey Christ our commander; and we put our heart and spirit into all He asks us to do. The Sabbath is a weekly re-commitment to be a loyal and responsible member of the Lord's army and all that it involves.

The hymn "Sound the Battle Cry" by William Sherwin (1826–1888) expresses it well:

Verse 1: "Sound the battle cry! See! The foe is nigh; raise the standard high for the Lord. Gird your armor on, stand firm, every one, rest your cause upon His holy word."

Verse 2: "Strong to meet the foe, marching on we go, while our cause we know must prevail. Shield and banner bright, gleaming in the light, battling for the right, we ne'er can fail."

CHORUS: "Rouse then, soldiers! rally round the banner! Ready, steady, pass the word along. Onward, forward, shout a loud hosanna! Christ is Captain of the mighty throng."

Questions: Do you consider yourself loyal to Jesus Christ no matter what? Are you standing under the Sabbath flag, willing to hold it up as the flag of your loyalty, without being a legalist but out of love to your heavenly Commander?

God's Foresight

Insights From Ellen White's Books *The Great Controversy*
and *Spirit of Prophecy*, Volume 4

NOVEMBER 8

"O Jerusalem, Jerusalem, you who kill the prophets and stone those who are sent to you! . . . Your house is left to you desolate!"—Matthew 23:37, 38, NET

The Destruction of Jerusalem. When Christ died on Calvary, Israel's day as a nation that was blessed by God would end and Jerusalem would be destroyed. From the ridge of the Mount of Olives, the very spot that the Roman general Titus and his army would later occupy, Jesus looked at Jerusalem, and His heart was moved with pity and compassion for His people. The Majesty of heaven was in tears! The Son of the infinite God was bowed down with anguish! The scene filled all heaven with wonder. Christ saw Jerusalem as a symbol of the world, hardened in unbelief and rebellion against God.

Questions: If you had been there that day and had seen the Majesty of heaven in tears over wicked people, would you have been in tears too? Would your heart have gone out to Jesus, or to the wicked people that He was crying over? What kind of love is this? How do you feel about lost people? What are you doing, directly or indirectly, to help those you can?

NOVEMBER 9

"If they persecuted Me, they will also persecute you."—John 15:20, NKJV

Persecutions in the First Centuries. The persecutions began about the time that Paul was martyred under Nero and continued with greater or lesser force for centuries. Throughout the ages, Christians were falsely accused of crimes, said to be the reason for God's bringing natural disasters, accused of being rebels against the government, not being willing to join other churches, and being troublers of society. Under the fiercest persecutions, God's people kept their faith and did not compromise. With words of faith, patience, and hope they encouraged each other.

When Satan saw that persecution did not accomplish what he thought it would, he changed his plans and worked against God inside the church. Persecution stopped, and in its place he substituted temporal prosperity and worldly honor. New Christians received only a part of the Christian faith. They had no conviction of sin, felt no need of repentance, and had no change of heart. But God's people stood firm and did not compromise their faith. However, as time went on, most of them did lower their beliefs to form a union of Christian and pagan beliefs. So the true believers decided to stop all union with the apostate church rather than sacrifice principle.

Questions: Are you loyal enough to biblical truth and God's people that you will not compromise even one point of your faith? Are you sure? What can you do to make sure that never happens?

NOVEMBER 10

"In vain they worship Me, teaching as doctrines the commandments of men."
—Matthew 15:9, NKJV

An Era of Spiritual Darkness. To accept converts from paganism, the church provided substitute idols of worship to which they could pray, such as the Virgin Mary, the statue of the apostle Peter, and the worship of departed saints, all of which did away with the second commandment. Next, Sunday was introduced in honor of Christ's resurrection, and disregard of the Sabbath followed. Prominent among all this was the belief in humans' natural immortality, their continued consciousness in death without the body, and eternal torment to those who did not repent. Purgatory was introduced as a way to purge sins and not have to suffer eternal torment. Full remission of sin past, present, and future was promised by various methods of payment of money to the church, which were called indulgences. Such payments could release loved ones from purgatory and have them be taken to heaven. A moral and intellectual paralysis had fallen on the Christian church. Such was the result of neglecting the full teachings of the Bible.

Questions: If you had lived during that time, what would you have done? Would you have believed all this and been willing to confess your sins to the priest, who supposedly had power to forgive them, or pay to have them forgiven? Does God accept faithful Catholics who do this today, yet live up to the best knowledge they have about salvation and God? How can you help them? Do you know how to do this without condemning them for their lack of knowledge?

NOVEMBER 11

But whoever keeps His word, truly the love of God is perfected in him. By this we know that we are in Him.—1 John 2:5, NKJV

The Waldenses. In every age, no matter how dark, there were witnesses for God who cherished their faith in Christ and held that the Bible was the only true rule of life, including the Sabbath. In lands far away from the jurisdiction of Rome, there were groups of Christians in Central Africa and in Asia who believed in the law of God and kept the Sabbath of the fourth commandment. But it was the policy of the papal church to do away with every trace of doctrine that differed from her teachings. Beginning in Europe, she did not hesitate to crush any opposition of those within her reach.

Christians committed to Christ and Scripture were forced to flee to the mountains and other isolated places, and the light of truth continued to burn. The belief of the Waldensian believers was in sharp contrast to what the Roman Church taught. These humble peasants, in their obscure retreats with daily toil, were committed to the faith of the apostles and the Bible Sabbath and thus made up the true church of God. But the Roman Church not only demanded that people keep Sunday but that the Sabbath be broken. Some believers compromised their faith, but many did not. They valued the principles of truth above houses, lands, friends, relatives, and life itself. The Waldensians sacrificed everything for the sake of the truth, and they educated their children to endure hardships for God.

Questions: Have you forgotten that there were faithful Sabbath-keepers before there were Seventh-day Adventists? What will happen when, at the end of time, you will be commanded to break the Sabbath or be killed? Is a day, the seventh-day Sabbath, worth giving your life for? Are you sure you would?

November 12

Let no one despise your youth, but be an example to the believers.
—1 Timothy 4:12, NKJV

Committed to Scripture. They committed the gospels of Matthew and John, as well as many of the epistles, to memory and used their time by copying the Scriptures, verse by verse and chapter by chapter. From the home schools in the mountains, some of the young were sent to institutions of learning in the cities. From their mothers' knees, they were trained for witnessing, and in spite of opposition, converts were won to the truth in those institutions. Missionaries were sent elsewhere as merchants, usually two by two, older and younger men together. Churches began to spring up, and only the day of God will reveal the rich harvest of souls gathered in by these faithful men. In spite of the crusades launched against these believers, they continued to send out missionaries to sow the seeds of truth that would eventually bring forth the Reformation.

Questions: Are you training your children to be missionaries for Christ, either here at home among their neighbors and friends or overseas in some mission field? How do you do that?

NOVEMBER 13

Study to shew thyself approved onto God, . . . rightly dividing the word of truth.
—2 Timothy 2:15, KJV

Luther's Separation From Rome. Martin Luther grew up in a humble peasant home in Germany, but God purposed to make him a builder of faith and advancer of the truth. At the age of eighteen, Luther enrolled in the University of Erfurt. One day he went to the university library, and as he was examining the books on the shelves, he noticed a copy of the Latin Bible. He had never seen one before. With mingled awe he turned its pages and started reading. Then he said to himself, "O that God would give me such a book as my own!" He began each day with prayer, and came under the conviction of sin. So to find peace with God, he entered a monastery and became a monk, where he devoted himself to a life of self-discipline and denial. The monastery had a Bible chained to the wall, which he was eager to read, and studied more and more. Because of such self-discipline, he lost strength and suffered fainting spells but still found no relief from the conviction of sin. He was on the verge of despair, so he went and talked to his superior, who pointed him to Jesus as the sin-pardoning Redeemer, which brought peace to his soul.

Soon Luther was ordained a priest and was called from the monastery to a professorship at the University of Wittenberg. There he applied himself to the study of Scripture in the original languages. He spoke from the Bible at the beginning of each mass, and the grace of God rested upon him. The people were captivated by his eloquence and were convicted by what they heard.

Questions: How much do you appreciate having a Bible of your own? Do you study it? How often? What benefit are you getting from it? Do you like to memorize Scripture? Have you tried? Did it help?

November 14

The righteousness of God, through faith in Jesus Christ, to all . . . who believe.
—Romans 3:22, NKJV

Visit to Rome. In the providence of God, he decided to visit Rome. When he got there and saw the city from a distance, he fell on his knees and said, "Holy Rome, I salute you!" While there, he attended the churches and listened to the marvelous stories the priests were telling the people. But as he mingled with the priests and monks, he was shocked at the iniquities and dissipation he saw on all levels. It seemed as if Rome were built above hell itself. A recent decree of the pope promised the people that forgiveness of sins could be had by going up the stairs of Pilate's staircase on their knees. Jesus supposedly walked down this staircase as He descended from the judgment hall, and it had been miraculously transported to Rome. One day, as Luther ascended the staircase on his knees, he suddenly heard a voice like thunder, "The just shall live by faith!" In surprise and shock at what he heard, he stood up, came down the stairs, and left the place. From that moment on, he saw more clearly than ever before the fallacy of trusting to human works for salvation. He turned away from Rome in heart and spirit and devoted himself to the study of Scripture as never before.

Questions: Do you trust in what you're doing to help you be saved? Why? Should you live totally by faith or depend on works for your salvation? What reasons can you give for either position? Or is salvation by both faith and works? If it is, can you clarify the right relationship from Scripture?

November 15

In whom we have redemption through his blood, even the forgiveness of sins.
—Colossians 1:14, KJV

Return Home. After his return to Wittenberg, Luther was given the honorary degree of Doctor of Divinity. Now he could more fully devote himself to the study of Scripture. He was no longer considered a mere monk or professor, but an authority on theology. He firmly taught that Christians should receive no other doctrines but those that are based on Scripture. He said to himself, "God is not guiding me—He's pushing me forward." The day before All Saints Day, Luther joined the crowds making their way to the castle church, and he posted ninety-five propositions on the door that he had written against the selling of indulgences for the forgiveness of sins. What he had done spread throughout Germany, and people recognized in these propositions the voice of God speaking to them.

Questions: Do you believe that you could recognize it when the voice of God is speaking to you? Can you make sure that's it the voice of God? How would you go about it?

November 16

Be of good courage, and He shall strengthen your heart.—Psalm 31:24, NKJV

Luther Before the National Assembly. When the new emperor, Charles V, came to the throne, the ambassadors from Rome went to congratulate him and suggested that he use his power against the Reformation. But the governor of Saxony, to whom Charles was indebted for helping him to become emperor, stood up for Martin Luther. He said that no one had shown that Luther was wrong and that he should not be put to death, but be given a fair hearing of what he believed. Luther was willing to appear before the emperor, but his health was not good at that time. So he wrote to the governor: "If I can't go there in good health, I'm willing to be carried there! If the emperor is calling me to come, then there is no doubt in my mind that God is calling me. Even though there be as many devils in the city of Worms as there are tiles on the housetops, I am still going there." On the way, Luther was surrounded by admiring crowds and was asked to preach to them, which he did.

The Roman delegates did not believe that Luther would dare to come. Word was sent to the emperor that Luther had arrived, and one of the Roman bishops suggested that Charles V get rid of this man at once and burn him at the stake. Now, Luther was weary after his two-week journey, and the very next day he appeared before the assembly still marked with the traces of illness, but with a kind expression and a courageous bearing. Standing in the presence of this powerful assembly, the lowly Reformer seemed awed. One of the noblemen who was there to witness the trial slipped up to Luther and whispered in his ear, "Fear not them which can kill the body but not the soul," giving him the words of Christ to strengthen him.

Questions: How would you feel about having to stand before such an important assembly to testify for your faith? How would you prepare for such an occasion? Do you know? Can you explain what you would do?

NOVEMBER 17

When they bring you unto . . . magistrates, . . . take ye no thought how or
what thing . . . ye shall say: for the Holy Ghost shall teach you in the same hour
what ye ought to say.—Luke 12:11, 12, KJV

Questioned. Then an imperial officer arose and, pointing to a collection of Luther's writings, demanded that the Reformer answer two questions: whether he acknowledged them as his, and whether he proposed to withdraw what he wrote. Luther moved wisely; he did not act from passion or self-defense but asked for time to think about it. He showed such calmness that it surprised the assembly and gave him the time he asked for. The next day would be the time for his final answer. He went back to his room, threw himself on the ground, and begged God for help and strength. An all-wise Providence permitted Luther to realize his danger so he would not trust to himself. Luther felt his insufficiency and pleaded not for his own safety but for the triumph of the gospel. He was given the assurance that he would not appear alone before the council.

The next day, when he was taken to the council, they demanded an answer. He said that his writings could be divided into three groups: in one group he wrote of faith and good works, in another group he pointed out the corruptions among the priests and the abuses of the Roman Church, and in the third group he exposed individuals who had defended such evils. Then he added, "If I have done wrong, please show me from the Bible, and I'll take my books and throw them in the fire myself." Luther had spoken in German—now he was asked to repeat it in Latin. This was according God's providence, because those present could not at first follow Luther's reasoning.

Questions: To explain your faith to someone, would you be upset that you have to repeat what you just said? Can you say it with patience and love the second time and make it clearer so there would be no misunderstanding? Are you sure? What can you do to prepare for such a situation?

NOVEMBER 18

If they speak not according to this word, it is because there is no light in them.
—Isaiah 8:20, KJV

Response to Emperor. Then the spokesman of the council demanded: "Will you or will you not take back the things that you wrote?" Luther addressed the emperor and said, "Your majesty, you wish a clear and precise answer, and I will give one. Unless I'm shown by Scripture and clear reasoning that what I wrote was wrong, I cannot and will not deny it, because it is not safe for a Christian to do so, help me God. Amen." Here we see an example of faith that overcomes the world. He was asked to withdraw from the council while the princes consulted on what to do. They decided to give him one more chance to withdraw what he had written and renounce his doctrines. He came back in and said, "I have no other reply." Several of the princes acknowledged the justice of Luther's cause, and later others took Luther's side. The Roman Church sustained a great defeat at this time and reminded the young emperor of the danger of giving in to such an insignificant monk. Nevertheless, the emperor decided that the promised safe conduct of Luther must be honored, and he ordered him to return home.

Questions: What do you think of Luther's response to the emperor? What is not safe for a Christian to do? Can you expand on Luther's statement? What else is not safe to do or not safe for you?

NOVEMBER 19

In the volume of the book it is written of me.—Psalm 40:7, KJV

Back Home. It was not long after Luther arrived home that the Roman ambassadors persuaded the emperor to issue a decree against Luther, and he was denounced as Satan himself in the form of a man. People were forbidden to shelter him or in any way help him. Those who openly supported him would have their property taken and they would be imprisoned. But the governor of Saxony devised a plan for the Reformer's safety by hiding him in the Wartburg Castle in the mountains, and for a long time no one knew where Luther was. However, during this time Luther's pen was not idle—he spent his time translating the New Testament into German for the people.

Questions: How would you feel if you were denounced as evil and others suffered because of you? Would you still remain true to Scripture? Are you sure? How can you be sure? What should you do?

NOVEMBER 20

"Men will rise up, speaking perverse things, to draw away disciples after themselves."
—Acts 20:30, NKJV

Progress of Reform in Germany. Luther's public disappearance caused concern throughout Germany. They looked for him everywhere, wild rumors circulated, and many believed that he had been murdered. The Roman Church leaders were shocked at the high pitch of feelings against them. Finally, the news that he was safe in the mountain castle at Wartburg calmed the fears of the people. His writings were read with even greater interest, many joined the cause defending the Word of God, and they pressed forward with new earnestness.

However, Satan was not idle, either. He now did what he has always done when God's work moved forward—he deceived people by introducing a counterfeit movement. Some men began imagining themselves to have received revelations from heaven and to be commissioned to complete the Reformation. They rejected the principles of the Reformation, that the Word of God is the rule of faith and practice, and the way was opened for Satan to control the minds of people as it pleased him.

Questions: What are some of the dangers that Satan is using today to deceive believers? Do you know? How can you keep from being deceived? What are some of the dangers for you that you need to be particularly aware of?

NOVEMBER 21

Take heed to yourself and to the doctrine. Continue in them.
—1 Timothy 4:16, NKJV

Neglecting the Bible. The Reformers were shocked as the people began to neglect the Bible. When Luther at the castle at Wartburg heard about all this, he said, "I always suspected that Satan would send us this kind of plague." From among his friends who supported the Reformation had come its worst enemies, but Luther had set himself against the use of force of any kind, and from the pulpit he spoke with gentleness, instructing and correcting those in error. Finally, God, through Luther and others, broke the spell of fanatical excitement and brought the people back to the way of truth, and they were seen with the Bible in their hands, in spite of the outbreak of the persecutions that followed.

Questions: Could you face persecution with the Bible in your hand? Do you think you could be that bold? Should you be that bold? Wouldn't that enrage the persecutors that much more? What is the best thing to do when persecution comes?

NOVEMBER 22

"Whoever loses his life for My sake will save it."—Luke 9:24, NKJV

Another Reformer. While Luther was opening the Bible to the people in Germany, Tyndale was led by the Holy Spirit to do the same thing in England. He fearlessly preached to the people, telling them that all doctrines must be brought to the test of Scripture. Twice his work was stopped, and England seemed closed to him, so he moved to Germany and made his way to Worms, where Luther had taken his stand on Scripture some years before. It was here that he printed the New Testament in English and secretly transported it to England. Tyndale was betrayed into the hands of his enemies, put in prison, and finally witnessed for the truth by a martyr's death.

Questions: How fearless would you be in declaring your faith and loyalty to Scripture, including the Sabbath, even if you knew what lay ahead? How do you prepare for that eventuality?

NOVEMBER 23

He shall give His angels charge over you.—Psalm 91:11, NKJV

Later Reformers. In Scotland, John Knox was a champion for the gospel. He was a true-hearted reformer and feared no man. The martyrdoms all around him only increased his zeal. Other Reformers followed, and with faith in God and His Word, they were willing to give up their lives for the truth. Unfortunately, the Church of England followed in the steps of Rome, persecuting the Reformers and their followers. Families were broken up and many were put in jail, including John Bunyan, known for writing *Pilgrim's Progress*. Others who were burned at the stake said, "By God's grace we will light such a candle in England that it will never be put out."

Later, Whitefield and Wesley appeared on the scene as light-bearers for the truth. They endured hardships as good soldiers for Christ and were subjected to scorn and persecution, including at the university where they were preparing for the ministry. Through their witness and preaching, thousands were convicted and converted. Again and again, John Wesley escaped death by a miracle of God's intervention. Often an angel in human form would come to his aid, and the mob would fall back to let Wesley pass on safely. The Methodists endured ridicule and persecution. Mobs went from house to house, destroying furniture, plundering whatever they chose, and abusing men, women, and children.

Questions: How can you light a candle of truth where you are and do it in such a way so as not to turn people against you? What would you do if a mob broke into your house and plundered and destroyed things, even abusing family members? Would you stand for truth in spite of it? Don't say yes so quickly. Are you that sure about yourself? If not, what should you do to prepare for it?

November 24

"Be faithful until death, and I will give you the crown of life."
—Revelation 2:10, NKJV

Fourth Commandment. Among the Reformers were those who saw the importance of the fourth commandment and the obligation to keep the Sabbath. There were such in many lands. No class of believers was treated with greater injustice by historians than those who honored the Sabbath. As the years continued, others began to honor the Sabbath. Under persecution some gave up the Sabbath, but others were true to God's commandments. One woman, a Sabbath-keeper, whom even her enemies said was a virtuous woman, was thrust into prison. She was often visited by her persecutors, who were trying to induce her by arguments to renounce the Sabbath. She asked them to show her from Scripture that she was in error and that Sunday was the day to keep. They simply asked her to smother her convictions because the church knew what was right. She refused to compromise, and for nearly sixteen years she remained a prisoner and endured great suffering until she died in prison.

Questions: In your mind, which would be worse, to be killed for your faith or imprisoned for your faith? If you had a choice, which would you prefer? How about the aspect of witnessing? Your courage as a martyr could bring others to Christ, and so could your witness to fellow inmates. Have you thought about this? Some Christians are facing death and imprisonment for their faith today.

November 25

Choose you this day whom ye will serve.—Joshua 24:15, KJV

The French Reformation. The Reformation in Germany was weakened by divisions among its supporters, followed by years of conflict and civil war. Finally, the emperor was forced to grant toleration to the doctrines that it had been his ambition to destroy. In Switzerland, as in Germany, there came dark days for the Reformation. In France, before the days of Luther, a man named Lefèvre, a professor at the University of Paris and a zealous Catholic, came across the Bible in his research into ancient literature and introduced it to the students. As he studied the Bible, the light of truth came upon him, and he wrote, "It is God who gives us faith, which by grace alone justifies us with the promise of eternal life." He translated the New Testament into French at about the same time that Luther's German Bible came from the press. Many witnessed for the truth, but persecution broke out, initiated by the papacy, and these humble Christians had to choose between being loyal to the truth and the flames.

Questions: How do you respond when you see divisions among believers? How should you respond? Should you try to get the two sides together, or do nothing? What would be another option for you?

NOVEMBER 26

"You are My witnesses," says the LORD. . . . *"Besides Me there is no savior."*
—Isaiah 43:10, 11, NKJV

In Paris. At one of the schools was a young genius named John Calvin, a staunch defender of the Roman Church. He heard that the Bible teaches that salvation comes from the free grace of God alone. At first he refused to accept this new doctrine that he had heard from his cousin and said, "I will have none of it." But one day alone in his room, he thought more about what his cousin had said, and the conviction came on him that all the ceremonies of the church and the penances required were powerless to atone for sin. Another day he was in the public square and witnessed the burning of a heretic. What he saw filled him with wonder at the expression of peace resting on the martyr's face. He determined to study the Bible more, found Christ, and cried out, "O Father, You placed the Bible before me like a torch. I now know that none of my own merits can save me except the merits of Christ alone."

While the universities were filled with theological arguing, Calvin went from house to house, opening the Bible to people. One day officers were on the way to arrest him, but friends detained the officers for a moment, while others let him down from a window to escape to another city to witness there. In the meantime, the persecutions continued in Paris. Calvin went to Switzerland, and for nearly thirty years he labored in Geneva, establishing a church built on the principles of Protestantism. From Geneva, publications and teachers were sent out to spread the new teachings. The persecuted from many lands needed instruction, counsel, and encouragement. Those who visited Geneva returned to their own countries—England, Scotland, Spain, and even France—to resist the tyranny of Rome.

Questions: Are you willing to go from house to house giving out literature or even giving Bible studies and personally sharing the truth with people? How deep is your relationship with Jesus Christ? What love and kindness would you project to those you would meet?

NOVEMBER 27

I am not ashamed of the gospel of Christ.—Romans 1:16, KJV

Netherlands and Scandinavia. The Bible was translated into the Dutch language, believers began to multiply, but soon persecutions broke out. From one of the provinces came Menno Simons, who was educated and ordained as a priest. He refused to read the Bible for fear of being pulled into heresy. After witnessing the beheading of a man who had been rebaptized, he studied the Bible in regard to infant baptism, for which he found no evidence in Scripture. Menno withdrew from the Roman Church and devoted his life to teaching the truth he had discovered. He traveled with his wife and children under great hardships, teaching people. Nowhere was the truth received more generally and where believers endured more terrible persecutions. To read the Bible, to hear it preached, or to talk about it was to incur death at the stake. In some cases, men died by the sword and women were buried alive, but they all bore it with unflinching courage.

In the countries to the north, the reformed doctrines received a peaceful entrance as Luther's writing spread the light. Hans Tausen, a young Danish student, entered the cloister and was granted permission to go to Germany. He first went to one of the strongholds of the Roman Church in Germany and became disgusted with its mysticism. Then he enrolled as a student in Wittenberg, where Luther had been, and accepted Lutheranism. On his return to Denmark he did not hide his new faith. He preached Christ as the sinner's righteousness and hope, leading his friends to a purer faith. When he was expelled from the monastery, he went out to preach to the people, and not long afterward, Denmark declared its acceptance of the reformed faith.

Questions: Can you imagine the result of a young person's witnessing like this and the whole country's becoming committed to the truth? If you're young, do you have such faith? And if you're older, what can you do to help and encourage the young people to share their faith? Any ideas?

November 28

The Lord is our defence; and the Holy One of Israel is our king.
—Psalm 89:18, KJV

Sweden. In Sweden, young men who had gone to Wittenberg, where Luther had been, took the truth back home. Two brothers who were leaders of the Swedish Reformation, Olaf and Laurentius Petri, sons of a blacksmith, shared with the people what they had learned. The Catholic priests stirred up trouble, and Olaf was attacked by a mob and barely escaped with his life. But the Reformers were protected by the king, and the leading men of Sweden, who favored the Reformed faith, declared that teachings which are in accordance with the Bible are to be declared in a simple manner so that people may understand them. Olaf translated the New Testament into Swedish, and soon the two brothers translated the whole Bible into Swedish. The king of Sweden accepted the Protestant faith, and the country became one of the strongholds of Protestantism.

Questions: Can you imagine two young men witnessing to others by sharing their faith and a king accepting the truth, or in our day the heads of government accepting the truth? How do you think these two young men witnessed to win people's hearts? What is your witnessing like, whether publicly or personally? Is it winning people's hearts? How about your neighbors and friends?

NOVEMBER 29

Let you light so shine before men, that they may see your good works, and glorify your Father [who] is in heaven.—Matthew 5:16, KJV

English Reformers. In England the New Testament had been published in Greek and Latin. Tyndale had studied these and began to preach the truth. His preaching created great interest, and many accepted the truth. There were threats and misrepresentations, but Tyndale was determined to translate the Bible into English and said, "If God spare my life, ere many yeares I wyl cause a boy that driveth the plough to know more of the Scripture, than he [the pope] doust." Driven from his home, he went to London, but when violence again threatened him there, he went to Germany and settled in Hamburg, where he translated the New Testament into English. Soon three thousand copies were printed, and though the English authorities guarded the ports of entry, by various means the New Testament came in to the country and made its way to London. Tyndale never returned to his own country but was betrayed into the hands of his enemies, imprisoned, and suffered a martyr's death.

Other Reformers in England followed, such as Latimer, the Ridleys, and Cranmer. To them the Holy Scripture was the infallible authority and the rule of faith and practice. These holy men gave up their lives at the stake, but faith in God and His word sustained them. Latimer said to his fellow martyr as the flames were about to silence their voices, "Play the man, Master Ridley; we shall this day light such a candle, by God's grace, in England, as I trust shall never be put out."

Questions: Do you consider the Bible infallible? What authority does it have in your life? How constant is it, or do you waver in accepting it fully? If you waver, what's the problem? How do you rectify it?

NOVEMBER 30

They that sow in tears shall reap in joy.—Psalm 126:5, KJV

Scotland. In Scotland, John Knox turned away from the Roman Church, fed his soul on the truth of God's Word, and joined the persecuted Reformers. When brought to the Queen of Scotland, he witnessed kindly and respectfully to the truth. The queen said, "You interpret the Scriptures one way and the Roman Church another way—whom shall I believe?" The Reformer answered, "The Word of God is plain. What is hard to understand in one place is made plain in another place."

In England, the papacy with its doctrines was rejected, and the Protestant faith became the national religion. The monarch became the head of the Church of England, known in the United States as the Episcopal Church. The right to worship according to the dictates of conscience was not acknowledged, and dissenters were persecuted. Thousands of pastors were expelled from their positions, and people were fined, imprisoned, and banished to foreign lands. In a loathsome dungeon with others, John Bunyan wrote his wonderful allegory, *Pilgrim's Progress*.

Questions: How much do you appreciate freedom to worship God according to the dictates of your conscience? Who or what is telling your conscience whom to worship and how? Explain.

DECEMBER 1

Blessed is the man whose strength is in You.—Psalm 84:5, NKJV

Wesley Brothers. Some years later, Whitefield and the Wesley brothers appeared and became God's light bearers, and they were led to see that true religion is situated in the heart. They lived a life of self-denial but did not find the peace they were looking for to break free from a sense of the condemnation of sin. After John and Charles Wesley were ordained to the ministry, they were sent on a mission to America. On board ship, they met a group of Moravians from Germany, who did not fear death in spite of the storms they encountered. They had a peace that the Wesley brothers did not have and sang songs to the Lord. When the ship finally made it to America, the Wesleys stayed with the Moravians in Savannah for a while. Before returning to England, they had received a better understanding of biblical faith, renouncing all dependence on works for salvation and wholly trusting in God.

Back in England, John Wesley preached with power, but the established clergy denounced him from their pulpits. Again and again, he escaped death by a miracle of God. Wesley said, "One man struck at me several times with a large oaken stick, but each time the blow was turned aside and I don't know how. Another time a stone was thrown which did strike me between the eyes, and a man hit me across the mouth with such force that blood gushed out, but either time I felt no pain." In those early days of Methodism, mobs went from house to house, destroying things, plundering whatever they could, and brutally abusing men, women, and children. John Wesley faithfully carried out the work God gave him. At the close of his life, his followers numbered more than half a million.

Questions: Have you had an experience where the faith of others brought you closer to God? Do you remember who they were and what spiritual benefit you received from them? When you meet people, is their acquaintance with you benefiting them? You may not know, but what do you think?

DECEMBER 2

The LORD shall preserve you from all evil.—Psalm 121:7, NKJV

The Bible and the French Revolution. In no country was the spirit of the rejection of Christ and His truth more strikingly displayed than in France. The king of France, urged on by the Roman priests and prelates, carried out a slaughter of Protestants known as the St. Bartholomew's Day massacre. The ringing of the church bell at midnight gave the signal for the slaughter to begin. Protestants by the thousands, sleeping quietly in their homes, were dragged out of bed without warning and murdered in cold blood. This continued for three days. The pope rejoiced and proclaimed a jubilee to celebrate the event. In addition, Bibles were burned in the streets, and symbolically the Old and New Testaments lay there as two dead witnesses. It only took a little time before France renounced the worship of the living God altogether and set up a worship to the Goddess of Reason, displayed by an immoral dancing woman. The young woman was paraded before the people and asked to stand next to the president as the fittest representation of what they now believed.

Voltaire and his associates cast aside God's Word and spread infidelity everywhere. The people now carried out their rejection of God on the Roman Church. Unprepared, Rome now felt the deadly power of those she had trained in the cruelty against Protestants. The scaffolds ran red with the blood of priests. No mercy was shown to gender or age; babies were tossed from spear to spear. The restraining Spirit of God to hold Satan's actions in check had been removed. About three and a half years later the government granted toleration of the Scriptures, and the Bible was translated into many languages and scattered to every part of the globe.

Questions: We know the expression, "We reap what we sow." The papacy sowed and reaped. Looking at your life, have you had sowing and reaping experiences? Do you remember them, and what did you learn from them? Would you feel comfortable passing these experiences on to others to help them not do the same?

DECEMBER 3

"If the Son makes you free, you shall be free indeed."—John 8:36, NKJV

The Pilgrim Fathers. The monarch in England determined to make the Puritans conform to the state religion. Hunted, persecuted, and imprisoned, they saw no hope for better days. Some determined to find refuge in Holland, but in their flight from England, they had left their houses, their goods, and their means of earning a living. But even here their purposes were hindered; they were betrayed into the hands of their enemies, and losses and imprisonment followed. These Puritans had made a covenant among themselves that they would walk in God's ways, no matter what happened. Here was the vital principle of the Reformation. Then a way opened for them to leave Holland to find a home in the New World. It was the desire for liberty of conscience that inspired the Pilgrims to brave the dangers of the long journey across the ocean and endure the hardships to live in America, as a new nation was being formed.

However, some did not have a true concept of freedom of conscience and made a regulation that only church members should have a voice in civil government. So a state church was formed, and magistrates were authorized to suppress any dissent. Roger Williams was a respected and faithful minister, and his refusal to accept the authority of the civil magistrates over the church led him to be banished from the colony. He fled to Rhode Island, where he helped to lay the foundation of civil and religious liberty, which became the cornerstone of America as guaranteed in the Constitution.

Questions: Are you ready to refuse the authority of the civil government over your conscience and commitment to Scripture? How far would you go to stand for freedom of conscience? Do you know where to draw the line? Are there areas where you would give in to the government and where you would not? What are they?

DECEMBER 4

Study to shew thyself approved unto God.—2 Timothy 2:15, KJV

An American Reformer. William Miller, an honest farmer, who at first doubted the divine authority of Scripture, was chosen by God to proclaim Christ's second coming. Early in life he battled with poverty and learned lessons of self-denial. His father was a patriot and a captain in the Revolutionary War. Young William did not have an opportunity for a college education, but he loved to study and was a careful thinker. He had a high moral character, but the Holy Spirit impressed him that in spite of this, he had a sinful tendency as all humans do and needed a Savior. He studied the Scriptures, and in Jesus he found His Savior and Friend.

Laying aside all preconceived opinions and dispensing with commentaries, he compared scripture with scripture, and to him the Bible became its own interpreter. With intense interest he studied the books of Daniel and Revelation. Angels were guiding him, and after a few years of study, he concluded that soon the Son of God would come and probation would close. At first he presented his views privately to others, and then he presented them publicly. He left his plow and opened to the people the mysteries of the kingdom of God without passion or excitement, but with kindness, calmness, humility, and self-control. With every such effort he gained new strength and courage.

Questions: Can you study the Bible and lay aside all your preconceived opinions? Which opinions would you hold on to, if any? What are they, and why would you hold on to them? Explain.

DECEMBER 5

"This same Jesus, who was taken up into heaven, will so come in like manner."
—Acts 1:11, NKJV

A Great Religious Awakening. In the prophecy of Revelation 14, the proclamation of Christ's soon coming is foretold. An angel is seen flying in the midst of heaven, proclaiming, "Fear God and give glory to Him, for the time of His judgment has come, and worship Him who made all things in heaven and on earth." This is a symbol of a worldwide movement proclaiming the gospel and the soon coming of Christ. Joseph Wolff, whose father was a Jewish rabbi, had become a Christian, and he began proclaiming the soon coming of Jesus in Europe, the Middle East, Africa, Asia, and India. Then he came to America and preached the same message in New York and other cities. In South America, Lacunza, a converted Jesuit priest, read the Scriptures and believed in the soon coming of Christ. In Scandinavia, the Holy Spirit moved on the hearts of children to preach the message. In the United States, William Miller began preaching the soon coming of Christ even more earnestly, and thousands from various churches joined what was called the Advent Movement.

However, when the time came and went when they thought Christ would come, and He did not come, there was great disappointment, and many went back to their former churches. This was not the time of Christ's return as expected, but the beginning of the end. While the people expecting Christ's return were disappointed, they were encouraged by the words of Paul, "Cast not away your confidence; be patient, the Lord will come" (Hebrews 10:35–37, paraphrase).

Questions: How would you respond if you found out that you had made a mistake in believing certain things from your study of the Bible? Would you be willing to change if, by a more diligent study of Scripture, you found that you had been wrong in your previous understanding? Be honest with yourself.

DECEMBER 6

*"I will come again and receive you to Myself; that where I am,
there you may be also."*—John 14:3, NKJV

What Is the Sanctuary? God had led in the great Advent awakening and would not let it end. Those who had so faithfully studied the Scriptures investigated the subject again and discovered that the coming of Christ spoken of at that time was not to the earth but to do His special work in the sanctuary in heaven. When Moses was asked to build a sanctuary for God's people on earth, it was to be a copy of the sanctuary in heaven (Exodus 25:8, 9; Hebrews 9:11, 12). So the sanctuary in heaven is the great original after which the earthly sanctuary was built. The temple in heaven is the dwelling place of God. It has two compartments just like the sanctuary here on earth, the Holy Place and the Most Holy Place. When Jesus ascended, He entered the Holy Place where the Father was, but then the Father rose from His throne, stepped into a flaming chariot, and went into the Most Holy Place, and sat down. Then Jesus stepped into His flaming chariot and followed the Father into the Most Holy Place to begin His final work. When He, by virtue of His blood, will erase the recorded sins of His people from the books of heaven, His work will be finished, and He will return to take His people home.

Questions: Do you believe that God led in the great Advent awakening? What gives you such confidence?

December 7

I will keep the commandments of my God!—Psalm 119:115, NKJV

A Work of Reform. The importance of the Sabbath was included in the preaching of Christ's return. This was foretold by Isaiah: "Blessed is the man who lays hold on the Sabbath and keeps it, to love the Lord and to serve Him" (Isaiah 56:1–7, paraphrase). But the Sabbath as a day of worship was changed by the papacy to Sunday. However, the Sabbath of the fourth commandment is a sign of God's authority. "To the law and the testimony; if they speak not according to this word there is no light in them" (Isaiah 8:20, paraphrase). The time had come for the divine institution of the Sabbath to be restored. As the claims of the Sabbath are being presented, many say, "We have always kept Sunday." What can a group of people keeping the Sabbath hope to accomplish with those who worship on Sunday? The reason why the Lord does not often work through men of learning is that they trust their own interpretations of Scripture and theological systems.

Unfortunately, in the beginning of the Advent movement, when Christ did not return as expected, many turned away from the light of the Sabbath and returned to their former churches. It was not the will of God that the coming of Christ should be so long delayed. In mercy Jesus delays His coming so that others may have an opportunity to hear the message of salvation and the Sabbath. The obstacle in accepting the Sabbath does involve difficulties. But as Paul says, "Our light affliction is but for a moment of time when we consider the glory to follow, when the Savior comes to take us home" (2 Corinthians 4:17, paraphrase).

Questions: Have you ever had difficulties keeping the Sabbath with your employment? Do you still have difficulties, or do you not have them anymore? If you don't have them anymore, are you grateful that they have worked out? Was it a miracle, or did God quietly help you? Do you know others who have had or are having Sabbath job difficulties? Have you prayed for them? Is there anything you can do to help them? If so, have you?

DECEMBER 8

"Take heed that you not be deceived."—Luke 21:8, NKJV

Modern Revivals. Wherever the word of God is faithfully preached, there are results that testify to the presence of the Holy Spirit. Deep conviction takes hold of the minds and hearts of people, and they see that nothing but the cross of Calvary and its sacrifice for their sins can reconcile them to God. With faith and humility they accept the Lamb of God who takes away the sin of the world, and they believe and are baptized. But it should be said that where there is only surface repentance, there will be no reformation of one's life. Unfortunately, many modern revivals may have large accessions to various churches, but without a corresponding increase of real spiritual life. Appeals are being made that excite emotions and imaginations, producing gratifications that spiritual growth has taken place. But converts have little desire to study the Bible for themselves. Unless a religious service has some attraction for them, they have no interest.

Notwithstanding, there are true followers of Christ in all churches, and the time will come when the Spirit of God will be poured out on all His people, and they will separate themselves from their churches. Both ministers and people will gladly accept the truth that God has caused to be proclaimed in these last days to prepare them for His second coming.

Questions: Do you faithfully attend church, even if the service is not what you would like it to be? Do you go to church only because you like the service or because you love God, even if the service is not always to your liking? Are you being honest with yourself?

DECEMBER 9

This is a deceiver and an antichrist.—2 John 7, NKJV

Counterfeit. Satan will introduce a counterfeit message. In the churches that he can bring under his deceptive power, he will make it appear that God's special blessing is being poured out, and many will rejoice that God is working marvelously for them. Under a religious guise, Satan will seek to extend his influence over the whole world. There will be a mingling of the true and false, which is well adapted to mislead. Whenever men neglect the testimony of the Bible and turn away from its plain testing truths which require some self-denial, we may be sure that God's blessing is not there.

It is the work of conversion and sanctification to reconcile men and women to God by bringing them into harmony with the principles of His law. Through Christ, the hearts of men and women must be renewed by divine grace, and there must be in them a new life from above. In this new birth their hearts are brought in harmony with God's law; the old life has ended, and a new life of reconciliation, faith, and love has begun.

Questions: How do you identify a counterfeit message? Do you know how to test a message to see if it's a counterfeit? What criteria would you use? What areas of faith would you test first? What other areas would you test? If you need help in doing so, where would you go?

DECEMBER 10

What is man. . . . You have made him a little lower than the angels.
—Psalm 8:4, 5, NKJV

Easy Religion. The sanctification gaining prominence in the religious world is to "only believe"—that is all that is needed to be saved and all the blessings will be yours. No further effort on the part of the believer is required. But at the same time, men and women are released from obligation to keep the commandments. The desire for an easy religion has made the doctrine of faith, and faith only, a popular doctrine. But the Scripture says, "What shall it profit a man if he says he has faith and does not have works. Faith without works has no meaning" (James 2:14, 17, paraphrase).

We should not forget that while the Christian's life should be one of humility, it should not be one full of sadness and self-deprecation. We are the sons and daughters of God, and through Jesus Christ we belong to the royal family of the universe. It is not God's will that we should be under self-condemnation or self-deprecation. Because of Jesus, we have been cleansed and stand before the law without shame and condemnation. Truly, God's servant Nehemiah said, "The joy of the LORD is your strength" (Nehemiah 8:10). And Paul said, "Rejoice in the Lord always; and again I say, Rejoice!" (Philippians 4:4).

Questions: Would you like an easy religion? What are some harder parts that you don't care about? How would you evaluate the harder parts to see if they are genuine and not just self-imposed? Can you help others who prefer an easy religion to accept the hard parts also? How would you go about it?

December 11

My defense is of God. . . . God is a just judge.—Psalm 7:10, 11, NKJV

The Investigative Judgment. In the book of God's remembrance, every deed of His people is recorded and immortalized: every temptation resisted, every evil overcome, every word of tender pity expressed, every act of sacrifice, every suffering and sorrow endured for Christ's sake, and every secret purpose and motive. Also, opposite each name, every selfish act, wrong word, unfulfilled duty, secret sin, untruthfulness, and unimproved opportunity is recorded, and the influence for good or evil with its far-reaching results to see if they have been forgiven, covered by the blood of Christ. If so, the person is counted worthy to be resurrected or translated when He comes, to be God's royal son or daughter, equal with the angels.

During this time of investigative judgment, Satan is there to accuse God's people and point to the record of their lives, the defects of their character, and their unlikeness to Christ. Jesus does not excuse their sins but shows him their confession, repentance, change of life, and faith, claiming forgiveness and acceptance. Then Jesus rebukes Satan and shows that His people are covered with His robe of righteousness. All this is to be done during the investigative judgment. The intercession of Christ in our behalf in the sanctuary above is as essential as was His death on the cross. For some years this has been going on, and soon it will close. Shortly before Christ's return, probation will silently close unnoticed. The unjust will remain unjust, and the righteous will remain righteous (Revelation 22:11, 12).

Questions: Do you believe that there will be a time when God will have to decide who His people are and who are not? Do you think such an evaluation time will need to take place before Jesus comes? Do you think it could be now? If so, what is the most important ingredient in this evaluation process?

DECEMBER 12

Do not be conformed to this world, but be transformed by the renewing of your mind.—Romans 12:2, NKJV

Neglecting Warnings. Among professed Christians, and even ministers, there is scarcely a mention of Satan from the pulpit. They overlook his continued activity and neglect the warnings given us in Scripture; they seem to ignore his existence. Satan is working the streets of our cities, using his influence in churches, and, wherever possible, in courts of justice. All who are not decidedly followers of Christ are influenced by Satan. But in the renewed heart there is hatred of sin and evil and a determination to resist it, and Satan has no power to control the will and force it to obey him.

When the church conforms to the world, hoping thereby to convert the world, the opposite will take place—the church will be converted to the world. Many think that courtesy and refinement are in some way associated with Christ, but men with cultured intellects and pleasant manners, who would not stoop to an immoral act, can become polished instruments in the hands of Satan, which makes it even more possible for them to successfully work against the cause of Christ than those who are uneducated. We must never forget that we wrestle not against flesh and blood but against the principalities and powers of darkness, against wicked spirits. So put on the whole armor of God, and you will be able to stand up against the subtleties of the devil (Ephesians 6:11, 12 and 1 Peter 5:8).

Questions: Do you think conforming a little to the prevailing culture is helpful in winning people to Christ? If so, how far would you go? Is there a danger in doing this? What is it? Do you know? Could this be like a slippery slope? Is it better not to conform to the prevailing culture even a little? If so, how do you reach people attached to the present culture? Have you thought about how you would do it?

DECEMBER 13

For He shall give His angels charge over you.—Psalm 91:11, NKJV

Agency of Evil Spirits. The connection between the visible and invisible world, the work of God's angels and Satan and the wicked angels, is plainly revealed in Scripture and interwoven with human history. We are told about the number, power, and glory of the heavenly angels and their responsibility in the government of God, and their relation to the work of salvation. The Scripture speaks about ten thousand times ten thousand, and thousands of thousands of angels, and Paul talks about innumerable angels (Daniel 7:10; Hebrews 12:22). Fallen because of sin, Satan and his angels have joined together to dishonor God by destroying the human race. We are told of their malicious designs against us. But we need to remember that a guardian angel is appointed to every follower of Christ to shield them from the power of the evil one. God's people, exposed to the deceptive power of the prince of darkness, are assured of the unceasing guardianship of heavenly angels.

None are in greater danger from the influence of evil spirits than those who deny their existence. They respond to their suggestions and suppose they are following the dictates of their own conscience. This is why, as we approach the close of time, Satan will be able to work with greatest power as he spreads the belief that he does not exist or lets himself be presented as a loathsome, misshapen being, and is pleased when those who consider themselves intelligent deny his existence. But the followers of Christ are safe, for they are under His watch-care. Angels are sent from heaven to protect His people, and the Wicked One cannot break through the guard that God has stationed around them.

Questions: How do you protect yourself from evil spirits or even from the influence of evil spirits? Do you know? Should you even be concerned about it? If so, what are the precautions you should take? Do you know? Are you taking such precautions?

DECEMBER 14

"The devil . . . is a liar and the father of it."—John 8:44, NKJV

Snares of Satan. The great controversy on earth between Christ and Satan has been going on for nearly six thousand years and will soon come to a close. This is the time when he will redouble his efforts to defeat the work of Christ on behalf of the human race. Satan wants to hold men and women in darkness until the Savior's intercessory work in heaven is over and there is no more opportunity to be saved. Like a skillful general he lays his plans, and as he sees the messengers of God searching the Scriptures, he takes note of the subject to be presented to the people. Then he tries to control circumstances by bringing about something urgent that requires their presence so they cannot be present for the message to reach them.

Again, Satan sees the Lord's servants burdened because of the spiritual darkness that hovers over the people. He hears their earnest prayers for power and grace to break the spiritual darkness. He tempts the people with some form of self gratification or gets them to focus on the faults of others, and thus they fail to hear the very things they need to hear. Satan leads them to put a false coloring on the words and acts of those who love the truth and point to the most earnest and self-denying servants of Christ as not trustworthy.

Questions: How concerned are you over the spiritual darkness that covers this world and the deteriorating world conditions? What can you do about it, if anything? What is the only solution? Can you help in bringing this solution about? What would it be?

DECEMBER 15

As for me, I trust in You, O LORD; . . . my times are in Your hand.
—Psalm 31:14, 15, NKJV

Suggested Doubts. The great deceiver has many ways to present every kind of error to ensnare the souls of men and women. It is his plan to bring into the church such as are unconverted or insincere to encourage doubt and hinder the work of God from advancing. Many who have no real faith in God and pass as being Christians are able to introduce errors such as it doesn't really matter what one believes, because a correct religious faith is unimportant. This is one of Satan's most successful deceptions. His intention is to confuse people's minds so that they will not discern the truth. Instead of carefully studying God's word with humility to discern God's will, many do so only to discover something original and different. They hold on to passages of Scripture separated from the context or quote only a portion of a text to make their point. This will happen whenever the Scripture is studied without prayer and without a humble, teachable spirit, and the passages will be taken from their true meaning. The whole Bible should be studied and given to the people just as it reads.

Satan says to his angels, "We must watch out for those who are bringing the importance of the Sabbath to the attention of the people; they are leading many to see the claims of the law of God. We must exalt Sunday, the Sabbath of our creation, and lead people to accept their minister's explanation of Scripture and not to investigate the matter for themselves. Working through ministers, I can control the people according to my will. But our main concern is to silence this sect of Sabbath keepers by leading those in authority to enforce Sunday laws and turn against those who will not swerve from their allegiance to God's holy day. But before these extreme measures, we must use subtlety to deceive those who honor the true Sabbath. We must make those who believe the truth to become careless; this will confuse their judgment and bring about their fall."

Questions: Have you become careless about your faith? How do you know? If not, praise the Lord. If you have become careless, how do you plan to stop it and become totally committed? Explain, and then do something about it.

DECEMBER 16

The King of kings, and Lord of lords; who only hath immortality.
—1 Timothy 6:15, 16, KJV

Spiritualism. The doctrine of natural immortality was first borrowed from pagan philosophy, and after the time of the apostles, it was brought into the Christian church. The teaching of men's continued consciousness in death included the belief that their spirits continue to live and minister to the living, but this false teaching has prepared the way for modern spiritualism. If the spirits of the dead are admitted into the presence of God and are given insights into things far exceeding the knowledge they had before, why should they not minister to the living, comfort them, and warn them of dangers that threaten them?

Satan has power to bring before men and women the appearance of departed loved ones and friends, and lead them to believe they have returned to help them. They claim to be happy in heaven, and no difference is made between the righteous and the wicked, which is contrary to Scripture. The spirits of dead loved ones foretell future events, which gives them greater reliability. By these manifestations many will be deceived, and this will be especially true before the return of Christ (2 Thessalonians 2:9, 10). Satan is able to pervert the senses of all who are not shielded by divine power. Our intellectual and spiritual nature is changed by what we see and hear. The mind gradually adapts itself to the subjects on which we dwell. The grace of God alone has power to protect us from this downward spiral.

Questions: How would you respond if you suddenly saw one of your dead loved ones? Would you be surprised, shocked, glad? What if they started talking to you and telling you things that only they and you would know? Would that convince you? If they asked you questions, would you answer? Would you start a conversation with them, or would you back away from them? Why?

DECEMBER 17

The dead know not any thing, . . . neither have they any more a portion for ever in any thing that is done under the sun.—Ecclesiastes 9:5, 6, KJV

The Apostles. Through the spirits of the dead, including the so-called spirits of the apostles, Satan will make them say things that are contrary to what these men wrote. So the Bible is made to appear as unreliable, or fiction, and not suitable for modern man. The Book that is to judge Satan and his followers is placed just where he wants it. The Bible is used and interpreted in such a way that it is pleasing to the unrenewed heart, and the requirements of God's law are kept out of sight. Isaiah warns us by saying, "To the law and the testimony; if they speak not according to this word, there is no light in them" (Isaiah 8:20).

The people of God are able to meet Satan as the Savior did, with the words, "It is written." But we need to remember that Satan can quote Scripture and misapply it. So each one who would stand true in the time of the end must understand the Scripture themselves. The blindness of the people today is amazing. Thousands reject living by what the Bible says about God's law and see those who go by the Bible upholding God's law as being narrow-minded. But "great peace have they which love thy law; and nothing shall offend them" (Psalm 119:165).

Questions: What if you showed from the Bible that dead loved ones who appear are not real but impersonations by evil spirits? What if some of the apostles appeared and contradicted what they wrote, telling you what they really meant? What would you do? Would you believe them, or would you stay with what is written in the Bible? How would you have the courage to do that? Tell me!

December 18

I will be their God, and they shall be my people.—2 Corinthians 6:16, KJV

Aims of the Papacy. The papacy is now regarded by Protestants with far greater favor than in former years. The opinion is gaining ground that there is not so much difference between the two faiths as in former years. Excuse is given for Rome's former cruelty against Protestants as the result of the times, but things have now changed. Any fear of Roman Catholicism today is said to be prejudice. Though the papal church has made some outward changes and has apologized for her cruelty to Protestants in the past, and Protestants have apologized for their uncharitable opinion of her, the Roman Church has never given up her claim to infallibility on the basis of her faith. The recent papal expressions of love and toleration for others do not imply a change of heart, for being tolerant is to her advantage. Every priest, bishop, archbishop, and cardinal takes an oath of allegiance to the pope.

It is also true that there are real Christians in the Roman Catholic Church. Thousands of them are serving God according to the best knowledge they have. God looks with tenderness on them, and He will cause rays of light to penetrate their hearts and minds. He will let them see the truth as it is in Jesus, and many will yet take their stand with God's people.

Questions: Do you personally know some wonderful Catholic people, maybe nuns and priests? Many people know about Mother Teresa, the nun, the kind person she was, helping and serving others—the poor, the hungry, and the needy. Have you ever been shown kindness by a Catholic and knew that he or she loved God? Would you share that experience with others?

DECEMBER 19

For ever, O LORD, thy word is settled in heaven.—Psalm 119:89, KJV

The Impending Conflict. From the very beginning of the great controversy in heaven, it has been Satan's aim to overthrow the law of God, and his purpose has not changed. He can achieve this by deceiving men to break the whole law by breaking one of the commandments—the result is the same. This is the battle we are facing today. Do we stay with what the Bible says, or do we not?

It will be said that the world's fast-spreading corruption is the result of not honoring Sunday and that enforcing it would solve the problem and the morals of society would improve. This claim will first be made in the United States, and every other country will follow. Moral reform is needed but not by disregarding the law of God and by sacrificing freedom of conscience for the overall "good" of society.

Questions: What if the whole world keeps Sunday to honor Christ and His resurrection? Would you continue to stand firm and keep the Sabbath? Where would you get the courage to do so? Explain.

DECEMBER 20

For they are the spirits of devils, working miracles.—Revelation 16:14, KJV

False Miracles. Satan delights in war, and in this way he can excite the worst emotions and sweep thousands into eternity to be lost. He will bring diseases on people and then remove the cause and make it appear as though he is the great miracle-working physician. Satan is also at work causing calamities by sea and land such as tornados, hailstorms, floods, tidal waves, droughts, and earthquakes. These things will become more and more frequent as we near the coming of Christ. Finally, it will be said that these things are happening because God's day, Sunday, is ignored and needs to be strictly enforced. Spirits of the dead will appear and say that God has sent them to persuade the rejectors of Sunday to obey the laws of the land. Commandment-keepers will be misrepresented, a false interpretation will be given to what they say, and false motives will be attributed to them.

When Sunday is first enforced, there will follow a brief time of peace and prosperity, and the response will be that God is blessing because people are honoring Sunday. However, this time of peace and prosperity will not last long. The final cataclysmic events will happen, and men's hearts will fail them for fear of what is coming on the earth (Luke 21:25–28; *Maranatha*, 259). But the servants of God will be sealed and kept by the power of God. They have been faithful to all of God's commandments, and the Sabbath is the outward sign that they belong to Him.

Questions: When this happens (as you have just read), will you stand for the Sabbath? Why? Is it just because the Bible says that you should? Is there an added, deeper personal reason for it? What is it?

DECEMBER 21

Let us . . . come boldly to the throne of grace, that we may obtain mercy and find grace to help in time of need.—Hebrews 4:16, NKJV

The Final Warning. It is during the time of the end that the Holy Spirit will be poured out without measure and God's people will proclaim the last message to the world with power. However, with every rejection of the truth, the hearts of the people will become more stubborn, and many will end up turning against those who keep God's commandments. The nations of the earth will unite to compel everyone to observe the false Sabbath, and those who refuse to do so will eventually be declared as deserving of death. The event so long doubted that it could happen, will happen. The true Sabbath will become the great test of loyalty to Jesus Christ. Those who are faithful to Christ and keep all of God's commandments will be thought of as being absurd and going to the extreme.

When this happens, a large number who have professed their faith in Christ and the commandments, who have not obeyed from the heart but only as an outward form, will choose the popular way and abandon their position and join the ranks of opposition. Men of talent and pleasing speech, who once rejoiced in the truth, will use their influence to mislead others, and when Sabbath-keepers are taken to court to answer for their faith, Satan will use these former believers to bring false accusations against them. It is at this time that the Lord's true servants will be tested. But they will know that to stand for the truth is beyond their personal strength, and in their helplessness they go to the Mighty One for help.

Questions: When you see some of your fellow believers, even those you highly respected, go with the popular flow of Sunday-keeping, what will you do? Follow their example? Are you personally committed to keeping God's commandments, even if you were the only one in the world? Are you sure about that?

DECEMBER 22

These are they which follow the Lamb.—Revelation 14:4, KJV

Decisions Are Made. While company after company of so-called believers will leave the Lord's side, tribe after tribe of those who are honest in heart and value God's Word above any earthly advantage will see the deciding issue. That's when they will decide to keep the true Sabbath and unite with God's people. They will take the places made vacant by those who left the true faith, and the ranks of God's people will never decrease (*Testimonies*, 8:41; *Selected Messages*, 3:422).

About this time, Michael (another name for Jesus, meaning "The One who is like God") will end His intercession in the sanctuary above, and He will announce: "He who is unrighteous, let him be unrighteous still, and he who is righteous, let him be righteous still" (Revelation 22:11, paraphrase). Every case has been decided for life or death.

Questions: How will you feel when you see many of your Christian friends start keeping the Sabbath? Some of these may have been kind and loving Christians but were not interested in leaving their churches and the friends they had there. But now they are willing to leave them and have done so. To what do you attribute this sudden change?

DECEMBER 23

Be not deceived: for many shall come in my name, saying, I am Christ.
—Luke 21:8, KJV

Ultimate Deception. As the crowning act of deception, Satan himself will appear, impersonating Christ. In different parts of the world, he will manifest himself as a majestic being resembling Christ whom the apostle John saw in vision (Revelation 1:13–17). The shout fills the air, "Christ has come! He has come!" In a soft and gentle voice filled with compassion, Satan repeats the same gracious truths that Christ taught and says that he changed the Sabbath to Sunday as a day of worship. He also says that those who persist in keeping the seventh day are dishonoring his name and keep refusing to listen to his angels sent to them with the truth.

This is an almost overwhelming deception, but the people of God will not be misled. What Satan is saying is not according to the Scripture. Those who have been diligent students of Scripture and have the love of the truth in their hearts will be shielded from this delusion. The people of God who are standing firmly on what the Scriptures say will not yield to what they see and hear, but will cling to the Bible, and the Bible only. The Lord will not forget His people during this trying hour. How can He forget them? They were carved on His hands when their sins were nailed to the cross for their redemption.

Questions: Can you imagine Christ saying that He changed the day of worship from Sabbath to Sunday? Could Christ do that? If yes, would He? If He would not, do you know why He wouldn't? Explain.

DECEMBER 24

I will hear what God the LORD will speak, for He will speak peace to His people.
—Psalm 85:8, NKJV

God's People Delivered. As God's people are earnestly praying for deliverance, the veil seemingly separating them from God is withdrawn. The heavens begin to glow with the dawning of eternity, and the words of music from angels fall on their ears: "Stand fast to your allegiance to God and His Son. Help is coming!" Christ's voice comes from the gates of heaven, "Lo, I am with you. Do not be afraid."

God will step in to rescue His people. Suddenly a dense darkness will fall on the earth, but a shining rainbow will span the heavens and each praying company of Sabbath-keepers. Then they will hear a clear and melodious voice saying, "Look up!" They do, and they see Jesus seated on His throne, notice the nail marks in His hands, and hear Him say, "Father, I would like for My people to be with Me where I am." Then God's voice shakes the heavens and the earth. Graves are opened, and all who have died in the faith come forth glorified and, together with the living faithful, will hear God's voice of peace.

God's people are now secure. Their voices break out in a triumphant song, "God is our refuge and strength," as they ascend to the celestial city. A hand appears in the sky, holding two folded tablets of stone. The hand opens the two tablets, and the words of God law are seen written with a pen of fire. God's ten words, brief and authoritative, are presented for all the inhabitants of the world to see. It is impossible to describe the horror and fear of those who turned against God's requirements. But it is too late. They see that the Sabbath of the fourth commandment is the seal (the stamp) of God ownership on His people that they belong to Him, and they hear the blessing pronounced on all those who have honored the Sabbath.

Questions: What will it feel like to be resurrected and hear God's voice of approval? And then to see Christ holding the two tablets of stone that had been written by His own finger? This whole experience will be incredible! Was your commitment to Christ and the Sabbath worth it? If the answer is yes, can you tell me the real reason for your obedience?

DECEMBER 25

They shall be priests of God and of Christ, and shall reign with Him a thousand years.—Revelation 20:6, NKJV

A Thousand Years. For six thousand years the great controversy has been going on, as the Son of God and His angels have been in conflict with the evil one and his warfare against God and His law. Now the time has come for God to vindicate His law. At the coming of Christ, the wicked are destroyed by the brightness of His coming, leaving the earth empty. The whole world appears like a desolate wilderness. The ruins of cities, uprooted trees, and ragged rocks are scattered everywhere. This will be the condition of the earth for one thousand years. It will be the home of Satan and his angels. Totally cut off from the work of deception and the use of his power that he had used against God's people, Satan will walk up and down on this desolate earth to see the results of his rebellion. All he has to look forward to is the final judgment and the punishment for all the sins that he had caused people to commit.

During this one thousand years, God's people will be in heaven and, in union with Christ, will judge Satan, his angels, and the wicked, comparing their actions with the Bible. As Paul says, "Don't you know that the saints will judge angels?" (1 Corinthians 6:3, paraphrase). Together with Christ, they will comprise the heavenly jury to make the decision of what final action should be taken against Satan, his angels, and the wicked. Then at the close of the thousand years, the wicked will be raised from the dead to appear before God and, together with Satan and his angels, to receive their sentence. Some will suffer longer than others, depending on the degree of their wickedness. Some will perish quickly and be as though they had never been (Obadiah 15, 16), while cruel kings and rulers will suffer longer, and Satan and his angels will suffer the longest.

Questions: How will you feel when Satan is no longer around to bother you, tempt you, trouble you, or threaten you? What a relief, don't you think so? What an actual blessing, in addition to being saved! Have you ever thought of thanking God for this? Why don't you?

DECEMBER 26

These shall make war with the Lamb, and the Lamb shall overcome them.
—Revelation 17:14, KJV

The Controversy Ends. Finally, the universe will be free from sin. God will wipe away all tears from the eyes of the redeemed, and there will be no more death, sorrow, or crying, for the former things will have passed away, and there will be a new heaven and a new earth (Revelation 21:1–5). The New Jerusalem in all its glory and splendor comes down from heaven and settles in the place prepared for it. Then Christ, together with His people and the holy angels, enters the holy city.

Before Satan is destroyed, he prepares for his last final struggle. When he sees the multitude of the wicked raised, his hopes revive, and he determines not to yield and give up the great controversy. He claims to be the rightful owner of the earth and represents himself to those raised as their redeemer, who brought them back to life. He makes the weak strong with his own spirit and energy. He tells them that they can take the holy city away from Christ and His people. There are unnumbered millions who have been raised from the dead, including kings and generals who had never lost a battle. Satan consults with his angels, and then with these mighty men, they lay their plans on how to take the city. At last the order is given to advance against the holy city, with Satan leading the way.

Questions: Can you imagine what it will be like to see the hordes of wicked attacking the place where you are? How will you feel as you watch all this? This is beyond our imagination, especially since the wicked had all been dead. Why would God raise them from the dead and allow this to happen? Can you explain it?

DECEMBER 27

He shall judge the world with righteousness, and . . . truth.
—Psalm 96:13, KJV

Video Replay. By the command of Jesus, the gates of the New Jerusalem are closed, and Satan and his army surround the city. Then Christ appears high above the city, sitting on His throne, the glory of which cannot be described. The glory of the Father surrounds His Son and shines beyond the city, covering the earth with its brightness. Then Christ is invested by His Father with majesty and power, and as King of kings, Christ pronounces His sentence against Satan and his army. Above the throne appears a blazing cross and then a view of the history of the human race, including the Savior's birth, His early life, baptism, temptation by Satan in the wilderness, life of ministry, His condemnation, and His death on the cross; everything is seen just as it was. Next is seen the history of the church through the ages to the very end. Every question of truth and error has been made plain, and God's justice has been fully vindicated. They see in Christ's hands the tables of the law, which they have disobeyed.

Questions: What a video that will be to watch and see the whole history of God's people from the beginning of time! There has never been a video like that and never will be. What parts of this video will interest you the most? Why?

December 28

What are these wounds in thine hands? . . . Those with which I was wounded in the house of my friends.—Zechariah 13:6, KJV

Satan's Response. Even though Satan acknowledges the justice and fairness of God, confesses his sin, and accepts the supremacy of Christ, his character is unchanged. His last desperate struggle has come to an end. Then the wicked, filled with hatred of Christ and God, see that their case is hopeless, and in anger and rage they turn against Satan and his angels in the fury of demons. That's when fire comes down from God out of heaven, and Satan and the wicked are destroyed. The earth is at rest and is quiet. There is only one reminder: the Savior will always have the marks of His crucifixion in His hands and feet and marks on His wounded head and in His side.

Questions: Imagine the whole wicked world of people turning against Satan and his angels. We know that humans can't kill them and that God will have to destroy them. Then the only reminders of the great conflict between good and evil, between Christ and Satan, are the wound marks of our great Freedom Fighter, scars that will remain on Him forever. How will you respond to such a great Warrior?

DECEMBER 29

"[God] will dwell with them, and they shall be His people."
—Revelation 21:3, NKJV

The City of God. There will be no night in the city of God, for God Himself will be there, and His presence is its light. His people will never feel tired and will be eager to sing praises to Him. They will have the privilege of seeing the Father and the Son face-to-face and of having open conversations with them. Also, there will be the sweetest and most harmonious social life with the redeemed of all ages, and there will be one whole family. With great delight God's people will take part in the joy and wisdom of unfallen beings throughout the universe. And as the years of eternity roll, they will bring greater and more glorious revelations of God and Christ, and the happiness of the redeemed will keep increasing. All things throughout the universe will declare that God is love.

Questions: All the questions you have or have had about your life here on earth will be answered by then. Won't that be wonderful? And to think that we will be learning new things throughout eternity! What things will you want to learn? What do you think the unexpected things will be that will stimulate you to want to learn even more? Can you tell me?

The Glorious Future

Insights From Various Ellen White Books

DECEMBER 30

Only those who are written in the Lamb's Book of Life.
—Revelation 21:27, NKJV

A Glimpse Ahead. Christ looks upon the redeemed, renewed in His image, with joy unspeakable, every face reflecting His likeness. We will hold open conversations with the Father and the Son. Language is inadequate to describe the glory of our new home. As Paul says, "Eye has not seen, not ear heard, nor have entered into the heart of man the things which God has prepared for those who love Him" (1 Corinthians 2:9, NKJV). Christ told His disciples that He would go home to the Father and prepare mansions for them and then come again to take them home so they could also can be where He will be (John 14:1–3). Some, not wanting to make the inheritance of God's people too literal, have spiritualized away this truth, which Jesus has promised.

Things that have been hard to understand will be made plain. We will see harmony in all that perplexed us and realize the love and care of God, even during the times that were most trying. He worked all things together for our eternal good (Romans 8:28). We will rejoice with unspeakable joy and praise His name forever. We will be able to meet and talk with our guardian angels, learn the history of interventions in our life and from the dangers we were preserved. But as the hymn says, "Holy, holy, is what the angels sing, and I expect to help them make the courts of heaven ring; but when I sing redemption's story, they will fold their wings, for angels never felt the joys that our salvation brings."

Questions: How literally do you take Jesus' words regarding your home in heaven and the glories there? How much of it should be taken as symbolic? When you talk to others about it, what do you tell them?

DECEMBER 31

They shall see His face, . . . and they shall reign forever and ever.
—Revelation 22:4, 5, NKJV

Joys Unimaginable. Music will be there such as we have never heard or conceived. Every power will be developed, and the highest aspirations and ambitions will be realized. Also, not restricted by mortal bodies, we will be able to fly to worlds afar. With telescopic vision we will be able to look at the glory of God's created universe such as the stars and systems, all in their order, circling the throne of our heavenly Father. As the years of eternity roll, they will bring more revelations of knowledge and insight beyond what we can ask or think. Our greatest joy will be found in sharing with unfallen worlds our personal story of redemption and salvation, and listening to them as they share with us all that they have learned through ages untold.

We will also meet and have fellowship with Adam and Eve; Noah; Abraham; Moses; David; Mary, the mother of Jesus; and the apostles, Peter, John, James, and Paul, not to mention our loved ones and our countless friends, and fellow believers and workers during the final days of earth's history. But best of all will be to see Jesus, our Savior; the Holy Spirit, who gave us our spiritual birth; and our heavenly Father, whose love is beyond words. As the hymn says, "The Love of God is greater far than tongue or pen can ever tell. . . . Could we with ink the ocean fill, and were the sky of parchment made, were every stalk on earth a quill, and every man a scribe by trade, to write the love of God above would drain the ocean dry; nor would the scroll contain the whole, though stretched from sky to sky."

Questions: What will you say and do when you meet men and women you read about in the Bible in both the Old and New Testaments? How about when you meet faithful Christians you read about in history, including Adventist history? What will you ask them? What will you want to know from them?